Deprivation, participation and community action

Deprivation, participation and community action

edited by Leo Smith and David Jones

Routledge & Kegan Paul

London, Boston and Henley

First published in 1981
by Routledge & Kegan Paul Ltd
39 Store Street,
London WC1E 7DD,
Broadway House,
Newtown Road,
Henley-on-Thames,
Oxon RG9 1EN and
9 Park Street,
Boston, Mass. 02108, USA
Printed in Great Britain by
Thomson Litho,
East Kilbride

ISBN 0 7100 0827 9

305.56
D442

Contents

Introduction
David Jones and Leo Smith   ix

1 A model for the development of public
   participation in local authority
   decision-making   1
   Leo Smith

2 Public participation in Islington -
   a case study   37
   edited and compiled by Leo Smith

3 Area management: Newcastle's Priority
   Areas Programme   97
   Chris Miller

4 Lambeth and neighbourhood councils   112
   Charles Allwright, Mark Brangwyn,
   Fiona Crosskill, Jo Osorio, Mary Turle

5 Organising in three neighbourhoods   125
   Marilyn Taylor

6 Promoting participation in planning:
   a case study of Planning Aid, Dundee Area   137
   Laurie Bidwell and Bill Edgar

7 Resource centres and participation   153
   Nick Bailey and Marilyn Taylor

8 The Normanton patch system   168
   Mike Cooper

9 Community education in Scotland   181
   Charlie McConnell

10 Negotiating a new tenancy agreement   196
    Dudley Savill

11 Promoting participation through community   207
    work
    Bryan Symons

Contributors

Nick Bailey is a lecturer in Town Planning at the Polytechnic of Central London. He has been employed by a number of local authorities and previously worked with Ray Lees on the research project monitoring resource centres, based at PCL.

Laurie Bidwell is course tutor for the Post-Graduate Certificate in Community Education (Adult Education, Community Work and Youth Work) at Dundee College of Education and secretary of Planning Aid, Dundee Area.

Bill Edgar is lecturer in Town and Regional Planning at Duncan of Jordanstone College of Art, treasurer of Planning Aid, Dundee Area and a management committee member of Hillcrest Housing Association.

Mike Cooper is Area Social Services Officer in Wakefield, covering the Normanton area. Formerly a senior social worker in Batley, West Yorkshire. Trained as a teacher and came into social work in 1968.

David Jones is Principal of the National Institute for Social Work. Director of the Southwark Community Project, 1968-72. Chairman of Gulbenkian Community Support Programme Advisory Committee.

Charlie McConnell is a lecturer in Community Education and Social Work Department, Dundee College of Education. Has written one book 'The Community Worker as Politiciser of the Deprived' (CEC, 1977). Chairperson - Scottish Association of Community Workers.

Chris Miller is a lecturer in community and youth work at Sunderland Polytechnic, and an activist in Newcastle where he has undertaken research for the Tenants Federation and helps produce the city-wide community newspaper 'Broadside'.

Dudley Savill formerly General-Secretary of the Association of London Housing Estates; Co-ordinator of the National Tenants Organisation and Consultant to the National Consumer Council on landlord/tenant relations.

Bryan Symons is Development Officer and Co-ordinator of Islington Voluntary Action Council. Previously head of the student training unit at the Association of London Housing Estates. Joint author of 'Principles and Practice of Community Work in an English Town'.

Leo Smith is Director of Society for Co-operative Dwellings, a Secondary Housing Co-operative. He was the first (and only) Public Participation Officer for Islington Council 1973-80. Joint editor of 'Collective Action'. Script consultant to the BBC Radio 4 series 'Community Work'.

Charles Allwright, Mark Brangwyn, Fiona Crosskill, Jo Osorio, Mary Turle were the staff of the Lambeth Neighbourhood Councils Office at the time the article was written in 1979.

Marilyn Taylor Senior Research Officer for the Community Projects Foundation. Author of the recently published report 'Street Level: Two Resource Centres and their Users'.

Introduction

David Jones and Leo Smith

The original intention for this book was not a theoretical
discussion of the philosophies and ideologies of participation
but to assume that, in appropriate circumstances, increased
participation was both feasible and desirable. In particular,
the assumption was that socially deprived populations should be
enabled to participate in decision-making affecting their lives.
It was hoped that an analysis of the factors influencing
participation and examples of practice might enable community
workers and others similarly engaged to increase their understanding and become more effective in fostering and supporting
such participation.

Now the political and economic context in which participation
and community work have to be considered has changed dramatically.
In addition, the disillusionment and scepticism of many community
workers and community activists has colluded with the obstinate
resistance of many institutions and services to the exhortations
of a series of reports, studies and statements commending
participation which have appeared regularly from the late 1960s
onwards.

By 1973, a group of some 70 people representing an extremely
wide range of opinion and including many people in official
positions was able publicly to endorse without dissent a suggested
declaration of intent that:

Central and local government authorities and other public
institutions should declare their intentions to involve in
decision making, in whatever ways may be most effective,
those who will be closely affected by their proposals and
policies; and to explain the reasons for the final decision.
(1)

Seven years later, our contributors reveal how confused and
problematic the matter still remains.

Participation does not necessarily have over-riding value and

people will have other values they wish to protect or promote.
There are always the highly practical questions of who benefits
and in what way? Participation can be used to divert, frustrate
and manipulate. The methods which community workers use to
promote participation can be used for undesirable purposes.
Existing or aspiring elites of all kinds may only be able to see
participation as an instrument to further their own interests.

Nevertheless participation remains central to any meaningful
conception of community work as distinct from proselytisation or
public relations. Even so, one line of thought assumes that
participation always results in defeat or co-option or is a
diversion of energy from the main task of promoting an effective
working-class organisation or other political or religious
cause.

Chris Miller reflects some of this ambivalence when he claims,
in relation to the Newcastle Priority Areas Programme, that:

> most political activists in the community saw it as an offer
> to participate in, and thereby condone a programme that could
> never realistically make a substantial impact on the problems
> of the inner city.

Laurie Bidwell looking at the other side of the fence sees a
similar outcome:

> From within government and the planning profession, criticism
> has been levelled at the costs to entrepreneurs of delays
> incurred in the development process, about the value of
> participation schemes in the face of low and unrepresentative
> levels of response and concern about the unlikelihood of
> planners being able to include adequately the diversity of
> public response into the plans under preparation.

He goes on to argue, however, that 'these pitfalls and
difficulties do not justify a policy of non-intervention by
community workers.... However marginal the potential for redistribution through planning, it should be noted that this redistribution could be progressive or regressive, the underprivileged
could be worse off if they opt out of the process.'

In Newcastle, in fact, it is reported that the participation
aspects of the Programme were to some extent increased following
discussion with voluntary and community organisations and the
dilemma is underlined by the fact that the city has funded or
initiated a whole range of schemes 'many of which have been
innovative and exciting and are likely to receive support from
community workers.'

Chapter 1 reviews the development of ideas about participation
since the late 1960s and then discusses the problems inherent in
extending participation in local authorities as we know them.
Not least that the long-standing division by function and the

more recent moves to much larger authorities and departments and
to corporate planning make it difficult to relate effectively to
local communities. A model scheme for local authorities (who
would clearly have to be already highly committed to promoting
participation) is then worked out in considerable detail. It
proposes thorough-going policies for the promotion of participation in decision-making in all aspects of local authority activity
and particularly emphasises that appropriate structures and staff
are essential to make these policies a reality. In addition to
working directly with groups, community work staff in fact have a
responsibility to try and ensure that suitable structures are
established and maintained. It also requires the development
and support of strong independent community organisations
employing their own staff. Collaborative and joint action between
these independent community organisations is to be encouraged, but
at the same time different groups to articulate different interests
should be allowed to develop. Throughout priority should be given
to the development of participation among the most deprived and
excluded populations.

The model focuses almost entirely on the local authority.
Issues of participation are, however, equally important in other
public services; in public utilities, in voluntary organisations
of all kinds and in the work place and market place. The case
study of the development of participation in Islington which
follows enables us to set this ideal statement against some of
the realities of day-to-day practice.

The original plan was that the Islington study should consist
of independent contributions from an appropriate selection of the
rich variety of activities and projects which have developed in
the area. This intention was overtaken by events and the account
has been produced collaboratively by a number of the people
involved. Not surprisingly, the developments are seen and
assessed primarily from the standpoint of the authors.

That the reality falls short of the model in various respects
is only to be expected. Islington remains one of the most
thorough-going and ambitious attempts to develop participation
by a local authority. Yet the case study discerns a steady
decline in impetus from 1975 onwards and by 1980 a number of
central features of the model had been dismantled. But although
depleted, Islington still has a larger investment in community
involvement than most areas.

Was the decline quite fortuitous? Or is it to be explained
in terms of personalities and group dynamics? Is it merely a
temporary eclipse? Was both the rise and decline of participation
just a fashion? Or are there other lessons to be derived from
the Islington experience?

Public expenditure cuts were clearly important but the authors
deny that the decline can be explained solely in these terms and
see the reasons as political rather than financial. Political in

this context, however, refers not to political party or ideology but to a struggle between factions. Participation is by definition political but the Islington experience indicates the danger of too close and exclusive an alliance with any one political group despit the prospect of immediate gains. It thus highlights the contra- dictory advice from our contributors to support the Labour party and to abhor it!

Established bodies, including political parties, are perhaps always suspicious of developments which might cut across existing allegiances or create new sources of action.

Did other factors contribute to the decline? Reference is made to the heavy demands the process made on the time and energies of leading councillors and officials. Perhaps extensive participation makes too great a demand on the resources and decision-making procedures of even such a responsive authority as Islington?

Much of the initiative throughout was taken by the local authority itself. It is clear that the authority provided relatively substantial resources. Was the consequence that community organisations never developed their own independent strength either individually or collectively so that the constitu- ency for participation was never strong enough to counter other pressing demands on councillors and the local authority when they ar

Pessimism about the uses of participation possibly derives from the fact that the outcome will tend to be determined by the prevailing distribution of power, influence and control of resources. As the Lambeth workers point out: 'it would be un- realistic to expect participation to work unless the Council which holds power, is willing to allow it to succeed'.

This willingness is heavily influenced however by prevailing values, assumptions, conventions and policies. Although in practice some are more equal than others, participation is supported by deeply held values in our culture and society. The demand can be made on those in power to live up to their own principles and visions of themselves.

Additionally the disparity in power that always exists in relation to socially deprived populations, can to some extent be redressed by organisation, solidarity, persistence, hard work and the acquisition of greater knowledge and skill. The ALHE work in relation to tenancy agreements illustrates this.

Such activity makes excessive demands on the participators, however, and is difficult to sustain over long periods. Dudley Savill and Marilyn Taylor both argue that community groups need their own support staff as well as other resources.

Nick Bailey and Marilyn Taylor summarise the role of resource centres as enabling

the community itself to organise, articulate needs and evolve

appropriate organisations to meet them. The aim is therefore
to encourage the development of effective community organisations and to ensure they have sufficient resources to pursue
their chosen strategy.

The Lambeth Neighbourhood Councils' were supported by staff
employed by the local authority and a variety of tensions are
indicated. Dudley Savill, while arguing that community groups
should employ their own staff, pointedly raises crucial issues
of accountability:

There is no doubt that trained and articulate community workers
can manipulate and direct groups. They may do so for a variety
of different reasons such as their own motivation, ideology,
shortage of time available or as a strategy for achieving
objectives.

Aspects of the worker's role are discussed by a number of
contributors. Laurie Bidwell says 'the planner involved in
advocacy or advice is not promoting demystification and citizen
learning, and retains the role of the expert urban manager' and
proposes a community development model. Similarly, Charlie
McConnell sees the need 'to elicit demand without pre-empting
response' and argues that 'to be committed to participatory
democracy the community educator must not indoctrinate or
condition'.

The need for groups to increase their impact and to respond
to more wide-ranging issues, leads a number of writers to argue
for federations, neighbourhood councils and umbrella organisations
of various kinds. Marilyn Taylor illustrates many of the strengths
and weaknesses of such combinations and Laurie Bidwell suggests
that in Scotland community councils might actually deprive people
of the opportunity to participate.

'Bureaucracy' in terms of the inappropriate structures and
procedures of organisation and 'professionalism' in relation to
the attitudes of behaviour of their staff are used pejoratively
throughout. Both are present in Mike Cooper's account of the
in-built obstacles to be overcome in converting an area office
of a social services department into a mutual aid network.

An analogous concern with participation at the micro-level
comes in Charlie McConnell's account of the process whereby an
'almost insignificant English class grew ... into a unique
experiment in Community Adult Education in Scotland'.

Indeed for a number of contributors, community education in
the widest sense is the way forward. This implies the education
of the community workers if they are to fulfil their task
adequately. Bryan Symons, in a critical down-to-earth and wide-
ranging review, picks up on these and other issues implicitly
or explicitly raised by the contributions. He insists on the
distinction between the community worker as such and other roles

of community activist, spokesman, community leader, councillor and
social scientist.

While demanding greater knowledge, skill and commitment from
the community workers he echoes Charlie McConnell in emphasising
that the worker's task is to support appropriately the group but
not to dominate it or impose his own views.

A crucial skill for the worker is the ability to intervene in
a variety of situations in ways which release and stimulate
individual and group capacity. The aim is not merely to cope
with whatever is immediately at issue but to develop in people,
individually and collectively, the ability to deal more effectively
not only with the present problems but with other problems in the
future.

He also stresses the analytical and assessment skills required
of the worker and the fundamental importance of sound and
realistic judgment in what are situations of great complexity and
uncertainty.

The worker has the duty of making his own best judgment
available to the group. Groups need a realistic appraisal of the
options available, and what might be achieved at what cost. As
Symons points out it will only demoralise a group to encourage
them to go into battles they are bound to lose. Interestingly
he also indicates the need for action to be as economical and
appropriate as possible. It is undesirable to burden already
hard-pressed groups. A major campaign may be quite unnecessary
and the use of dramatic acts, such as demonstrations, however
useful on occasions, may if repeated too frequently be devalued.
Throughout he sees the process as educational although in no
sense didactic. The community worker is seen essentially as a
resource and enabler.

In order to meet these demands the worker needs not only
personal ability and commitment of a high order but appropriate
initial training, continuing staff development, skilled
supervision and an appropriate organisational base.

As far back as 1921, Lindeman was writing:

The Democratic Process expresses itself, or is personified
in the total community membership. The Specialist expresses
himself, or is personified, in the division of labor which
produces highly skilled persons and agencies, organizations,
or institutions, equipped to do one thing effectively .... The
Democratic method is slow, cumbersome, halting and beset with
many back-eddies which seem to be antiprogressive. The
specialist becomes impatient with all of this and desires to
to straight toward his goal. He *knows*. The constituents of
Democracy do not know, and must be shown the way. (2)

An era determined to reduce public expenditure constitutes a
hostile environment for community work.   It may well stimulate
better off sections of the community to organise themselves even
more effectively or to create alternative self-help arrangements
quite possibly at the expense of deprived populations.   Community
workers could have a crucial role in enabling the most deprived
and excluded members of our society to have a voice and achieve
a greater degree of justice for themselves.

1   'Current Issues in Community Work: A study by the Community
    Work Group', Calouste Gulbenkian Foundation, 1973, p.138.
2   Lindeman, Eduard C., 'The Community - An Introduction to the
    Study of Community Leadership and Organization', New York:
    Association Press, 1921.

1 A model for the development of public participation in local authority decision-making

Leo Smith

INTRODUCTION

Interest in public participation in government decision-making grew from the late 1960s onwards, due to the needs of government itself, and in response to community action. The growth of community work is a manifestation of this development. Partly because people are more highly motivated by issues that affect them directly, partly because of their ability to draw lessons from personal experience and partly because of community workers' own efforts, most work to develop participation has been done at a local level. Local government services have thus been the main arena for debate and experience, though very few councils attempted to work out in a systematic and rational way what they were trying to do.

Further, community workers themselves have paid little attention to the performance and structure of local government, and the changes that have taken place. Much community work involves helping groups influence local councils, but there are few examples of attempts to change the way councils actually work so they can be influenced more easily. By accepting the status quo, community workers are ignoring one of their main roles - to increase local democracy and to increase the community's control over the factors that affect it. This chapter therefore analyses the origins of participation, recent trends and the practical problems encountered in trying to make it work. In the light of this analysis it suggests the basis of a model for participation in local government decision-making and the programme of work needed to bring it about. It also discusses the role of community workers and the demands that should be made by them and others of local government if partici- pation is to be significantly increased. It does not attempt to cover the related questions of the development of community organisations to exploit the situation thus created; this is dealt with in other parts of this book and elsewhere. It is not based on a theoretical approach but a practical analysis of the real issues and problems which will confront people trying to make local government more open and participatory based on the experience of community work in the 1970s.

Though the policies of the Thatcher government have created an unfavourable climate for the extension of participation and community work at the local level, it is essential that the lessons of the 1970s are analysed and understood, so that when and if a more favourable climate occurs in the future, we can build on past experience rather than repeat the learning process. Even in the current climate many of the lessons have immediate application.

THE ORIGINS OF THE PRESSURE FOR PARTICIPATION

Pressure for public participation in decision-making by national and local government has largely arisen in the last fifteen years. It has grown from the inter-action between government and governed during the period when state intervention in people's everyday lives has increased tremendously. As government has played a larger part in economic and social management, so the institutions of government and politics have evolved. People's attitudes have responded to these changes and they have made demands of their own.

THE GROWTH OF STATE INTERVENTION AND LOCAL GOVERNMENT

The Macmillan era was typified by a landslide victory in the 1959 General Election on the slogan 'You've never had it so good'. However, this was followed by increasing public attention on the social inequalities of the affluent society. Poverty became an issue and working-class children were shown to be still at an educational disadvantage. Television became widely available and focused attention on these and other issues. The 1964 election returned a Labour government committed to major reforms through direct intervention on many economic and social issues, consequent increases in public expenditure and the National Plan. The education and road-building programmes of the Conservatives were supplemented by housing programmes (involving substantial compulsory purchase, clearance and redevelopment), increased land-use planning powers and big increases in social services. Secondary education started going comprehensive.

Most of these reforms were managed by local authorities. Apart from hospitals, major roads and defence, the vast majority of public expenditure is channelled through them. Consequently, their powers and the size and scope of their programmes increased substantially during the 1960s. Bennington has drawn attention to this dramatic growth of local government:

Between 1948 and 1968 Local Government's share of the Gross National Product (GNP) doubled, its revenue expenditure quadrupled and its capital expenditure quintupled - all in real terms.... With a total annual expenditure nearing £10,000 million and employing 10% of the total working population, Local Government has become big business in its own right. (1)

State intervention led to the rapid growth of planning at all levels of government. One of Labour's election slogans in 1964 was 'You know Socialist planning works'. The first local authority planning department was established as recently as 1960. Planning evolved from land-use planning to planning the complete society. State intervention needs a planned better future as its justification and its goal. As the plans were no use if other departments did not carry them out, corporate planning and corporate management took increasing hold of local authorities.

As this extension of state power took place, concepts of participation developed with it or in opposition to its manifestations.

For many years legislation had given people a statutory right of objection to compulsory purchase orders and major planning proposals, but by the late 1960s government realised that it was better to consult people on some issues before decisions were finalised, rather than give them the right of objection after the event. Thus in two of the main areas where local authority powers were extended, official reports also made recommendations to increase public participation - the Skeffington Report on planning (1968) and the Seebohm Report on social services (1969). Both these reports also recommended local authorities to employ people- community development officers or community workers - to promote this participation.

Obviously these developments did not take place in isolation; they were a response to several different social trends, all of which increased the pressure for greater participation.

COMMUNITY ACTION

As government intervention became more frequent and more local, and increasingly followed a pre-set plan, it became easier to focus attention on it and mobilise people. The factors which facilitated trade union organisation in factories - a common interest, a high level of personal and social contact, a focus for negotiation and campaign, enough members to throw up an effective leadership and a tradition of struggle - became more common in cities. Opposition to council plans was reinforced by the belief that the council was elected to meet people's needs, not to ride roughshod over them.

Direct action increased - people refused to accept decisions and resisted their implementation. The most spectacular and

well-publicised examples included resistance to the clearance of
houses for redevelopment, objection to urban motorways (particularl
in West London), squatting by some of the growing number of homeles
in the increasing number of empty houses, and occupation of empty
office blocks produced by property speculation.

This refusal to accept arbitrary and unjust government was
part of a wider social attitude at the time, illustrated by the
large number of unofficial strikes (mainly against management
decisions that workers did not like and had not been consulted on),
followed by a campaign against 'In Place of Strife', and the studen
revolt against paternalistic college authorities and social
injustice.

Students' militancy also contributed to the growth of community
action in a secondary way. It was this generation of students
who became employed by the rapidly expanding local government
departments and voluntary organisations, and many took their
beliefs in participation and social justice with them.

CHANGES ON THE LEFT

Many significant changes within the political left also generated
support for greater participation. With the defeat of unilateral
disarmament in the Labour party, and consequent decline of the
Campaign for Nuclear Disarmament and the Committee of 100, many
activists turned to grass-roots activity which had more
immediacy and importance to ordinary working people. Their
organising experience and commitment to direct action provided
a focus and leadership for community action.

The left became further disillusioned with party politics
following the failure of the Labour Government to carry out its
promises. The Labour party itself is a broad coalition. While
the vast majority of members support greater equality of power
and wealth, they disagree fundamentally about how it should be
achieved. One wing believes in government management of economic
growth in a mixed economy to direct increased resources for the
benefit of the less well-off through high public expenditure on
housing, social services and income support. The other believes
in the expropriation of power and wealth through a wealth tax
and nationalisation. The writings of Crosland and Bevan had
clearly articulated the two alternatives, but while in opposition
it had been possible to confuse and blend them. During the
'Thirteen years of Tory misrule' the Labour party became
respectable to the left. However, in government the party showed
no real inclination to challenge the power and wealth of private
enterprise. While it broadly tried to follow the Crosland
strategy, it was unable to do so to any extent because it refused
to take control of the economy, and responded to economic crisis
by cuts in public expenditure. The hopes and aspirations of both
sections of the party were largely dashed. Consequently, the
legislation for social reform (and with it increased state power

and responsibility) was put on the Statute Book without the
necessary resources to enable it to work effectively. Nevertheless,
the 1964-70 Labour government significantly extended the range of
state powers.

The socialist left became involved in alternative forms of
political action. It has always been part of their belief that
those who have power and wealth will not give it up readily.
If a redistribution of it is to take place it cannot be done solely
by a party with a majority in parliament. It requires the active
participation of most of the population committed to fighting
(perhaps physically) for change. Many supporters of this ideology
also believed that the point of taking power is not to hold on to
it themselves, but to give it back to the powerless, those from
whom it was taken in the first place. They are thus committed to
a decentralisation of power and responsibility rather than the
extension of state power and bureaucracy, and put great store on
grass-roots political activity. To them the failure of government
to carry through its programme demonstrated the need for mass
popular support for social change. They saw community action as
contributing to this process, and supported it vigorously.

This contrasted strongly with the approach of the Labour
leadership throughout the Wilson era. His aim to make the Labour
party 'the natural Party of government' was an elitist commitment
to management of the economy, rather than any significant level
of participation.

The consequence of these developments in the Labour party has
been to increase the number of left-wing people involved in
community politics, community action and community work. Many
of these people are outside the Labour party, but many have
remained in it and some have considerable influence in local
Labour parties and as councillors. Thus, some Labour councils
developed a far-reaching commitment to participation at the same
time as other people were working for it outside the political
framework.

These changes in political thinking were not confined to the
left. People of other political persuasions also supported the
need for participation, as shown particularly by the commitment
of the Liberal party to its version of community politics.
Though these political changes provided much of the active
leadership for community action, the pressure for increased
participation was much more widespread. It permeated the
institutions of government.

CHANGES IN THE INSTITUTIONS OF GOVERNMENT

The extension of government power and the challenges to it had
an effect on the ministers, councillors, civil servants and local
government officers who wielded it. Any government depends for
survival on a combination of the consent of the people to be

governed and the use of force (police and prison) against those
who refuse to obey the rules. In our society, with its social
democratic traditions, if people were refusing to be governed
and public opinion was supporting their direct action, government
had to vary its approach. Elected representatives - MPs and
councillors - often reinforced the need for change by supporting
the people with grievances and using their positions to modify
the governmental process.

Thus, national and local government both looked for machinery
to avoid public confrontation. Public relations became established
in local authorities and participation became fashionable. Other
changes reinforced the trend. As state intervention increased,
so the roles of politicians and officials changed. Each election
is fought on only a few issues. As the range and number of
issues on which decisions have to be taken increased, so did the
number which had not been decided by the election. Thus,
politicians could not speak on behalf of their electors to the
same extent. This was compounded by the increasing amount of
time politicians were spending in taking decisions which obviously
reduced their contact with their constituents (or made the lack
of contact more apparent). Further, government became more
concerned with issues and special-needs groups outside the
politicians' normal range of interest. Many politicians were not
willing or capable of changing their role from case-work and the
immediate issues of their own experience to the new demands of
the more powerful and extensive local authorities, such as long-
term planning and the management of a multi-million-pound
building programme. As the inability of politicians to represent
the different sectional interests within their electorate became
more critical, officials had to find out directly what the people
would go along with and what they would object to. They too saw
the value of some form of public participation.

At the same time the number and scope of officials was growing
rapidly and politicians were becoming more dependent on them for
information and recommendations. Politicians found it increasingly
difficult to cope within the limitations of their own experience.
Many realised that they had no check on the advice of officials
and saw public debate before decisions were taken as the only way
of providing it.

Thus, many politicians and officers wanted participation for
different reasons, at the time when a leadership for community
action was being provided by people disillusioned with party
politics; and many ordinary people were reacting against increased
state intervention in their own lives.

OFFICIAL BLESSING FOR PARTICIPATION

Planning was the first area where institutionalised participation
was largely accepted in principle. The Skeffington Report (2)
was not a revolutionary document, but it gave government and

professional blessing to 'public participation'. The planners' concept of participation has permeated the government system in the wake of the growth of planning. In considering the future of the social services, the Seebohm Committee (3) wanted to extend both the voluntary sector and the state role. A few of the former children's and welfare departments and many long-established voluntary organisations encouraged voluntary work to help people in need. Here participation largely meant helping individuals in need, rather than influencing policy, but the people who were motivated to help also believed that the state provision should be extended. They had a detailed working knowledge of the problems, so consequently voluntary organisations put proposals and policies of their own to central and local government.

Further, unless more elderly and handicapped people were to be institutionalised, the fast-disappearing extended family had to be replaced by 'community care'. Partly for these reasons and partly because it was recognised that many social work cases were the symptom of social deprivation or bad policies and plans of other government departments, Seebohm recommended the extension of participation in social services in several ways. These included the development of consumer participation 'the maximum participation of individuals and groups within the community in the planning, organisation and provision of social services', encouragement of volunteers, and help and grant-aid to organisations able to assist with community work.

Seebohm also recognised the inevitable conflict between participants and government agencies. 'Mutual criticism between Local Authorities and voluntary organisations may be essential if the needs of consumers are to be met more effectively and if they are to be protected from the misuse of bureaucratic and professional power.'

Thus, by the end of the 1960s two of the main growth areas in local government had official reports recommending participation. By the early 1970s some politicians and housing managers had begun advocating tenant participation in estate management. They felt the need to 'improve communication' and develop 'a community spirit on estates' and saw tenants' associations and tenant participation as a means to this end. There were many reasons for this development - the big increase in the number of estates, the poor design of many of the estates built with no consideration of tenants' needs or wishes, the consequent vandalism and social problems, the mood of the tenants themselves who were becoming more critical of bad management and maintenance and more willing to stand up for themselves, and the loss of regular contact with tenants after the demise of personal rent collection.

The general climate of opinion permeated all areas of local government - parents were added to school governors and managers, the youth service became more community-based, adult education set out to cater for a wider range of people, and community run pre-school playgroups and adventure playgrounds were established in many areas.

Although these developments were encouraged by official reports and government policy, actual implementation depended upon the willingness of councillors and staff in different local authority departments. Attitudes varied widely, growth was sporadic and there was no previous experience of successful practice to draw on. Nevertheless, by the mid-1970s some departments in many local authorities were trying to develop participation to a greater or lesser extent.

WHO IS PARTICIPATION FOR?

It is obvious from this analysis that pressure for participation came from many diverse sources, but a substantial part of it has come from within government itself. The success of community action and direct action, the need for government to avoid regular confrontation and the political views and needs of politicians and officials have combined to create official support for the idea of participation in local government.

However, this apparent consensus was based on different interests. Their reasons for supporting it varied and were often mutually incompatible. Their view of what it meant differed. These differences led to shifting attitudes as the interests of each group changed in response to more recent trends.

RECENT TRENDS

The popularity of participation as a concept continued until the middle of the 1970s. Since then official attitudes to it have become much more ambivalent or hostile. The change was partly due to the experience of trying actually to develop in practice (which is dealt with in the next section), partly due to the fact that it had become established in a limited way and was thus no longer an issue, and partly due to changes in the main social issues and the way the country is governed.

First, central government partly blamed the failure of the social reforms of the 1960s on the small-mindedness and lack of managerial ability in the local authorities, rather than the limitations of their bureaucratic approach and enabling legislation, and inadequate public expenditure. All government advice to local authorities and all reforms of the institutions of government have since been based on the principles of retaining central government control of the finance and programmes, strengthening corporate management and inter-departmental co-operation in local authorities, making local authorities less local so they can deal with the issues through planning on a large scale, reducing political representation to allow professional management more scope and removing control of services from local government altogether so they can be controlled by professionals as well as managed by them. Government policy to cut public expenditure has also led to increased central control

of the amount local authorities spend and what it goes on; but
although the Conservative government has substantially extended
controls, the process was undoubtedly started much earlier.
These changes have reinforced the bureaucratisation of local
government, but the professional managers hide behind the elected
representatives, protecting themselves from public scrutiny by
blurring the divisions of responsibility. Real participation -
a sharing of power - is a political process. The depoliticisation
of local government has tended to limit public involvement to
providing data for the management process.

Second, official encouragement for participation has continued
to some extent and some new structures for it have been created.
In particular, central government still advises local authorities
to undertake participation in some areas of work, and requires
it in others. While this is partly a reflection of earlier
attitudes, it is also a means of putting pressure on local
councils from below to complement that of the government from
above. Again, the Conservative Government has continued a trend
started by its predecessor.

Third, the continued failure of the government to manage the
economy effectively has replaced the hope and expectancy of
people in the 1960s with a despondency and self-centredness.
If people have no confidence in the institutions of government,
they are not going to waste their time trying to influence it.
Cuts in public expenditure from the mid-1970s onwards have
reinforced this. Given the chance, people demand better services
from government which does cost more. If cuts have to be made,
public demand has to be discouraged.

Thus, the national mood has turned against participation, while
changes in the system of government have discouraged it. At the
same time, the factors which gave rise to it have continued.
Government intervention in society grew further under Labour,
and although the Conservative government has set out to reduce
it, it is highly doubtful that it will succeed to any great
extent. On some issues the government is encouraging participation as an aspect of this policy. Community projects, many of
which were initiated to promote participation when it was
fashionable, also keep the debate alive to some extent.

Within this general context, several specific changes have had
an important influence.

CONTINUED GROWTH OF STATE INTERVENTION

The main factor in the growth of local participation - the
extension of local authority powers and activities - continued
until the defeat of the Labour government in 1979.

Only local government (and to a lesser extent government-
funded housing associations) had the means both of raising finance

and of acquiring land to provide new housing in built-up areas. It is not uncommon for local authorities to own over half the housing in inner-city areas. Comprehensive redevelopment was largely replaced by rehabilitation and housing action areas, partly to avoid breaking up whole communities. The change obviously facilitated participation and the government advised local authorities to involve people in housing action areas.

Government policies to regenerate employment through the inner-cities programme involved local authorities in the direct encouragement of employment for the first time. Planning powers were supplemented with new expenditure and a new branch of local government opened up. Community projects are already challenging these policies and often providing new jobs from their own initiatives.

The inner-cities programme led to new participation machinery being set up in some areas at least, and community groups were encouraged to help it.

LOCAL GOVERNMENT RE-ORGANISATION

The re-organisation of local government which came into effect in 1974 made it even more distant. Powers and responsibilities previously held by cities and town councils were transferred to new county and metropolitan county councils. Planning and some services were thus carried out at a regional level rather than a more local one. The division of responsibilities was confusing to people, not least those trying to operate the system. This was exacerbated by frequent policy and status conflicts between the tiers.

Many new local authorities built up centralised corporate management structures and strongly hierarchical departments. At the same time the level of political representation on district and county councils was effectively decreased. The constituencies of county councillors were much bigger, so they became more out of touch with their constituents, and the number of councillors on the district councils was reduced. These factors have substantially increased the professional and bureaucratic nature of local government and made it much harder for people to relate to.

Realising this, some authorities tried to counter-balance the trend by trying to encourage greater participation. The greater emphasis on planning by the new authorities, coupled with the planning profession's acceptance of participation, has reinforced the trend.

CUTS IN PUBLIC EXPENDITURE

The expansion of local authority services came to a fairly

sudden end in 1975-6. The Labour Government held local authority
spending at roughly the same levels, and the Conservative
government has reduced it. But if a local authority has a large
building programme, it must have made cuts in other services,
even if its expenditure stays the same - its capital expenditure
is paid for by borrowing money and repaying the principle with
interest over 30-60 years.   If it builds the same number of new
houses each year, it has to increase its borrowing (and hence its
repayments) each year to pay for them. It also has to employ more
people to manage the new houses when they are tenanted. Its
expenditure increases although the programme remains the same.
It thus has to cut programmes if it wants its expenditure to
remain constant. The same problem occurs with all aspects of
the capital programme - new schools and nurseries, social service
homes, parks and community centres. So, local authorities were
cutting services for some years before the election of the
Conservative government.

This process has strengthened centralised corporate management
still further. Re-arranging programmes and evaluating their
value for money is part of its role. In this situation community
projects are particularly vulnerable to cuts. Although participation may be of considerable value to the professional managers
of the public services when there are choices to be made, it is
unimportant to them compared with the need to defend their own
organisational and sectional interests against cuts.

Participation is a further embarrassment because it focuses
demand for new initiatives and expenditure on the outstanding
problems.

RE-ORGANISATION OF THE NATIONAL HEALTH SERVICE

The creation of regional and area health authorities to manage
the National Health Service also gave rise to centralised
planning and distant administration of a vital public service.
It was different from local government re-organisation in two
respects. First, the governing committees of the authorities
are not elected by the general public. They are mainly appointed
by local authorities and the government. Second, token
participation was institutionalised through the statutory creation
of community health councils. The community health councils
contained representatives of the local authorities in the area,
but also representatives of local community interests. The role
and importance of CHCs has varied considerably from place to
place. In some areas they have been staid bodies of establishment
councillors and professional voluntary organisations, while in
others they have adopted a much more dynamic approach, using their
resources and position to mobilise community action on a wide
range of health issues.

Again, more bureaucratic and distant public services were
coupled with an official participation structure.

THE GROWTH OF QUANGOS

Another growth area in the management of public services was the creation of quangos - bodies created by parliament to manage specific programmes and based more on the model of a private company than democratic accountability.

The Housing Corporation is probably the most significant quango as far as impact at a local level is concerned; it funds housing associations. Tenant co-operatives and other experimental forms of tenant participation in housing management have been developed by a few housing associations, while others have reproduced the worst aspects of local authority housing management. Some community projects have developed tenant co-operatives, using Housing Corporation funds.

Though the Conservative government promised to cut quangos as part of its attack on bureaucratic waste, it abolished relatively few. Quangos again reflect the increased bureaucratisation of government, accompanied by limited attempts to stimulate forms of participation.

THE EFFECT OF THE CONSERVATIVE GOVERNMENT

The 1970s were characterised by a growth of government responsibilities and organisation which was less and less accountable through political processes. To some extent, participation was seen as a counterbalance to this trend by politicians, officials and the general public. Though the Conservative government has set out to reverse the trend, in many respects it has not done so. It has reduced the powers of local authorities to determine their own expenditure, cut local authority housing programmes much more than those of the Housing Corporation, and established non-elected authorities to manage the docklands and Liverpool inner-city programmes. At the same time, it has extended the rights of council tenants to participation through the Tenants' Charter, increased people's rights to know how local government organises and pays for its services, and encouraged self-help welfare programmes.

While in other areas the government is cutting services and reducing the opportunity of people to object, it still sees some form of participation contributing to its own objectives. But this reinforces the preceding analysis - participation has been supported to various extents for their own purposes by sections of society with differing and often incompatible objectives and beliefs.

The biggest change results from the Conservative public expenditure policies. Cuts in local government services are much more extensive than under the previous government so the factors listed above become much sharper and damaging to participation.

WHAT SHOULD PARTICIPATION MEAN TO COMMUNITY WORKERS?

Government at any level is not a single self-conscious body with a clear sense of direction and purpose. Its powers are limited and within those limitations it tries to manage competing and conflicting interests. But one of those interests is the electorate itself, and the political bodies, pressure groups and community associations that seek to represent and involve it.

Because different national and local governments have encouraged participation to make the process of government easier, we should not conclude that it cannot be used by the community to obtain change desirable to them.

If participation is to be developed as a style of government, we must be clear on what it means. The term is so ambiguous because it is used from a number of different standpoints. In common usage it has a clear and unambiguous meaning - to have a share in decision-making.

Definitions of participation favoured by community workers are of the type 'giving people more control over the events that shape their daily lives' and 'strengthening local democracy'. In A Ladder of Citizen Participation in the U.S.A. Sherry Arnstein (4) defines eight broad levels of participation:

8	Citizen control	
7	Delegated power	Degrees of citizen power
6	Partnership	
5	Placation	
4	Consultation	Degrees of tokenism
3	Informing	
2	Therapy	
1	Manipulation	

She illustrates this:

The fundamental point is that participation without redistribution of power is an empty and frustrating process for the powerless. There is nothing new about that process, since those who have power normally want to hang on to it. Historically it has had to be wrested by the powerless rather than proferred by the powerful.

The same conclusion could be drawn about the exercise of real power in our own society. Thus, although some progress can be made through administrative reform and some groups of power-holders will be prepared to share their power more widely, the development of participation will involve a constant struggle to increase the range of issues on which it is possible and to change the rules by which decisions are taken.

Expressed another way, it means getting as high as possible up Arnstein's ladder on each issue. However, it must also be

recognised that in any society some issues must be decided
nationally or regionally rather than locally and even at the
local level many conflicting factors exist. Thus, the level of
attainment up the ladder will vary from issue to issue, and
several different levels will co-exist in the same locality on
different issues.

Some community workers argue that it is wrong to try and
institutionalise participation machinery in the local authority.
People will be absorbed into a decision-making structure which
acts fundamentally against their interests and which they should
be fighting.

This position is basically untenable, because it misrepresents
both the nature of 'the Council' and the process of social change.

'The Council' is not the single homogeneous body that its
name implies; it consists of councillors and officers, all
separate individuals that interact in particular ways. They
hold different political views, professional opinions and
personal prejudices. They change and they are replaced. Their
responsibilities and powers evolve and change. They will have
different attitudes to participation. Within the limitations
of what they are allowed to do by law, the resources at their
disposal and their vision, they do what they believe is best
for people. In this ever-changing kaleidoscope who can define
what is 'the Council's interest' in any absolute, permanent way?

How can participation be against the interests of people?
It is clearly true that government, big business and the unions
co-operate in the management of our mixed economy; that the
economy is still based on the values and objectives of
capitalism; that the largest companies are multinationals
effectively outside national control; and government programmes
to eliminate poverty and equalise power and wealth were
ineffective even before the Conservatives put them into reverse.
It is equally clearly true that working people are much better
off than a hundred years ago. The improvements have been won
through struggle within the government framework and through
direct action. The Labour party, the unions and pressure groups
have participated in the system, but also campaigned outside it.
The demand for universal suffrage - the first stage of participation - was both an end in itself and the means to an end. The
welfare state, the social wage and other gains have flowed from
it. Irrespective of the choices that may have existed in the
past, people do not have the choice of opting out of government
any more. The role of the state has increased tremendously,
particularly in the last fifteen years and is continuing to
increase. It will interfere in people's lives whether they like
it or not. There is no evidence to suggest that if they don't
participate now they are more likely to overthrow it later.
They may be jolted out of despair and engage in violent anti-
social dissent at some stage, but revolutions do not arise
from the demoralisation of despair, they arise from the self-

confidence of rising expectations and good organisation. They
arise also when the prevailing social order has evolved through
internal conflict and re-organisation and developed to a stage
where it can no longer contain events and demands and has to
give way altogether.

We do not know for certain whether our system is capable of
indefinite reform. Certainly the last revolution in this
country - the transfer of power to the capitalist class - took
place over many years and was embodied in the 1832 Reform Act.
The only way we will find out how far we can go is to keep
pushing. We will not find out by saying every demand is
reformist and therefore not worth pursuing.

Thus we help community groups to advance their own interests.
Participation is the process through which they try and the
greater the opportunity for it the greater the chance of making
improvements in their living conditions.

The process itself is in the main neutral - it is neither
good nor bad, it depends on the use made of it in terms of
both proposals put forward and its effectiveness in giving
people what they want. It is potentially good in the sense
that an extension of democracy is good. In many cases it can
be harmful in that it is set up to meet a particular need by
the local authority and it is incapable of being used by the
community in its own interest. This is not an extension of
local democracy but a device used by the council to collect
information or placate protest without compromising its power
to take decisions. In these cases it should be boycotted -
but this is a tactical decision, not one of principle.

It has been argued that participation is harmful in that it
may divert attention from the key political issues, but there
is no evidence to suggest that people will be more interested
and determined to tackle those issues if they ignore the local
and mundane ones. If anything, the converse is true. When
demands for local improvements are met with the answer 'no
money', the response 'why?' can soon lead to discussion of
national public expenditure policy. Further the experience of
organising a group and the self-confidence it can bring are
useful in wider political fields.

Most importantly the establishment of participation machinery
does not mean people have to use it for everything. They
always have the options of demanding changes in the rules, or
withdrawing. The main challenge of institutionalised
participation to community action is how to develop strategies
and tactics which utilise the official machinery to maximum
effect and at the same time continue to use the alternative
campaigning methods - the media, demonstrations and direct
action. As so many of the factors which affect people are (or
could be) under state control, maximising people's control over
their own lives must still require improvements in the official
participation machinery.

It follows from this analysis that while community workers
and groups should try and extend participation machinery in local
government as much as possible, they should have a clear idea of
their own objectives and ensure that they can be pursued through
the machinery available.

Thus, to develop participation in local government needs an
analysis of the practical attempts to develop it so far.

PARTICIPATION IN LOCAL GOVERNMENT

The problems inherent in participation at local authority level
come from five main sources.

First, the real issue - the extent to which power of decision
is delegated to the participants - is never confronted. Second,
people are not consulted on the issues they want to discuss.
Third, the methods used are not suitable for any meaningful
involvement from the participants' point of view. Fourth, the
organisation and structure of local authorities make it virtually
impossible to develop a coherent approach. Fifth, council and
public have unrealistic expectations of what can be achieved.

WHO HAS THE POWER?

All definitions of participation have one thing in common; they
express (or assume) a relationship between those with the power
to take decisions and those who ought to have a right to
influence them. As politics is about the exercise of power, then
obviously participation is a political activity. This gives
rise to two problems.

First, there has been a shift in power from elected councillors
to full-time paid officers for reasons explained earlier.
However, officers maintain the myth that councillors decide the
policy and they only carry it out. While this is technically
true, most decisions are taken on the basis of officers' reports
where they define the issue and recommend what the decision
should be. Many other decisions are taken in departments as
management decisions but are never reported to committee. Thus
the real methods of decision-making and power relationships are
heavily disguised.

This has the effect of de-politicising discussion, tending to
make the council see participation as a contribution to the
management of its programme by officers. It is very difficult
in this context to isolate the key questions - who defines the
issue, who has the power to decide and on what basis the
decision will be taken.

Second, and following on from the first, issues are presented
on the basis that rational discussion will lead to a consensus

which the council can implement. The very real questions of
conflicting interests and ideologies are lost in the 'professional
judgment' that leads to an 'objective solution'. Of course, if
officers admitted that they made political value judgments, much
of their power would be taken by the councillors. The consequence
is that most of the debate on key issues is reduced to marginal
questions of professional organisation conducted in a jargon
that makes it unintelligible to most people.

As participation is about power and the control of power is
surrounded by mystification, obviously most participation that
the local authority offers of its own volition is tokenism on
Arnstein's ladder.

THE ISSUES ON WHICH THE PUBLIC IS CONSULTED

More attempt has been made to stimulate participation in planning
than in any other local authority activity, but it is the one
to which people are least likely to respond. Most of the
creative energy of councillors and officers in the local authority
goes in devising new policies, programmes and plans and
monitoring existing performance. This is co-ordinated through
the management system described earlier, which thus largely
defines the issues on which consultation is to take place.
Thus, people are rarely consulted on the issues they want to
talk about. Many of these issues are outside local government
control. Of the remainder there is a rough hierarchy of social
need. People will only respond positively to issues at one
level if their needs in respect of the previous levels are more
or less satisfied. The most important need is a good standard
of living accommodation inside the front door - no sharing of
facilities or overcrowding and no repairs needed. These are
followed by a decent environment outside the front door - no
vandalism, well-lit streets and passages, efficient refuse
collection and street cleaning and not too much traffic -
somewhere for the kids to play where an eye can be kept on them,
and somewhere for the older kids to play. All these are very
local issues. They are followed by concern over neighbourhood
amenities - a park, shops, pubs and other recreation. Underpinning it all is a decent wage and the number of hours that
have to be worked to earn it.

Unfortunately, 'participation exercises' are much more likely
to be about county structure plans, so it is not surprising
that people faced with major problems in daily life are not
prepared to tackle issues in such an abstract and long term way.

THE METHODS USED

In the main 'participation exercises' are defined and presented
from the local authority viewpoint; the public response will
be only one factor taken into account; it will be assessed and

assimilated within the council by some filtering process
(usually the officers with responsibility for the report); and
the normal decision-making process (officers' report to a formal
committee) will not be altered. In practice the council is not
offering participation, but a limited form of consultation.
Not surprisingly, there is little public interest in this process.
Even if people were prepared to get involved in such an irrelevant
process, the way issues are presented makes them incomprehensible.

Envisaging the effect of someone else's proposals requires
considerable ability to think conceptually. In practice, only
few people have this ability. As it is one of the factors that
our educational system discriminates in favour of, most people
who have the ability are well-educated and consequently have a
good income and have reached the top end of the hierarchy of
social need referred to earlier. The tendency is thus for the
better-off and more highly educated to participate. This is
reinforced by the level and presentation of background material.
Whereas the authors are used to reading reports and the quality
press, most people read the popular press and little else. The
publicity and background material for the average planning study
has to deal with issues that are not commonly discussed in even
the quality press, and thus use unfamiliar concepts and
vocabulary. Explanations are much more detailed than even a
quality newspaper's in-depth analysis. Maps are used
extensively though they are not understood by most people.

Attempts to persuade planners to present plans in a more
concrete and easily understood way are resisted. If their work
can be readily understood by laymen, they would lose much of
their professional status. If the precise consequences of plans
are made known, those affected adversely will fight them while
others may take little interest.

Further, participation necessitates thinking about and
discussing alternatives, identifying the further information
needed and making choices. The communications skills needed to
involve large numbers of people have not been developed. Our
media - press and TV - are virtually all one-way. Other people
talk or write and we listen or read. We can't ask our own
questions or enter debate, we just have to hope that one of
the 'experts' involved will represent our views. Much of the
media's effort is engaged in the exact opposite of participation -
trying to persuade people to buy something or agree with someone
else's point of view. The main communication skills available
to local authorities through Public Relations Departments are
based on advertising and journalism and are inappropriate for
participation; new methods need to be developed.

Public meetings are used as the main form of participation
but they are inadequate in many respects.

First, it is unreasonable to expect people to come to a
meeting, listen to a proposal or series of options, clarify

any misunderstandings and seek any further information necessary,
assimilate the issues and formulate a clear response all in a
space of two to three hours.

Second, skills of public speaking and debate in a formal
gathering are rare and inexperienced people will fear ridicule
at the hands of the councillors and officers.

Third, the time available does not allow for a reasoned
response - any one speaking for any length of time limits the
number of other people who can speak at a meeting.

Meetings are thus either dominated by a few people who
already understand the issues and have the confidence to argue
their position, or they are negative - objections are stated
but no alternatives are discussed. They will only be useful if
they are the culmination of a consultation process, rather than
the only part of it. There must be adequate opportunity - a
period of several weeks - for issues to be discussed in a
locality through community groups before a reasoned response
is possible.

Councils argue that this causes delay. However, the issues
have been discussed within the council for months or years
before any consultation is organised. They are really saying
that they are not prepared to alter their own work to allow a
realistic chance for consultation to be effective, and they
are not prepared to allow public discussion on the issue as
it evolves; in particular, giving the public a chance to comment
on the definition of the issue.

The type of participation usually offered by local authorities
is thus poorly attended and reinforces social inequality - some
of the 'haves' participate and influence change in ways
desirable to them, whereas the 'have nots' are effectively
prevented from participating.

The usual response of the council members, particularly of
planners, is to blame apathy rather than their own choice and
presentation of issues, so they reduce any opportunity for
participation by replacing it with questionnaires and surveys.
It is ideal from their point of view - they define the questions,
everybody answers and no one gets a chance to say that there are
other solutions or the wrong questions have been asked. The
political process is reduced to the collection of management
information and the opportunity for new ideas and proposals
to emerge and evolve in discussion is lost.

The purpose of participation in council decision-making is
supposed to allow public discussion on issues before decisions
are taken. In practice, the way it is usually organised defeats
the objective because those who may participate are effectively
prevented from doing so.

THE ORGANISATION AND STRUCTURE OF LOCAL AUTHORITIES

Although substantial changes have taken place in the organisation
and structure of local authorities over the last fifteen years,
little consideration has been given to changes needed if
participation is to be extended.

The roles of councillors and officers and the way in which
they relate to one another through committees and departments
can militate against participation. First, the councillors'
role may be directly threatened. They were elected on a party
platform and believe they have a mandate for their policy and
programme. To them the election is the part of the participation
process which circumscribes the rest. They automatically reject
public proposals which conflict with the party policy. But
while they have justification for this, councillors also have
the power to take decisions on behalf of the electorate on all
matters. Participation often challenges this political role.

The councillor's role is also threatened by the increasing
power of officers. If community projects set up to facilitate
participation ignore or undermine councillors, and at the same
time develop close working relationships with officers on
particular issues that affect their ward, the councillors will
feel doubly threatened. If the community project/group provides
an advice service too, the councillor may feel another function
has been usurped. Participation and community work must
establish a proper working relationship with the elected
representatives.

Apart from these problems, councillors are also different
as individuals. They become councillors because they are
motivated by the status or power entailed, or they want to
take decisions and change things, or help people, or be popular
and famous. They don't like criticism (who does?) especially
if they have to seek re-election. They spend their time as
councillors on different things, they have different ambitions
and they have different attitudes to their role. Some aspire
to power and believe they were elected to govern. Others
believe they are there to represent their electorate and go to
great lengths to find out their views. Some see themselves
as advocates against the full-time bureaucrats. Others are
case workers, helping individuals get a better deal. Some will
welcome more participation, and some will oppose it. Those in
each camp will have a different view of what it means. Thus,
it is unlikely that there will be a clear political definition
of participation.

Second, the principal officers in departments have a
substantial degree of power. Most issues decided by the council
will be identified and brought up by the officers rather than
the councillors. The officers have power of deciding what is
discussed and their reports provide the background information
and recommendations on which the decisions are based. They can

sometimes prevent the councillors' policies being carried out.
They may convince the council the policy is wrong or deliberately
not carry it out when they disagree with it, or not grasp the
reason for a policy or have no sympathy with it and thus do an
inadequate job although doing their best, or feel that other
policies are more important and so not allocate resources. Thus
officers too have a power which is threatened by public participation as it provides another way for issues to be brought to
councillors' attention. It also disrupts their home life –
evening meetings may be the only opportunity for attendance by
councillors and residents, but for officers it is an extension
of work.

Officers too are all different. Though they are employed to
be experts, they disagree as much as politicians – not
surprisingly, because they are arguing about the same issues.
Which issues are important and what should be done about them
have to be decided on assumptions and prejudices just the same.
There are very few issues confronted by a local authority to
which there is only one correct answer, and there is no
objective way of determining priorities. They are determined
by value systems and officers have them the same as everybody
else. Thus, they too have different attitudes to participation.

Third, there is the problem of professionalism; that because
Sir Joseph Bloggs is a professionally qualified architect, he
knows how a house should be designed better than the people
who will live in it. Most local authority departments are
staffed with professionals of one sort or another. The more
matters become 'professional' matters (i.e. not subject to
public debate or democratic control) the less participation
there will be. It is a means of defining a sphere of influence
which cannot be penetrated by outsiders – of increasing the
power of the professional. Professional disagreement within a
department is constrained by the very hierarchical management
structure. Professionalism and hierarchical management combine
to create some very powerful officers. If there was always
professional unanimity and no public criticism of the results,
this might be acceptable; however, many of the problems of
modern society are the result of a previous professional
judgment. The growth of professionalism is a major threat to
participation as well as democratic control by elected
representatives.

Fourth, the committee system itself creates problems.
Although councillors are elected on a geographical basis (i.e.
to represent the electors of a ward) most council decisions are
taken by a committee with a particular responsibility (e.g.
housing, planning) rather than the full council. Thus, if
they are not members of the appropriate committee, councillors
have no vote on an important issue which affects their ward.
They may not even be present to put the case, as many councils
have no arrangements to ensure that councillors know the items
on the agendas of the committees of which they are not members.

As outsiders to the committee they may not be made welcome
anyway. In addition, the power of the council may be held by
a small clique, or the councillors for the affected ward may
be more interested in case work than the issue under discussion.
They may even be members of a different political party to that
in control of the council. All these factors mean that
councillors are frequently unable to represent their constituents
on important issues decided by the council, so groups develop
alternative forms of representation. Further, officers cannot
rely on councillors putting forward the view of the residents
in their ward, so they need to build up an alternative
intelligence system. Both these factors contribute to the
demand for participation, but both further undermine the role
of the councillor.

Fifth, the committees themselves are not a suitable forum
for real debate. They are too large to be able to discuss
issues thoroughly, and thrash out a policy on every issue. The
longer the agenda for each meeting, the less each item is
discussed. While two or three issues may be discussed in depth,
the remainder are dealt with very quickly. Thus, most
recommendations in the officers' report are adopted, often
without any discussion at all. Sub-committees and working
parties are the forum in which policy is evolved and many
important decisions can be taken there. If there are few of
them it means either that there is little innovation going on
under the direction of the councillors, or it is being directed
informally by a very small group or the committee chairmen only.
If there is not an extensive system of sub-committees and
working parties with substantial back-bench councillor membership
then it is unlikely that back-bench councillors have any real
influence in the council.

Sixth, officers do not have equal power. The structure of
each department is very hierarchical. Technically all the
power is concentrated in the hands of the head of department -
the chief officer. All reports from his department go to
committee in his name and he speaks to them there. He also has
the power to appoint most of the staff of his department, thus
the style and policy of the department largely depend on him.
His authority may be delegated in a planned way as part of his
management technique or he may not exercise effective control.
If the department is involved in many issues, the chief officer
cannot deal with them all personally, and if he is weak the
effective responsibility will be held by one or more principal
officers in the department. This markedly affects participation
in the department's work - it is pointless trying to convince
particular officers of a point of view if they do not have any
influence or the delegated authority to act on it.   Further,
a department in which authority is centralised and controlled
hierarchically is unlikely to be responsive to pressure from
outsiders (i.e. the public) expressing views on its policies.

Seventh, the departments do not have equal power. There is

increasing emphasis in local authorities on 'corporate management'.
Basically, it ensures that departments co-operate with one
another and agree on common policies so the council functions as
a whole rather than a collection of individual departments all
pursuing different and maybe conflicting policies. They also
try and see the council as a whole, as the public see it. Some
local authorities have very centralised corporate management
structures with formal officers' working parties reporting to the
director's board (which consists only of the chief executive and
heads of the most important departments). Every major report to
any committee has to be approved by the director's board first.
Other councils still have virtually no corporate approach and
each department ploughs its own furrow. In some authorities,
only the chief officers are involved in inter-departmental
meetings, and in others a large number of officers regularly
meet their counterparts in other departments. In highly
centralised councils individual departments may have little
freedom of action, particularly if their own chief officer is
weak or not respected by the others. A few officers may
effectively control the general policy of the council through
a corporate plan, a director's board and/or control of budget
making. If the director's board is very powerful it will
function as a united body. The bargaining and compromise
necessary to maintain this unity will involve all members in
the sacrifice of many policies and projects to strengthen their
hand on issues they feel to be more important. Proposals that
originate outside the main departments, especially public
proposals, are particularly vulnerable in these circumstances.

Local authorities have been consistently advised by the
government to adopt a corporate planning approach in the
interests of efficiency. Cuts in spending have reinforced this
process. The council needs a way of evaluating its priorities
and taking decisions that consider all its policies and services
together. The centralisation of decision-making inherent in
corporate management grew rapidly throughout the 1970s.

On the other hand, there are different problems if there is
no machinery for adopting an overall approach. The public is
being misled if the planning department is encouraging participation but hasn't got the muscle to ensure its plans are carried
out by the other committees and departments.

The extent and nature of corporate management obviously
affects the ability of the council to cope with participation
because it determines where the real power in the council lies.
A strong corporate management structure can only work if power
at the political level is also highly centralised, so back-bench
councillors are further excluded from influence.

Lastly, secrecy makes participation impossible. Information
required to make valid judgments is often confidential. There
is no reason why councils cannot be more open. The experience
of those with a well-established open government policy is clearly

that the forecasts of doom from those resisting change are ill-founded. The only reason for retaining secrecy is to avoid public knowledge and scrutiny of what's going on. While those who maintain secrecy may well have a reason - to avoid having to explain or defend what they are doing - they cannot possibly hold that it is in the public interest.

UNREALISTIC EXPECTATIONS

Council and public each have unrealistic expectations of the other's attitudes and responsiveness to participation.

First, and most importantly, the general experience and expectations of most people militate against participation and acceptance of responsibility. Half the population have not got control of their own living conditions, they are tenants. The family structure, school and job all socialise an acceptance of authority in many subtle ways. To challenge it may mean eviction, the sack, a beating or other punishment. Even politics is not a participatory process. People usually have the choice between two or three candidates who are standing on party platforms. They have no say in the selection of candidates, nor can they accept some parts of the platform but not others. The choice is often between the lesser of two evils.

Against this background - virtually the whole of people's lifelong experience - comes a planner (or a community worker), who tells them they have the right to control their own lives, without recognising that the skills, experience and self-confidence needed for participation on the council's terms are not possessed by most people.

In so far as the public takes any notice of the council, most people are concerned about the efficient delivery of essential and basic services and improvements to their own immediate surroundings. Residents who can't get the council to provide decent roads and pavements, or repair council housing, are not going to take seriously an invitation to participate in preparing a plan. Planning by its nature is concerned with the future. But the council is going to be judged on past and present performance. Even if there are major differences in attitudes to participation between the different departments, the public won't differentiate between them. In fact, the council would be judged on all aspects of its relations with the public, not just those it chooses to present. If the council is held in low esteem, people will obviously believe that participation is futile. This is rarely recognised by politicians or officers. People don't differentiate between individual departments, they judge the council as a whole. If they see the housing maintenance and refuse collection every week and planning officials once during the life of a plan, then their view of the council will be based on the former.

Apart from the reasons outlined above - the wrong issues
presented in the wrong way - people often believe that participation will have no effect. In some ways they are right. The
powers of local government are defined by central government.
Whereas individuals can do anything as long as there is no law
against it, local authorities can only do those things that the
law specifically allows. Many things that affect the locality
are outside the council's control. Most important, the
government decides how much the council can spend and many other
council decisions require the specific approval of a central
government department. The one limited loophole in this
constraint is rarely used to the maximum. Under Section 137 of
the 1972 Local Government Act, local authorities can spend up
to a 2p rate on anything they consider to be in the interests
of the borough or a section of it.

There is an assumption amongst people who are interested in
politics (in any sense, including local participation) that
everyone should be interested in it because it affects them.
This is partly due to the nature of politics and partly because
everyone believes that the things important to them are
important to everyone else. However, the practical experience
of community workers and the evidence of many research projects,
is that people are not apathetic so much as cynical or bewildered.
However, there are many important issues that are decided by the
local council, and as we have seen earlier, the powers and
responsibilities of local authorities have grown considerably
in the last fifteen years. Many people are not aware of the
powers and duties of the local authority and it is frequently
judged on outdated criteria.

These factors - the constraints on local authority power and
the time lag in the public's knowledge of local authority powers -
create substantial public ambivalence to local authorities. It
is reinforced by the council's attempt at involving people.
They bring local issues and the powers of the council to the
public attention, yet they can alienate as much interest as they
create. Genuine participation involves the redistribution of
power in the locality. In practice the council usually envisages
something different - two-way communication or consultation.
The power to take decisions is not shared. As this obviously
is not participation in the commonly understood meaning of the
term, public cynicism is increased.

Surprisingly, many people accept the invitation to participation at face value. They often think it means that they
personally will get their own way. Paradoxically, the more
people participate the less likely it is that any one person
will do so. In fact, the local authority usually means that
people can participate as long as they agree with their
definition of the problem, and major aspects of the proposed
solution.

When all these factors are taken into account, the very

limited response to official 'participation exercises' appears
better than can be reasonably expected.

THE BASIS OF A MODEL FOR PARTICIPATION

As shown in the earlier section on recent trends, it is likely
that some attempt will continue to be made by national and
local government to develop participation in a limited way.
Further, community workers have a duty to advance it to enable
the groups they work with to have more influence over the
policies and events that affect them. If there is no support
for any form of open government and participation within the
local authority, obviously a campaign needs to be mounted to
achieve it. Assuming that the local authority concerned has
accepted a commitment to some level of participation, the
remainder of this article sets out the basis for developing a
participatory approach as a policy and style of government in
the light of the preceding analysis.

REALISTIC EXPECTATIONS

It is imporant that any attempt to develop participation starts
from a realistic assessment of the situation.

     Local authorities are considerably constrained by the higher
tiers of government and by economic and social forces that
the government does not control. Thus, participation at a
local level must have clear and limited objectives based on the
nevertheless considerable powers and resources that councils
have and may or may not use.

     We have seen earlier that local authorities are not structure-
less monoliths. Councillors and officers each have different
views and roles, operate within a complex framework, and have
a limited accountability to their electorate. The interaction
of these different factors will probably mean that the attitudes
to participation will vary from committee to committee and
department to department in the same local authorities. These
inconsistencies will create frustration in each area but they
also provide an opportunity for exploitation by the local
community. There will also be wide differences in policy and
attitude from one local authority to another.

     In this situation, participation will be offered by each
council on some issues, on some it will respond to public demand
and on some the community has no choice but to try and force
the council's hand or wrest away its power to decide.

     Any strategy for increasing participation must thus concen-
trate on, first, decentralising power so issues can be decided
at the most local level possible; second, on identifying
precisely who has what power and increasing their responsiveness,

sensitivity and accountability to those over whom they have the
power; third, to ensure that each power is shared as widely as
possible; and fourth, by developing people's knowledge and skills
so they can exercise power more effectively.

The strategy must also be based on the clear recognition that
many of the people who have power at present will resist losing
it, or being held more accountable.

THE BASIC PRINCIPLES

If participation is to be institutionalised to any great extent
within a particular council, it must approve a number of
principles. They are:

1 People have a right directly to influence or control their
   own environment and local government is one of the institutions through which that right is exercised. The council
   therefore has a responsibility actively to promote open
   government; informing the public of what it is doing, and
   why. Public access to information must be guaranteed and
   secrecy avoided if at all possible. As the size of wards
   increase and local government becomes more complex, the
   council and individual councillors need to ascertain the
   views from people themselves rather than assume that because
   councillors have been elected they automatically represent
   the electorate's views on everything.

2 One of the reasons why there is so little interest or
   involvement in local government is the council's own
   structure and machinery. It evolved over many years, and
   apart from the last fifteen years, public involvement has
   been positively discouraged, except at election time. It
   is complex and confusing to most people. The most recent
   changes of bureaucratisation, centralisation and corporate
   management have restricted the role of councillors and made
   participation harder still. Further, proposals are usually
   described in a technical jargon, incomprehensible to everyone
   except those of the same professional education. To enable
   public involvement in its affairs, the council needs to
   change its own practices and machinery. These changes must
   be carried out from the point of view of the participants
   and for their benefit rather than that of the council.

3 Many councillors and officers assume that if the council
   wishes to consult people, virtually everybody concerned
   should respond. This ignores people's other commitments,
   their right to be interested in other issues, public
   cynicism about the council's sincerity bred by years of
   secrecy, followed more recently by sporadic attempts at
   'participation' (during which the public view was perhaps
   ignored anyway), and the experience, self-confidence and
   length of time needed to formulate a view and articulate it.

It is unrealistic to expect large-scale participation.
However, everyone has equal rights so the participation
machinery must provide an equal opportunity for everyone.
People will only respond on issues of concern to them, and
only when the council's good faith has been well established
and the consultation machinery specifically designed to enable
and encourage them to play a part.

4   The issues on which the council wishes to consult are usually
different from those which the community feels to be
important and wants to discuss. More attempt has been made
to involve people in the planning field than any other.
However, most people are concerned with more immediate issues.
They are unlikely to become interested in long-term planning
issues until these more immediate problems are resolved.
Participation machinery needs to relate to all areas of the
council's work (not just planning). Crucially, it must also
provide for people to raise issues they feel are important
and have those issues dealt with.

5   Frequently the perception of a problem by people affected by
it is different from that of the council. Obviously, the
council's solution will be inappropriate if it is not
tackling the right problem. Thus, participation must involve
the definition of the issue as well as possible solutions.
Participation is thus a continuous process. Adequate time
must be allowed for community groups to digest and respond
to issues.

6   Accurate terminology should be used. 'Participation' embraces
many different levels of involvement (e.g. Arnstein's ladder
lists eight). Apart from the provision of basic information
which is an essential base for all levels of participation,
there are four general, separate arrangements embodied in
the term: consultation, where the council identifies an
issue and seeks public response; direct involvement or power
sharing, where community representatives are full members
of the decision making body; community action, where groups
put forward their own demands; and community self-management,
where groups have control of facilities or resources.

7   Each level of participation necessitates different machinery
which must be integrated into the council's decision-making
structure. It is pointless involving people if their views
are then filtered and processed. People must know what is
being said on their behalf and have the opportunity to put
their own case if their views are being ignored or mis-
represented.

8   Participation will thus only become effective if it becomes
a style of government - an attitude of mind - of the
council. It is not something that can be turned on and
off like a tap, it must be based on strong independent
community organisations that are able to represent local

views to the council and campaign in the interests of their area where necessary. The council cannot synthesise the views of all the residents separately, and the extent to which views change in the light of discussion and information is part of the political process. Groups which enable a local view to evolve or to be thrashed out are essential to the participatory process. However, there is a lack of experience of participation in community affairs, particularly in the worst off section of the community. Resources to organise groups are also lacking. The council must therefore promote the formation and development of strong independent community groups and ensure that the necessary resources of information, advice, technical support and funds are provided.

9   In many areas there are irreconcilable differences of interest between different sections of the population. In others there are very divergent views on priorities. There are also cultural and social factors which affect the level of involvement in a group - people will only join it if they support what it is doing and if they feel at home in the company of the other members. In these areas a number of different groups should articulate the different interests rather than one group try to represent the interest of the area as a whole. These groups will have different structures and degrees of formality depending on the experience of the people involved and the issues being dealt with.

10 Participation machinery could be dominated by the educated and articulate, who already know how to play the system, and use this additional machinery to their further advantage. Those already left out are unable to use the new machinery to campaign for the various forms of urban and social deprivation to be rectified. Support for community activity should therefore include the same degree of positive discrimination in favour of the disenfranchised and disadvantaged as other aspects of public authority programmes.

11 The council should delegate the operation and control of community services that affect particular areas to a community group rather than run them itself. This is partly because the local community can identify and meet its needs more effectively than the council, and partly because the experience gained by a community group in running a project will enable it to organise more effectively on other issues.

12 Participation is part of the political process. It is therefore essential to increase control of the council by the politicians, and strengthen the role of the ward councillors (however terrifying that might be in the case of some sitting tenants!). This involves a decentralised power structure and the recognition and containment of the role of officers. The interests of councillors and officers are different and participation machinery must involve both

of them at once with community groups to avoid the officers playing the groups and councillors off one against the other.

BRINGING PARTICIPATION ABOUT

Having adopted the basic principles, the council must adopt a systematic programme of work to make them a reality. In practice the general policy will still be interpreted in different ways by different people. A separate decision will be taken on each issue in an ad hoc way on whether and how the council encourages public involvement. The factors influencing this decision are the inter-action of established policy and precedent (has the council any rules governing the situation?), personal attitudes of the people taking the decision (how much or how little do they want to do? are they already convinced of the final decision?), and known public opinion and level of organisation (what can they get away with?).

If there is no precedent and the people affected by the issue do not actually know that it is being considered, public involvement will only occur if someone within the council argues that it should. Thus the council must employ its own staff because:

1 Only council officers have the right to present reports to committee and speak to them.

2 Given the in-fighting within departments and in officers' working parties, the case for public involvement needs putting at that level. This includes arguing for more effective forms of participation and funding for community projects.

3 Proposals for altering the style of work or objectives of council departments will be more effective as they will be based on a practical working knowledge of the current situation and its inadequacies.

4 Access to information is easier - on a formal level, officers have the right of access, and on an informal level they find out what's going on through their everyday working situation. Thus a council employee is more likely to find the right question to ask; know who to ask for the answer; receive the answer and, most importantly, find out before the decisions are all cut and dried.

5 It is easier to establish working relationships with other officers than for an outsider to do it. Council officers are more likely to be asked for advice on how to involve the public and can be less ignored when they intervene in an issue or advise a particular course of action.

It is also important as a matter of principle to get the
council to back its commitment to participation by putting
people on its payroll. They are a daily proof to other officers
that the council have committed the time and resources to
participation, and expect it to be reflected in everyone's work.

There is a danger that a local authority will fund voluntary
groups to promote participation, and see that as discharging its
commitment. In practice this is a way of avoiding the main
issue - how to change the way in which the council works on a
day-to-day basis.

Without the constant pressure from within for reform, the
demands from the community can be pushed aside. Thus the council
must define the responsibility for developing participation as
the jobs of specific officers.

Further, it is important that they are the primary or sole
part of the job for several reasons. The work requires
particular skills - particularly being able to put oneself in
the position of the affected community and identify what should
be done from their point of view. On many occasions pressure
of work means something must be neglected - if the participation
work is subsidiary it is that which will be left. There will
often be a conflict of interest between some sections of the
council who want to push through particular proposals and the
right of the public to be involved - a person who is more
concerned with the mainstream work of his department is less
likely to stand up to the department in the interest of public
involvement. Most importantly, it increases the chance of the
person appointed to the job in the first place having the
ability and commitment to do it effectively.

THE DUAL APPROACH

While it is necessary to have people working for the local
authority to develop participation machinery, there will
obviously be some restraints on their activity. It is therefore
also essential to encourage the development of strong independent
community organisations with their own resources and staffing
to develop their own proposals and campaigns for increased
participation.

This dual approach - pressure from both inside and outside
the council for change - has a much better chance of success
than either without the other.

THE ROLE OF THE COMMUNITY WORKER

The preceding analysis presumes a commitment to participation
on the part of the local authority. Community work has a role
in both bringing that commitment about, and establishing the

organisation to implement it. It is an integral part of the
model. It should 'encourage greater democratic control of
policies and services for which groups can fight through public
participation and community action'. (5)

However, the contribution of community work to the extension
of participation has been severely limited, partly due to the
influence of the employing agency. Even where the worker has
an apparently open-ended brief his work is influenced in subtle
ways.

Training and employment situations for community work in
social welfare have not absorbed the role of promoting participation as a means of extending the influence of community groups.

First, the employing agency may colour the community worker's
perception of issues. It can do this in several ways: by
recruiting someone who shares its values and its partisan view
of issues and problems; by specifically limiting or directing
the programme of work; by the type of information, resources and
support services provided; by the expectations of other workers
in the agency and by the results they expect. Thus the community
worker employed by the social services area team might work on
a particular estate because the team has a lot of referrals
from there; might form an under-fives group or a pensioners'
group because that is the area of responsibility of his agency
rather than form a tenants' association to tackle more pressing
social issues (e.g. the repairs service) caused by other
agencies; or develop an adventure playground or youth club
rather than challenge the building design and lettings policy
of the council which concentrates so many kids on an unsuitable
estate. In this way the community worker can actually divert
attention from the most pressing issues.

Second, the self-help tradition of community work encourages
the workers to throw the community back on its own limited
resources. Presumably the worker is present because the
particular community is 'deprived'. By this we mean it is
basically deprived of appropriate public expenditure and private
investment to provide proper living conditions, welfare services
and well-paid jobs. But these key resources are controlled
outside the neighbourhood. The community worker who encourages
people to expect solutions to their problems through their own
actions within the neighbourhood without encouraging them to
look at the external forces which also affect them, is doing
them a disservice. The social inequalities are actually being
reinforced by the community worker.

Third, although community workers are supposed to identify
with and relate to the deprived working class, they are mainly
well-educated middle-class people themselves. They have been
socialised by an elitist educational system to accept at least
some of the values of the managerial elite in local authorities.
Some even want to become part of the same elite by seeking

professional status for community work. There is an inevitable
tendency for community workers to encourage groups to play by
the rules - rules basically designed by people with power to
ensure that their power is not eroded. The rules must also be
challenged if the interests of the deprived sections of our
community are to be advanced.

If we are to be true to basic community work values, we must
develop a set of objectives and style of work to avoid these
traps. There are two key necessities.

First, identify the factors that affect the particular
community. Who controls them? How can their decisions be
questioned or challenged? What plans have they for the future?
How can those plans be influenced? Community workers should
know the answers to all these questions and have an intelligence
network that gives advance notice of potential changes. All
too often they do not, they are in the same position as the
community they are supposed to be helping. They have to react
to someone else's initiative.

Community workers must thus argue for the freedom of action
to work on what their community believes is important, and the
information, resources and support structures to be able to
work on the external factors that affect the neighbourhood as
well as the people within it. In so far as the local authority
affects the neighbourhood - both in terms of the action it takes
and the actions it could take but does not - the community
worker must understand its powers, what it is doing and why,
and how the community can influence or change it. If their
working situation also militates against this approach (e.g. if
they are at the bottom of the social services departmental
hierarchy in an area team office and get no information on the
work of other departments in their neighbourhood), then either
the agency or the employment situation should be altered. If
the council is secretive about its plans and policies, and the
basis on which it arrived at them, and if there is no opportunity
for public questioning and debate, then community workers cannot
do their job.

Thus, second, we need to argue and campaign for open government
and public participation as a necessary precursor to effective
community work. This means helping groups argue and campaign
for improvements in the council's flow of information to the
community, and opportunities for involvement. However, while
people can be motivated around particular and specific issues
which directly affect them, it is much more difficult to get
them worked up on the actual machinery of government. The
federations of groups that cover the whole borough or city may
make up these issues, but it is important that community
workers themselves confront the issues and make proposals of
their own either to the federal groups for endorsement and
action, or direct to their local authority. Without doing this,
community workers would be effectively hamstrung, and may in
fact increase the powerlessness of their community.

THE DEMANDS TO MAKE

The public expenditure situation obviously has a crucial bearing on the nature and timing of demands. In all but a very few areas it would be unrealistic to campaign for additional funds until central government channels more money into local authorities. However, community workers in particular areas may feel that they would be much more effective if they were organised in a different way with different objectives. More participation can be brought about in many areas by changing the methods of working rather than the amount of work (and hence cost). Many of the attempts by councils to develop participation have also not made the best use of money - expenditure on printing vast planning studies, glossy presentations, exhibitions and public relations, could have been used more effectively on community development. Thus, some demands could be made immediately.

Although many councils will be afraid of participation generating demands they cannot meet, some will welcome it as an additional weapon in the campaign against government's public expenditure cuts. Most people who share community work values will look forward to a change in national policy and an increase in local authority spending. If and when that happens community workers ought to have clear proposals worked out based on an analysis of what happened in the 1970s.

The precise nature of these proposals will depend on the individual circumstances of the local authority - the level of support or opposition from influential councillors or officers, what exists already, local experience and prejudices and the extent of support amongst community groups, back-bench councillors, the official opposition and the local political parties.

As we have seen, participation is essentially a political process, and it will not survive for long without support amongst councillors. It may be a lengthy task to win that support, but it is necessary and may include persuading councillors to accept any changes entailed in their own role. Where demands are made which involve the appointment of staff to the local authority, it is essential to define the job and the type of person necessary to do it, accurately. In particular, it must be clear that the job is to increase the direct contact between councillors and council staff and community groups interested in their work, rather than act as a channel of communication or buffer between them.

It is even more essential to ensure that the selection committee that makes the appointment is sympathetic to the objectives of the job. It may be necessary for community workers or community groups to seek representation on the selection committee, or even make the appointment on behalf of the council.

It may also be desirable to establish a permanent support group, advisory committee or management committee for particular posts.

Where demands are made for funds for projects to be independent of the council, the extent of the project's freedom of action must be defined at the outset, otherwise it will spend most of its time justifying itself against constant criticism, or it will be so cautious as to be ineffective.

The main demands should be:

1   Adoption of the basic principles outlined earlier (see pp.27-30).
2   A set of rules and procedures governing access to and distribution of information to community groups and the general public.
3   A committee of the council to be responsible for community development. This could be a special committee or sub-committee which could devote a lot of time to issues, or the Policy and Resources committee which is able to take an overview and give directions to the other committees.
4   A community development team located in the chief executive's department (or equivalent) of the council charged with:
    (a)   translating the 12 principles into specific policies and procedures for adoption by all the council's committees and departments;
    (b)   constantly reviewing progress of implementation of policies and procedures and recommending improvements;
    (c)   ensuring access to information for community groups. This will involve both anticipating information that would be useful to groups and providing it for them, and also ensuring the groups' own information requests are met;
    (d)   advising community groups and workers on how the council actually works and how they can best influence it;
    (e)   extending the community development programme particularly through facilitating or initiating new projects under community control.
    The team must have direct access to committees of the council (particularly the one with community development responsibility), individual councillors, the chief executive, any corporate management structure and each department.
5   Community liaison officers appointed to the central team and seconded to each of the main departments charged with enabling the community to participate more effectively in decision making in that area of the council's work through information and advice to community groups and advice and training on public involvement for the staff in the department.
6   Properly staffed and equipped neighbourhood projects where the project is controlled by the people in the neighbourbood rather than any council department (or an outside voluntary organisation).
7   A means for community groups to get together to share their own experiences and develop policies and proposals of their

own. This may be through a single co-ordinating committee
or resource centre or through a number of federations (e.g.
a tenants' federation, a council for voluntary service or
a play association). These agencies will also need resources,
particularly staff of their own.

8 Resources for a community workers group, particularly for
development of in-service training and research to enable
workers to identify and understand the influences on their
neighbourhoods.

CONCLUSION

In terms of the increasing open government and public participation in local government decision-making, the 1970s were a
decade of missed opportunity for community work. Some progress
was made as reflected in the following case studies, but much
of that was initiated by radical councillors or community
activists. Full-time community workers took the jobs created,
and those created by the management of the welfare services,
but did little to advance the frontiers of participation
themselves. Hopefully, the lesson will be learned so that if
and when another opportunity arises it will be taken.

Nevertheless, the experience gained and the analysis put
forward in this article should be useful to everyone trying to
improve local democracy - councillors, community workers and
community activists - in future.

NOTES

1 John Benington, Local Government Becomes Big Business, in
'Coventry Community Development Project', Final Report,
part 2: 'Background Working Papers' (obtainable from West
End Resource Centre, 85, Adelaide Terrace, Benwell, Newcastle-
upon-Tyne 4).

2 Committee on Public Participation in Planning, 'Public
Participation in Planning' (Skeffington Report), HMSO, 1969.

3 Committee on Local Authority and Allied Personal Social
Services, 'Report' (Seebohm Report), Chapter 16: The
Community, Cmnd 3703, HMSO, 1968.

4 Sherry Arnstein, A Ladder of Citizen Participation in the
U.S.A., 'Journal of the American Institute of Planners',
35(4), 1969, pp.216-24.

5 Extract from the definition of community work on the
recruiting leaflet of the Association of Community Workers
(c/o Community Centre, Colombo Street, London, S.E.1).

2 Public participation in Islington — a case study

Edited and compiled by Leo Smith, based on contributions and comments from the following people who, whilst not necessarily agreeing with all aspects of the case study, agree in general with its description and analysis:

Sue Einhorn, Nadine Finch, Bob Gilbert,
Ann Holmes, Chris Holmes, Emily Hope, Simon Kaplinski,
Martin Lipson, Gill Martin, Mick Mulloy,
Carlos Ordonez, James Pitt, Margaret Pitt, Jim Pollard,
Anne Power, Rosalind Ruck, Bryan Symons, Helen Ward,
John Ward and Bob Williams.

INTRODUCTION

By the mid-1970s the London Borough of Islington had done more than any other local council to encourage and support community groups and develop participation in council decision-making. Much of the initiative for this achievement came from councillors themselves. They created the opportunities and made available the funding for the work to be undertaken.

The more significant factors included:
1 The establishment of a council committee specifically to promote public participation in *all* areas of the council's work.
2 Paid staff - the Participation Office - to carry out the committee's work: encouraging the formation and development of community groups and recommending changes in council policy and procedures to enable groups to participate more effectively in decision-making.
3 A systematic attempt to minimise secrecy in decision-making and actively provide information to groups. The decisions taken over a number of years were drawn together as a council 'code of practice on open Government and public participation ' - a sort of local Freedom of Information Act.
4 Grants to community controlled neighbourhood projects with the primary objective of promoting participation in local affairs and council decision-making.
5 Encouraging all groups to comment on council policies and services (including providing grants for running costs and community newspapers).
6 Developing local control of some services by funding community groups to run them.
7 Employment of Liaison Officers and community workers in council departments to facilitate participation.

At the beginning of 1979-80 the council's budget was running at an annual level of £1.8 million in grants to community groups

and voluntary organisations (including about 70 people who could
be described as full-time community workers); and about 15 people
were employed by the council itself to encourage, support
and/or liaise with community groups and voluntary organisations.
As this included no provision for youth work or other Education
Department activities (ILEA is the education authority for all
inner-London boroughs) and the borough is fairly small (only
170,000 total population) it represented a substantial attempt
to involve the community in an area with little previous record
of community activity.

However, by the end of the decade the energy and vision which
initiated community development in the early 1970s had largely
disappeared, and during 1979-80 a large part of the money and
resources that were being put into it was cut.

This case study describes and analyses the origins, development
and ensuing decline of the process - the roles and work of
councillors, officials, community workers and groups. Although
many of the factors inter-connect, the study is written in
specific sections for ease of presentation. Further, the
development of participation established a momentum of its own
so it was still continuing as the forces which limited its
growth and eventually defeated it were themselves growing.
These forces are described in the later parts of the study. It
concentrates on those areas where Islington was unusual or
innovating and to which community projects contributed. Because
of pressure of space many significant events and projects are
not referred to and complex issues are over-simplified.

The successes and failures of the different approaches are
discussed. Hopefully, the conclusions will lead to more
realistic attempts being made to develop participatory democracy
at the local level in Islington and elsewhere, and a clearer
understanding amongst community workers of the issues and factors
involved in an often neglected side of their work.

WHY ISLINGTON?

The borough was formed in 1965 as part of the London government
reorganisation by amalgamation of the old Metropolitan Boroughs
of Finsbury and Islington. The councillors were mainly older
working-class men who accepted a hierarchical command system
and rigid Labour party group discipline. Bad housing was the
main problem they faced - the old Islington Metropolitan Council
had virtually no housing programme, in spite of having the
worst housing conditions in England. The new borough inherited
Finsbury's wealth and experience of managing a redevelopment
programme and applied both to the housing problem. Clearance
of large areas was started without regard for the people who
lived there. Their insensitive treatment led to a public
backlash against the council's policies and efforts, but there
was no way for any objections to be received and dealt with.

Officers were inaccessible, committees were held in secret, the full council meeting was only a rubber-stamp for their decisions, councillors controlled the moribund Labour party, and community groups were discouraged or opposed. People could not find out what was planned, or the reasons, and little attempt was made to keep them informed.

The borough was a large twilight zone with a huge population turnover and continuing decline. The 1971 census showed that only 10 per cent of the adult population had lived in the borough for more than ten years, and the population had declined from a peak of 407,000 in 1911 to 201,000 in 1971.

There was no tradition of community organisation or militancy. The trades council was inactive and many of its members were in fact councillors. Most of the housing was privately owned Georgian and Victorian terraces, providing badly maintained, overcrowded furnished rented accommodation, and the council had actively discouraged tenants' associations on its own estates. There was no tenants' movement to speak of.

In spite of this some community action did develop against the council in the early years of the new borough, and people had another outlet. Although the local council election in 1968 was mainly determined by the unpopularity of the Labour government, there is little doubt that public outcry against the insensitive bulldozer policy and intolerance of criticism contributed to the election of a Conservative majority.

During their three years in office the Conservatives set about modernising the council's machinery. Management consultants streamlined the administration, most committees were partially opened to the press and public, a public relations officer was appointed and liaison forums were introduced - representatives of community groups were invited to discuss the work of council committees with their chairmen.

Meanwhile, another crucial change was occurring. Central Islington had become a trendy place to live. Run-down Georgian terraced houses were being bought very cheaply by owner-occupiers and property speculators and modernised. Increasing numbers of young professional families were moving in. Many of these people joined the Labour party and, having chosen to live in an inner-city area, they wanted to improve it.

At first the established Labour party members tried to prevent the newcomers joining and they had to make a concerted effort to get into the party at all. This drew battle lines along antagonisms that already existed. Basic political disagreements were reinforced by class and cultural divisions and a generation gap. Bitter conflict between relatively young radical professional middle-class people and older conservative working-class councillors has been a feature of the Islington Labour party since the late 1960s. This conflict had a crucial bearing on the evolution of participation and community development in the borough, and we shall return to it several times during the course of this case study.

The two factions struggled for control in the meetings to select Labour candidates for the 1971 local elections. At the same time a number of study groups were set up to produce a manifesto and a lot of work went into developing proposals to tackle a whole range of borough problems.

The 'new guard' had a very small majority in the Labour group on the new council, but with it they were able to take all the committee chairmanships. They held the initiative, and, through the detailed work that had gone into the manifesto, they knew what they wanted to do. Many of them were very able and professionally qualified, so they were able to compete successfully with the officers for control of the council.

They embarked on a radical and ambitious programme to improve all aspects of life in the borough, and were prepared to invest substantial amounts of public money to achieve their goals. Open government and public participation were seen as an integral part of this programme, and the manifesto (1) included a specific and strong commitment to do so.

However, there were extensive disagreements amongst the new guard councillors on the extent to which participation should be promoted, and how it should be organised. While a few of them had thought through many of the implications and wanted to see participation as a continuous way of work for the council, their colleagues had a more limited view. The old guard, and many of the senior officers, could also be relied on to oppose any extension of participation when there was dissention in the new guard ranks. Thus, participation in the Council's work advanced in a fairly disjointed way.

THE COMMITMENT TO PARTICIPATION

As well as the general reasons why participation was fashionable at the start of the decade (see Chapter 1, p. 2) there were a number of additional reasons specific to Islington:

1 The Conservatives had introduced open committee meetings and machinery for consulting community groups in response to public criticism of the previous Labour council's secrecy and heavy-handed style. Labour had now to advocate a more progressive policy.
2 The huge problems of the borough could not be tackled by council action alone. A large-scale mobilisation of voluntary effort was also needed. Given the high population turnover, there was a prior need to establish a community identity. Encouraging community groups and involving them in the direct provision of services helped both objectives.

3 Projects could be initiated immediately without waiting for
   reform of the outmoded and conservative officer structure.
4 Many councillors had no previous experience of council work.
   Because they were highly critical of the old guard Labour
   group and the three-year Tory administration, they were not
   at all defensive about the council's previous performance,
   and in fact encouraged public criticism.
5 As the officers in the council's employment at the time were
   hired by the previous administrations, they were partially
   responsible for the situation the new council wanted to
   change. Strong community groups would challenge both
   existing policies and the quality of service provision.
   They were seen by many councillors as potential allies in
   the struggle with officers for control of the council.
   They were an alternative source of local knowledge, advice
   and expertise.
6 In the continuing struggle for control of the local Labour
   party, members recruited from community groups could provide
   a political base for the 'new guard' who were still in a
   small minority amongst the borough's predominantly working-
   class population.

These views were all held consciously by new guard councillors
at the time, though the emphasis and extent of the commitment
varied considerably.

In January 1972 the council accepted all the recommendations
of the 'liaison forum working party' to implement the manifesto
commitment. They included:

1 A definition of participation - 'the participation by the
   public in the discussions that lead to council decisions'.
   While this form of words appears limiting, it encouraged
   discussion of the implications of decisions before they
   were finalised and thus gave people a chance to shape them.
2 Guidelines to all the council committees on improving
   participation in their own areas of responsibility.
3 The establishment of a special committee on participation
   with its own staff and budget.
4 The promotion of experimental neighbourhood forums -
   similar in objectives to neighbourhood councils.
5 Holding liaison forums on borough-wide issues and on a
   neighbourhood basis.
6 Distribution of a new quarterly borough newsletter.

THE PARTICIPATION COMMITTEE 1972-6

The Special Advisory Committee on Public Consultation and
Participation, to give its full title, was responsible to the
policy committee for implementing these proposals and advising
the other committees on how to increase public participation
in their work.

Unfortunately, it took over a year to recruit the staff to support the committee. The bureaucratic delays in getting the posts on the establishment advertised and filled were a fair indication of the officers' attitude to the work. During this time the committee was very limited by not having staff directly assigned to it, and it gained a reputation for being a talking-shop. Some of the momentum created by the electoral commitment to participation had already been lost by the time the staff finally started work early in 1973.

The leading members of the participation committee were clear that one of their objectives was the reduction of political power of the officers and thus the participation officer had to be free from direct control by other officers, and strongly motivated and personally committed to the committee's position. They wanted the post to be directly responsible to the chief executive, but had to accept it being placed in the public relations division. They only agreed on condition it was reviewed after a year, and strengthened their resolve to make the post directly responsible to themselves in practice. They successfully insisted on being involved in the selection process and as vindication of their view the person appointed was not included in the short-list drawn up by the chief officer, or supported by him after the interviews. Without the chairman's involvement, the officers would have been able to appoint a safe candidate.

It was recognised that the participation officer's work would involve conflict as he was given a political brief - to argue for the extension of participation from within the council framework, expose the way decisions were taken to scrutiny by community groups, and advise groups what was in their best interests, even when in conflict situations with the council.

With the committee's approval, the participation officer and information assistant immediately set out to:

1 Create a climate of opinion in which strong independent community groups could grow and flourish and in which they would be supported and listened to by the council.
2 Help with the formation and development of new groups, especially in areas of council intervention.
3 Develop more open government and increase access to information about council decision-making.
4 Provide information and advice about what the council was doing and how it worked so groups could influence it. This involved a regular flow of information to all groups; responding to requests for information, advice and help from groups; and advising groups on how to pursue their own interests, even if they were contrary to those of a council committee or department.
5 Enable groups to function through provision of resources (material help and cash grants).
6 Recommend changes in council policies and procedures to increase the opportunities for participation.

The new borough newspaper 'Focus on Islington' was used to
help create a favourable climate. Councillors' names, addresses
and home telephone numbers, how the council works, the role and
address of the participation office and access to all the
information and advice centres and law centres was included in
an annual information supplement (1) distributed to every
household in the borough. This supplement was one of the main
sources of basic information for community groups and workers.
Early issues of 'Focus' described the council's participation
policy and practical attempts to involve people in decision-
making, the work and role of the participation staff and the
work of community groups. There was also an article in each
issue about an aspect of council policy or practice written
by someone outside the council, usually a community activist,
which was not edited and to which the council replied.

The other main vehicle which was used to build up a favourable
climate of opinion was a series of local forums, special forums
and tenants' forums.

The local forums each covered a small area - anything from
a whole ward to a few hundred households. Everyone in the area
was invited by leaflet, and all community groups were given
three weeks' notice by letter. The forum was an open-ended
opportunity for people to discuss any issue that affected the
area with their councillors (and officials).

As an experiment a comic (1) was used to publicise the
forums. Council leaflets are usually off-putting in their
style and language and are written from one point of view
the other hand a comic is simple to read, is attractive
unusual, and the reader can identify with any one of the
several different characters. Research showed that the
created a more favourable initial impression, and was
likely to be re-read than the more common style of lea
People had a better recollection of the comic's conte
they were more likely to grasp the purpose of the fo
the value of community groups. This was particularl
people who did not read newspapers, or who read tab
than the quality press, so the comic made more impa
usually excluded from positions of influence and w
tion programme must attract. About half the house
borough received one of these comics inviting the
so many people gained some idea of the council's
encourage community groups. Video was also used
to encourage interest and enable tenants to wor
approach to issues on several estates during th
programme.

In all, fourteen local forums, followed by
estates to form tenants' associations, were
month period. All the issues raised were fo
letter was sent to everyone who attended ea
happened about the issues raised. The for

people had clear and constructive views about what ought to be done
in their neighbourhood, and this experience subsequently influenced
the council's method of preparation of local plans and its
consultation procedures in general. The tenants' forums were
specifically to discuss the role and value of tenants'
associations, and to identify people who were interested in
initiating them in their own estates or areas.

The council had a long history of discouraging tenants'
associations so there were virtually none on council estates.
There was a need to get across the change in policy. At the
same time, the council was trying to protect private tenants
from bad housing conditions and harassment, and tenants'
associations could have an important role in this work too.
A leaflet explaining the council's wish to encourage independent
tenants' associations to represent the interests of their
members, irrespective of their landlord, was circulated to every
household in the borough with an invitation to the appropriate
forum. A new comic discussing the role of tenants' associations
was distributed in addition to every council tenant. Although
very few new tenants' associations arose specifically from these
forums, they encouraged and consolidated the general tendency
that led to tenants forming over sixty estate associations
during the year.

Forums were also held on particular issues. Though mainly
for representatives of community groups, they were also advertised
in the local press. They covered the development of services
for the under-fives, play provision and policy, and the
participation committee's own work. Each was the first step
in building up the opportunity for community groups to influence
council policy.

This concerted attempt to create a climate of opinion
favourable to community groups and participation was coupled
with increased help to groups. While they could get grants
from the social services or recreation committee to run
activities within the terms of reference of those committees,
they could now also get grants from the participation committee
for the purpose of formulating or campaigning for the policy
the organisation or providing the administrative resources
so do'.

Most applications were for community newspapers, publicity
administration costs of meetings, and the basic running
s of the group (postage, stationery and telephone calls).
t 130 different groups had been funded by the end of 1979.
grants were for single specific projects or items of
ment; many were annually recurring. The budget for these
s had reached £9,600 by 1979-80.

ups were specifically encouraged to produce community
pers or newsletters by the participation committee to
e information and promote debate on local issues, services

and groups; develop a community identity; and provide a vehicle
for community group campaigns. (3) These publications also
contributed to the favourable climate of opinion which the
committee tried to achieve in other ways. However, it was made
clear that each group had complete editorial freedom. They
could criticise the council in the paper if they wanted to, and
many did. By the end of 1974 about a quarter of the borough's
population were receiving a community newsletter.

To encourage newsletters, and also provide for the other
communications needs of groups, a network of centres where groups
had access to a typewriter and duplicator were set up. This
involved encouraging existing organisations to make their
facilities available to groups and also buying equipment for
some new places. Experience showed that most community groups
were reluctant to approach other organisations to use their
facilities, unless there was already close contact and a friendly
relationship between them. Thus, community projects that
positively encouraged groups to use the facilities made the best
centres.

The provision of resources for groups was complemented by
the provision of a regular flow of information. 'Info', a
printed newsletter, was mailed out to all the community groups
in the borough every six weeks. It was designed to give them
the basic background information they needed to participate in
council decision-making, enable them to communicate with each
other, and debate criticisms and alternatives to council policy.
One section contained articles by local groups on their own
activities, ideas and policies, which the council undertook
not to edit, but to which it could reply if it wanted. Perhaps
more importantly, 'Info' acted as a frequent reminder to groups
that they could get information and advice on anything else
from the participation office, and such requests came regularly
by phone, letter and personal visits. The mailing list of
groups had reached 800 by 1979.

A directory of community groups was sent out with 'Info'. It
was used by groups to contact others in the same area or field
of interest when they wanted to exchange information or take
action on a common problem. The directory was periodically
updated and redistributed.

Committee agendas and reports were available to groups on
request. The group registered an interest in one or more
specific committees; the agenda sheets for each meeting of each
committee were then posted to the group who could ring the
office to ask for copies of background reports in which they
were interested to be posted to them. Groups could thus find
out what was going to be discussed in advance and if necessary
lobby committee members before the meeting. About eighty
groups received agendas for one or more committees.

Groups could also register an interest in planning matters,

in which case they were sent the weekly list of all planning applications received by the council. They could then get further information from the planning department on particular issues.

In addition, an information pack was sent to each new group as it was formed. It included a description of the way the participation office could help the group, the current 'Info' and 'Focus' information supplement, and a collection of advice notes and other useful publications including the directory of community groups.

This information and advice to groups was complemented by attendance at their meetings to explain the thinking behind the participation programme, or advise on particular areas of concern to the group.

Initially, the participation staff were based in the town hall, but by the end of 1974 they were in shop-front premises in front of the town hall. This shop, the participation office, became a resource centre for groups. A photocopier, electric golfball typewriter, stencil cutter and duplicator were provided for their use. Stationery was available - anything in the council's stock at cost to the council plus 5 per cent to cover administration costs - thus giving groups the advantages of the council's bulk buying. An information resource centre and library were also developed. (4)

Although mainly based on council committee papers, other reports and publications of potential interest to groups were collected. Thus groups and community workers were able to study past papers in the office (working space was provided) to obtain background information for their own activities.

Most of this foundation work took place in the fifteen months between the staff coming into post at the beginning of 1973 and the May 1974 local council elections. Many projects were initiated during this period which depended on the appointment of additional staff for fulfilment. Provision was made in the 1974-5 budget for an additional information worker and two field workers. Although the former was eventually appointed, the appointment of the two field workers was subject to a number of delays, and was then frozen in 1974 as part of the panic response by the council to the rate forecast for the following year. These delays also meant that eight months in April to November were lost at a crucial stage in the development and establishment of participation work. Because of increasing pressure of other work, the programme of local forums could not be continued without these extra staff, and had to be abandoned; and inadequate support was given to groups arising from the first series. No follow-up work was done on the tenants' forums and the initiative was lost to the housing department on work with tenants' associations. Work on the 'Action manual' - envisaged as a collection of looseleaf advice

notes on every aspect of how the council worked and groups' own
organisation - came to a halt, though it has re-emerged
sporadically since.

The full council debated the staffing level of the participation office in July 1975. The debate clearly reflected the
disagreements about participation amongst the councillors. The
leader and chairman of the personnel committee supported a
compromise proposal to fill one of the frozen posts, on the
grounds that they supported the participation policy, and the
programme of work which had been agreed could not be implemented
by the existing staff. But one of the other leading councillors
argued that participation had to be developed through the main
service departments, and that it was counter-productive to
build up a central team; while the old guard argued that they
were in favour of participation, but didn't see why they needed
to employ people to promote it. The leader's proposal was
defeated by one vote.

The lengthy delay and uncertainty over staffing levels
obviously affected the ability to plan work, and morale. It
also meant the office was unbalanced in having both its information workers and neither of its field workers. Contact with
groups diminished and little time was available to initiate and
support new groups in areas of council intervention, or help
other groups make the most of opportunities to influence events
that affected them.

This tendency for the office to lose contact with groups was
reinforced by increasing pressure from the committee on the
Participation Officer to concentrate on the other aspects of
his work - to advise them on ways of improving the opportunities
of people to influence council decision-making by changing the
way the council itself worked. The committee started by taking
up the issues and proposals raised by community groups at the
public forum on the committee's own work.

The number of secret committee reports had been attacked by
groups, so recommendations were made which led to very limited
conditions being adopted by the council in July 1973 for any
report to be labelled 'confidential'. (5) The remainder - the
vast majority - had to be made publicly available and discussed
in public at committee. Any report to any committee which
directly affected a community group had to be posted to them
by the originating department, prior to the committee meeting
at which it was to be discussed. Sub-committees and councillors'
working parties were open to the public and items could only be
discussed in secret if they conformed to the same limiting
criteria laid down for the main committees.

It was this access to information, and the active role of the
participation office in disseminating it, which provided one
of the main foundations for the high level of community involvement in council decision-making.

After the 1974 election (after which all members of the
council were Labour) the traditional right of the official
opposition - to table written questions for answering at the
council meeting - was given to all ratepayers.

The committee took up the role of public meetings as a means
of public consultation, drawing attention to their limitations
both in general terms and the specific ways the council was
using them. After discussion a set of guidelines was drawn
up and adopted by the Council. (6) They required: a clear
definition of the issues to be discussed; early provision of
the necessary background information to the community groups
and individuals concerned, so they had a chance to discuss and
think about the issues beforehand; conduct of the meeting to
maximise public input; a clear explanation of how the results
of the meeting were to be taken into account; and notification
of the final decisions taken on the issue, with reasons, to people
who attended. They also required that consultation took place
early enough for decisions to be influenced, and consideration
to be given to whether in fact public meetings were the best
form of consultation for the issue concerned, and if so, whether
they would be needed at several stages in the evolution of the
decision.

Proposals were made and accepted for more effective publicity
to be given to planning applications, and the machinery for
public comment before they were decided.

The need to involve ethnic minorities more (by specific
encouragement and provision of information in their own first
language) was recognised. It was agreed to translate the most
important publications into five additional languages (though
implementation of this decision was poor and sporadic).
Councillors' surgeries were made more accessible. It was
agreed that they should be held in community buildings within
each ward and publicised by the council, rather than be seen
as a Labour party function.

These matters were all aspects of the general relationship
between the council and the public. The host of other issues
that the participation committee took up, which related to public
involvement in specific policy or service areas, are dealt with
in that context later.

Meanwhile, in the spring of 1974 the chief executive set
up an officers' working party to resolve conflicts between the
participation office and public relations over priorities and
resources, and to enable councillors to review the conflict
that had arisen in the development of their policy so far.
The working party's recommendations were adopted by the council
in March 1975, after discussion with community groups and
community workers. They included a clear policy statement that
people should be able to influence decisions and events affecting
their daily lives, and that groups should be encouraged to take

community action to achieve their aims; that a participation
programme will only be effective if it is supported by a
community development programme to provide the resources and
experience for people to become involved on their own terms;
that the community development programme should be based on the
principle of positive discrimination in favour of the non-
organised and worse-off sections of the community; that if
local views are genuinely to be discussed and heard, then a
whole range of groups with particular and partial interests
will need to be supported in each neighbourhood; that many
different levels of participation need to be recognised and
accepted; that community workers and other resources need to
be provided for the community development programmes; and the
need for a regular review of policy and progress.

However, the working party recommended that the participation
office should be separated from the public relations office and
co-ordinate (but not have any managerial authority over)
community workers in other council departments and the voluntary
sector. Community workers would be based in other departments
as they each needed to make their own arrangements for community
involvement, but a working group of all community workers should
be established with the right to report directly to the participation committee. Unfortunately, the chief executive did not
accept the recommendation to split participation and public
relations, so all the working party's recommendations on organisation and structure were deferred while he reviewed this issue
in the context of the whole of the council's relations with the
public.

Thus, although this review established a sound overall policy,
it did not lead to the creation of organisational machinery
within the council to enable it to be properly implemented.

In April 1975 the policy committee decided to wind up the
participation committee. It was given a year to 'advise Policy
Committee on their functions being carried out by the relevant
programme committees'. There were several reasons for this:
the committee had been seen as initiating a new development and
was not needed now participation had become established; it was
a lightweight committee - many of the more able supporters of
participation held office on other committees - so its existence
was not doing the cause much positive good; and the number of
other demands on councillors' time were growing.

This was accepted by the committee (and the participation
office) provided that a suitable position could be found for
the participation office in the council's organisation, to give
it the freedom of action necessary to carry out its delicate
and difficult task, and gain access to other committees to
ensure the existing policy was implemented and developed. In
fact, if such arrangements could be established, winding up
the committee was seen at the time as a distinct advantage -
the time and effort spent in preparing reports and bolstering

the committee's importance could be spent in working with other departments to develop day-to-day procedures and staff training.

During 1975-6 participation in the areas of responsibility of each committee was reviewed in detail, (7-12) and recommendations forwarded to each of them on specific improvements that could be made. It was agreed that these reviews would also form the basis of an ongoing annual review of progress by each committee in its own work. They would be structured so that participation could become an integral part of each committee's activities and programmes, an essential objective if participation was to become a way of work for the council and its officers.

A 'code of practice for open government and public participa-tion' was drawn up. It pulled together all the rights of the public and community groups to information and access to councillors and officers (and the supporting procedures) that had been agreed at different times over the previous five years, and was adopted by the council in October 1976.

A sub-committee of policy committee took over the responsi-bility for those parts of the participation committee's work that did not fall into the terms of reference of other committees. This included making grants, monitoring basic procedures and progress across the council as a whole, and annually reviewing the code of practice.

These arrangements satisfied the needs of the situation provided that the participation office was given the standing and authority to apply effective pressure on other departments. In the event, this did not happen and the procedures were never implemented.

The chief executive's review (13) of the council's whole 'relations with the public' had taken on the task of defining the participation office's role when the committee was wound up. He basically argued that the council could not have conflicting public relations and participation policies, so all the council's policies on participation were in effect its public relations policy as well. He proposed the reorganisation of the public relations division (including the participation office) into a new borough information office. His initial proposals included some quite specific benefits to the participation office, but contained only outline decisions - the final detailed arrangements had to be agreed by the personnel committee. The personnel department would not accept an arrangement whereby the divisional head (the borough information officer) was not responsible for all aspects for the work of the information office - the corollary of the proposed direct link for the participation officer to the chief executive. They proposed that the participation officer should have no executive responsibility, and that most of his previous responsi-bilities should pass to the borough information officer. The outcome of a bitter struggle through two personnel committee

eetings and several officers' meetings was an unsatisfactory
compromise' not significantly removed from the personnel
epartment's original recommendations; all the advantages in
he chief executive's original report had been removed, except
he creation of an inter-departmental council community workers'
roup with the authority to plan its own work programme and
raining, and report direct to any committee on community
evelopment issues (thus enabling the community workers to by-
ass their own departmental hierarchy), as proposed by the
arlier review. However, the new information office structure
reduced the staff engaged in participation work by two so the
roup could not be serviced properly and was therefore ineffective.
t functioned sporadically as a discussion group, and occasionally
ook up issues on which it presented reports to committees, but
ts vast potential - to report regularly to committee to ensure
hat issues were not swept under the carpet and were discussed
rom a community development perspective - was never developed.

To survive and flourish the participation office needed some
ndependence from a departmental hierarchy. Initially, the
councillors had realised that and provided (through the participation committee) a suitable framework. The chief executive had
recognised the need to preserve the office's freedom of action,
but had not been prepared to establish it outside the normal
departmental framework. The personnel department had not even
been prepared to allow that.

The councillors obviously had the power to override both
these points of view, but after considerable lobbying from all
sides, were in the end unwilling to do so. After this defeat,
the participation office felt that they did not have a
sufficiently secure base or political backing to continue to
advocate changes in council policies and procedures to facilitate
participation. Thus, apart from becoming involved in one or two
specific issues, and a major contribution to the research by the
Islington Economy Group (14) that demonstrated the real reasons
for the decline in the local economy, the participation office
did not significantly develop its role and functions from that
defeat (April 1976) until its closure four years later. Several
conclusions can be drawn from this experience.

Establishing a climate of opinion favourable to the growth
of community groups was seen as a political propaganda exercise.
The councillors most actively involved wanted to carry through
a sort of cultural revolution and neither they nor the participation office initially appreciated the need for a community
development programme to motivate and support the groups. By
the time they did, the fragmented pattern of community work
(described later) had already been established. In some cases
the people who volunteered to initiate groups weren't representative and in others groups quickly collapsed because of lack of
direct support in the initial stages. Thus, while the campaign
to establish the climate of opinion was essential, it should
have been accompanied by more direct support to groups through a
planned development of community work.

This difficulty was compounded by the cutting of the proposed additional staff to build up the programme, so much of the initial momentum was lost. The way the council budgeted made it impossible to plan a growing programme of work. In the last analysis, the budget was the only council policy statement that mattered, because it determined the resources that were put into implementing the other policies.

There was some resentment of the participation committee as the other committees felt it was interfering in their responsi- bilities. This, coupled with the participation officer's direct responsibility to the committee in practical terms, and continual disagreements over objectives and priorities with the public relations officer and departmental head, left him in a fairly isolated position. He was not significantly involved in officers' working parties, and in the main was not consulted on proposals for public consultation that officers were making in their own areas of responsibility. His brief that he should actively intervene in such matters caused further resentment.

Locating the participation office in the public relations division inevitably caused continuous conflict. The former was helping groups argue their own case while the latter was presenting the council's. Without the backing of the participation committee, the office would not have been able to function, but with it the public relations officer felt constantly undermined. Thus a number of functions that had been public relations' responsibility before the creation of the participa- tion office - particularly public meetings and consultation arrangements - were outside the office's sphere of influence. On the other hand, because participation was viewed as a communications issue, the office was prevented from evolving into a central community development unit. Ideally it should have undertaken both tasks, but it was largely prevented from doing either. In practice it was the worst possible location for the participation office. The proposal to include it in the borough information office was an attempt by the chief executive to create the best of both worlds, but in practice did the opposite. Given the choice, the councillors would want to appoint a borough information officer who would get them a good press, rather than an experienced community development worker; and it was obviously unlikely that anyone appointed to such a job would be a strong advocate for the development of participation in the work of other departments. There was no reason why a participation and community development office should be more closely associated with public relations than any other council department, but the creation of the borough information office effectively stopped any further advocacy for the extension of participation amongst the council officers.

The lack of uniformity and clarity of policy on participation amongst the new guard councillors also created difficulties. The participation officer had been given the brief of developing policy in a controversial area that directly impinged on the

councillors' own roles. Some of them, even in the 1971 council,
resented an officer who openly questioned their views rather
than manipulated them as other officers did. This may also have
been a factor in some of them opposing the expansion of the
participation office. This situation became worse after 1974,
when new councillors were elected who had not been involved in
the discussion about his role, as they tended to view him in
the same role as other officers.

Thus the political support given to the participation office
declined, and it largely disappeared after the committee was
wound up. Its future had still not been resolved when the
committee had its last meeting. It should have requested an
extension, but there probably would not have been sufficient
support to keep it going by that time.

While the participation office's role was under threat it
sought support from other community workers and groups, but the
issue was largely seen as an internal procedural wrangle. While
people can be mobilised on issues, it is much more difficult
to get them interested in the structures that would make it
easier to win the issues.

In general, the participation officer's role was a fairly
isolated one and suffered because of the absence of someone
to share the workload and thinking.

The combination of the participation committee and office
was able continually to raise new issues and extend groups'
opportunities to influence council decisions; without them the
council's general commitment to participation would have
remained a paper policy without the structure and procedures
to give it a reality. Many of the events described later arose
directly, or indirectly, from the participation committee's
work, and it thus played a crucial role in the development of
participation in Islington.

PARTICIPATION IN THE MAIN COMMITTEES' RESPONSIBILITIES

When the participation committee was set up the council clearly
established that each committee was responsible for participation
in its own areas of responsibility; that it was expected to do
what it could to develop it; and the participation committee
should advise and assist it to do so.

It was this attempt systematically to increase participation
in all areas of the council's work that distinguished Islington
from other local authorities, but it was not equally successful
in all areas. It depended on the nature of the work, the
commitment of the officers and councillors working on those
topics to inform the public, their ability to pitch public
information and debate at the right level, and the interest and
response of the community itself.

It was fairly easy for the council to pass broad resolutions but much more difficult getting councillors, and more difficult still getting officers, to change their personal beliefs and way of working to apply the broad concept in specific terms in their own everyday work.

Many attempts at developing 'participation' in particular programmes boiled down to informing people of what was happening, or collecting their views as one of a number of factors to be taken into account in forming a 'professional judgment' on the best course of action. Elitism, arrogance and cynicism about the ability and willingness of ordinary people to grasp issues and have a coherent view on them was prevalent amongst both councillors and officers (including many of those who professed support for participation).

It was in this context that attempts were made by particular councillors and officers to develop new patterns of work in key areas of the council's policy and programme.

HOUSING

Housing was the issue that dominated the borough throughout the 1970s. The council rapidly expanded the redevelopment programme in 1971 but the people affected by this process were informed of their fate after the decision at a public meeting. Virtually nothing was done to help tenants exercise any collective influence over the redevelopment, or their own rehousing. However, increased emphasis was being put on rehabilitation rather than redevelopment, partly due to the work of the North Islington Housing Rights Project and the Barnsbury Forum referred to later. By 1975 Islington had the largest rehabili- tation programme in the country, and housing action areas (HAAs) became its main thrust. A separate sub-committee of the housing committee was set up for each area consisting of housing committee members, ward councillor and residents' representatives. In the initial rehabilitation areas, where all the property had been bought from a single landlord, only tenants were affected by the programme and all residents' representatives were therefore tenants nominated by the tenants' association. However, the housing action areas included some housing that was solely owner-occupied, some occupied by owner and tenants, and some occupied by tenants of absentee landlords. In this type of situation it was notoriously difficult to involve tenants. To encourage them, separate tenant and owners' associations were promoted with roughly proportional representation (five tenants and two owners) on each sub-committee. (15) This was agreed on several grounds:

(a) The interests of owner-occupiers with tenants, and the tenants, were often in conflict. The owner still had to find at least 10 per cent of the cost of any improvement the council required to his house to give the tenant the

required standard, so the tenant could be harassed to
leave quickly or to tell the council he did not want the
improvements.
(b) Owners without tenants were usually satisfied with their
housing and wanted to use the HAA to secure environmental
improvements. Early concentration on this issue diverted
attention from the primary aim - improving the housing
conditions of the tenants.
(c) Even where the owners excluded landlords and wanted to
help the tenants as much as possible, the association was
likely to be run by people with whom the tenants could
not identify socially and culturally, so in practice they
would be excluded from it.

In the first HAA there were four separate street groups
already in existence prior to declaration. Though the type of
housing and social mix in these streets was more or less the
same, two were residents' associations and two were tenants'
associations. The contrast between these groups - in who
belonged to them and what they stood for - was both the reason
and the justification for the policy. It did not preclude the
tenants' association from agreeing to co-operate with the
owners on some issues, or even merging if they wanted to. The
important thing was they could decide for themselves. A single
association in practice removed the choices.

There have been two main difficulties in developing participation in the HAA programme - the weakness of many of the tenants'
associations and the nature of the joint sub-committees.

Tenants' associations existed in all the HAAs (except one
where there was a joint association) largely because the
housing rights project or the participation office helped to
establish one if no other community project was involved, but
to a large extent they were artificial creations. The areas
had only 300-500 houses and rarely had any focal point or
community activities specific to the area. Although a few
tenants' associations had continuous support from a neighbourhood project most had little back-up after the initial
formation. The housing department's HAA project leaders gave
the tenants' associations what help, advice and encouragement
they could, but they did not have the time or the community
development skills needed to help the tenants' association
achieve substantial active involvement.

The argument that the council ought to invest in community
activities and development at the same time as physical urban
renewal, to ensure continued commitment to the area from the
people living there, was accepted in 1978, but proposals to
systematically develop new neighbourhood projects in these
areas was cut before it could be implemented.

The joint sub-committees considered all officers' reports
on the HAA, the project leader had to report progress to each

meeting and the tenants and owners representatives could table
any issue for discussion. Councillors, officers and residents
sat round the same committee table - there was no opportunity
for officers to filter residents' views or advise councillors
without the residents having a chance to put a counter-argument,
or for councillors to plead ignorance or bad advice from
officers. As residents could raise issues and require information
or reports to be produced, there was the beginning of direct
accountability of the officers to the people they served.

On the other hand, there were reservations about the sub-
committees amongst the tenants' associations and community
workers. Any recommendation that was contrary to the basic
policy or could set a precedent was unlikely to be accepted by
the housing committee straight away. Attention was focused
on those recommendations that were not accepted; the feeling
grew that on important issues the sub-committees had no power.
However, the vast majority of recommendations were accepted
without discussion; decisions were taken by the sub-committee
that would not have been taken without residents raising the
issues and arguing their own case; increased awareness of local
feeling influenced the advice the officers gave in the first
place, and their subsequent advice to the housing committee;
councillors were under pressure to stand by the recommendations
of their sub-committees; and the controversial issues were not
necessarily those that were objectively important. More
importantly the housing committee was prepared to alter policy
as a result of joint sub-committee recommendations. They were
thus responsible for many changes in the HAA policy and
programme.

The second main reservation concerned the additional
difficulties the sub-committee created in terms of the development of an active, broadly based tenants' association. The
tenants representatives found it difficult to follow the jargon
and formal meeting style. As they got more involved they
became isolated from the people they represented. Proposals
that agenda papers should be circulated two to three weeks in
advance to give representatives time to consult on issues were
refused on administrative grounds. Thus, although the tenants
collectively could decide what issues they wanted on the agenda,
only the representatives could comment on the issues the
council tabled. Further, as they were full members of the sub-
committee they received confidential papers which they were
not supposed to discuss outside. While there were actually
very few confidential papers, they added to the general
isolation of the representatives from their constituency.
Thus, there was a tendency for the representatives to become
absorbed in the council machinery.

To make effective use of this form of representation requires
a lot of time and effort to organise activities and involve
new members, which was often not available to the tenants'
association. Consequently representatives tended to become

preoccupied with council business rather than neighbourhood
activities, further shutting themselves off from local people.
As the number of tenants likely to be interested and involved
in such a small area without substantial encouragement and
support was very low, the tenants' association could not achieve
substantial involvement without a lot of community work support.

The Islington Federation of Tenants' Associations tried to
work out a common approach to some of these problems and ensure
that tenants' associations were aware of the pitfalls, but they
had only limited support amongst the tenants' associations.

In spite of the difficulties and disadvantages of the joint
sub-committees, they were generally regarded by tenants'
associations and community workers as a good base on which to
build. No one argued that they should be boycotted.

Attempts to develop participation in the other main housing
responsibility, management of estates, was much less successful.
Before 1971 tenants' associations had been actively discouraged
by both councillors and housing department. Although the
councillors changed in 1971, the officers did not. In response
to pressure to develop tenant participation in estate
management, the housing manager proposed the establishment of
a tenant liaison officer. But while the councillors had been
actively involved in the brief and selection of the participation officer, through the participation committee, they were
not involved in the appointment of the tenant liaison officer.
Consequently, the housing manager was able to water down the
brief to a liaison role between tenants' associations and
housing management and appoint (in 1973) a person who accepted
that brief and had no wish to challenge housing management's
paternalistic attitude to tenants.

The tenant liaison officer was made responsible to the head
of the management division and rapidly became a roving
ambassador to tenants' associations. While many of them found
her helpful - she was after all the only housing department
person they could get to meetings - she did not try to change
the way management worked or their attitudes. In particular
she did not try to increase contact and dialogue between the
tenants' associations and the people responsible for their
housing, but acted as a channel of communication - a buffer
and a bottleneck - between them.

As the council had a policy in favour of tenants' participation in estate management, they had to establish machinery for
it. The chairman of the Housing Committee decided that the
best approach would be the formation of a Tenant Liaison
Committee. In spite of objections from the participation
committee chairman, he called a meeting with representatives
of all the tenants' associations on council estates, and, with
their agreement, obtained housing committee approval for
setting up a tenant liaison committee.

The participation committee argued against this approach and put forward an alternative 'bottom-upwards' strategy to the housing committee: (17)

The basic issue to be resolved is what proportion of tenants should be involved and at which level in the decision-making/ management structure.... The vast majority of tenants would be far more concerned about conditions on their own estate than those elsewhere, or on general housing or management issues. Thus tenants involvement must provide in the first instance for all tenants to be involved in the management issues on their own estate.

The participation committee report identified several issues that tenants could thus reasonably expect to influence or control - environmental improvements, minor rehabilitation, major rehabilitation, conditions of tenancy, estate management and caretaking - and recommended a programme of work to create strong independent tenants' associations with whom these issues could be discussed.

Although the question of tenant participation was discussed at several liaison committee meetings in 1975, most tenants' associations said they were not interested until the council improved the repairs and maintenance services. They believed participation was a 'con', a means of getting the tenants to shoulder the unpleasant aspects of estate management on the cheap. The detailed work of helping tenants' associations understand the management system and its advantages and disadvantages; identifying things they would be interested in managing; working out the powers and finances necessary to match the responsibilities; and negotiating an agreement with the housing department/committee, was never done. During this whole period tenants' associations had no one to undertake detailed work on their behalf, and who they could perceive as acting in their interests rather than the council's. The tenant liaison officers never fulfilled that role, though their numbers increased.

Unfortunately, the existence of the tenant liaison section enabled the housing department to resist external pressure for tenant participation on the grounds that they had their own experts who advised them what to do. The chairman of the housing committee, herself a supporter of increased participa- tion, confused the correct belief that participation will only be effective when the housing department positively accepts it, with the view that proposals and impetus for change should therefore come from within the department. This was a long, slow process and not until 1979 did the department bring forward proposals of its own for joint council/tenant committees to consider estate management, to be tried on one or two estates on an experimental basis.

The budget for tenant participation was used in practice to

limit the autonomy of tenants' associations. Rather than
allocate it on any fixed criteria, or distribute as grants
(either approach would have needed a committee decision, and
given associations an opportunity to contest it), the tenant
liaison officers spent it on some of the materials, equipment
and estate management that associations asked them for, thus
reinforcing the paternalistic relationship.

The participation office was unable to carry out the
proposals to develop strong independent tenants' associations,
because of their staff shortage. The Islington Federation of
Tenants' Associations never had substantial support among
council estate tenants' associations, and never got to grips
with their problems. It was a fairly political body, in that
it included the few politically active tenants' associations
from all housing sectors (Trust, GLC, Islington and private)
and was most concerned with issues like fighting cuts in the
housing programme and increasing direct labour and municipalisation. In the main, estate tenants' associations have been
isolated without any co-ordination or community work support.
They were preoccupied with the problems of their own estates,
and the predictions of the participation committee about the
inadequacies of the tenant liaison committee were borne out
by events. The liaison committee was broken down into five
district forums in 1976 to enable more time to be spent
discussing each estate.

Although the formal opportunities for tenant participation
were not successful, they did give tenants' associations the
encouragement to say what they thought, and the opportunity to
make contacts or make representation direct to the housing
committee which led to limited improvements on their individual
estates.

The only success in tenant participation in estate management was the housing department's own initiative to establish
co-operatives on a few estates - a direct result of the success
of the Holloway Tenants' Co-operative and other co-operatives
initiated by the North Islington Housing Rights Project and
the Mildmay Forum (which are described later).

Substantial resources were spent, but not on the activities
likely to bring results - sustained community work on particular
estates where the tenants were interested, by a worker who had
a grasp of housing management issues and could gain the trust
of the tenants. Instead, by appointing 'safe' tenant liaison
officers with an unclear brief, refusing to respond to pressures
from outside the department, not providing tenants' associations
with any real resources and not encouraging co-ordinated
activity, the housing department effectively stifled the growth
of strong independent associations and any real participation
in estate management.

How did community workers respond to the opportunity of the
council's tenant participation policy?

First, many believed that tenants' associations should campaign to force the council to improve management and maintenance rather than try and take control of it themselves. Some believed the development of co-operatives was diversionary - the main issue being the level and structure of housing finance and public expenditure generally.

Second, the role of most community workers was limited by their employing agency, so while they may have worked on estates, it was more likely to be on playgroup, pensioners' clubs or youth activities.

Third, it required long-term work and planning. The length of time to achieve results was unacceptable to the worker, who did not stay in the job that long; and to the funding body, which wanted immediate results. The style of work required and the objectives were different from those of most community workers who chose to work on housing issues, who saw themselves as activists.

Fourth, it was difficult to get tenants interested, and workers found it hard to work with them over any period of time, because of major cultural and political differences between them and the tenants.

Fifth, acceptance of community work was most prevalent in the new local authority departments - planning, social services and recreation. Jobs for community workers were established in those areas, the brief and pressure from the employing agency encouraged workers to concentrate on them, and many of their staff sympathised with community work values. However, housing management had a long paternalistic tradition of its own with completely different values, which provided a hostile environment for community work.

So, although participation in estate management was the area where community workers might have made the biggest impact on giving people more control over their own lives - after all, their home is one of a person's major concerns in life - in the main they were not willing or able to devote much time to it as an issue.

One significant campaign on housing policy must also be mentioned. Just as the council's municipalisation and housing action area programmes were getting under way, the government cut the money available for housing rehabilitation. A joint campaign between the new guard councillors and the community groups affected (led by the Islington Federation of Tenants' Associations) successfully fought the cut. It was probably the largest mobilisation of mass opinion during the 1970s and culminated in a joint council/IFTA meeting of over 600 tenants. It showed how strong the combination of councillors and community activists could be when they were acting in defence of tenants' interests, and it also showed that councillors

could circumvent the conservatism of their own bureaucracy by
working through tenants' and community organisations. Significantly, it was also a campaign by a Labour council against a
Labour government. Many councillors were opposed to it for
this reason, and subsequent government policies were not opposed
in the same way, and the councillors became isolated from
community activists again.

Throughout the period the housing committee was receiving
deputations from tenants' groups. Some of them were concerned
about the conditions of particular estates or areas, but many
were concerned about broad policy issues. In particular, the
lettings policy was changed by providing accommodation for
young married couples who had been brought up in the borough
and would otherwise have had to move away from their families
because of the absence of anywhere to live, and for young single
people, who could not find anywhere to live when furnished flats
were taken off the market when their tenants were given security
of tenure.

Deputations frequently took up the first two to three hours
of a housing committee meeting, and most were successful in
securing an improvement in conditions on a particular estate
or a change in council policy.

SOCIAL SERVICES

The social services department was fully committed to the
proposals in the Seebohm Report to develop community self-help
and volunteer schemes. (18) It was particularly necessary in
Islington with the high population turnover, and lack of social
cohesiveness. The field work services were established on a
very decentralised basis with ten separate area teams, and
community groups were established and helped to take responsibility for providing particular services. Programmes were
built up with active community involvement to provide for the
under-fives (day nurseries, pre-school playgroups, mother and
toddler clubs), the elderly (particularly lunch clubs), the
handicapped and disadvantaged families. Adventure playgrounds
were an important part of the same process, although responsibility for them was transferred to the newly created recreation
department in 1974. The department's major achievement in
developing this type of work was fully described in a report
to the participation committee in March 1976. (10) However,
the departmental management confused this with public participation in decision-making over the extent and objectives of
services. While there is no doubt that people involved in
community groups or in providing services had an influence on
the department, it mainly operated at an informal level. They
generally resisted attempts to institutionalise public comment
on their policy and performance. To some extent this was
inevitable - the social control role of the social services,
particularly in the children's, family and mental health areas .

gave many people a view of social work that was incompatible
with the community development role to which they aspired; the
severe incapacity or preoccupation of many clients obviously
limited their participation; residential establishments were
often unwelcome intrusions into particular neighbourhoods and
while they rarely became crystallised issues at the political
level, it was not in the department's interest to establish a
framework for discussing them; in other ways too, community
involvement may have been against the interests of clients; the
social workers themselves were trying to increase their status
by establishing reserved areas of professional expertise on
topics on which most people claimed knowledge and had views -
the field of personal relationships; the philosophy and practice
of social work put more value on informal relationships than
formal ones; and the additional resources that Seebohm argued
should be put into social services were never there in sufficient
quantity for the department, so it had to select priorities and
they conformed to its statutory duties and mainstream activities.

Proposals agreed by the social services committee in May
1973 to establish a formal advisory committee on the under-
fives programme, including representatives of voluntary
organisations, were never implemented. The department believed
that its informal relationship with all the groups concerned
meant there was no need for such a body, so a number of subsequent
disagreements on policy and direction between the department and
community groups were brushed under the carpet.

Further, the committee accepted that the views and experience
of voluntary organisations given a grant to provide services
was no less valid than that of the department, but proposals to
establish machinery to enable the voluntary sector to make its
own proposals to the committee were not acted on. To some
extent this need was rectified over the years by the creation
of under-fives forums, Islington Age Concern, Islington
Disablement Association and MIND, who were each subsequently
involved in the committee's review of policy and services for
their client group. However, none of these federations was
adequately funded for their own policy development work and
they established close working relationships with the
department's research and development team. While this obviously
enabled them to influence the department's thinking, the converse
was at least equally true. In general, the department was
successful in limiting the independence of the voluntary sector
and directing its resources.

Although the Islington Council for Social Services (ICSS)
made an important contribution to establishing the voluntary
sector in the early 1970s, it was unable to develop its role
to keep ahead of the council as a creative thinker, or advocate
for voluntary organisations, after the establishment of the
research and development team and voluntary organisations'
liaison officer in the social services department and the
participation office in the town hall.

After an extensive review in 1976 the social services committee cut ICSS staff from 4½ to 2½. But the argument that ICSS should be allowed to retain its staffing level to enable the voluntary sector to pool its own experience and policy, and contribute to council policy-making, was not accepted. They had had the resources to do so already, but had not proved the need.

Other proposals (10) to establish a framework for genuine participation in different aspects of the department's work were made by the participation committee, agreed by the social services committee but never implemented - formal management structures for residential establishments and day centres, involving, where possible, clients, relatives, voluntary organisations, staff and the general public; the publication of a leaflet setting out the role, powers and areas of discretion of social workers and the rights of their clients; and a number of experimental approaches to community management of the work of area teams.

The biggest difficulty was the attitude of the social services department to community work.

As part of the strong community-based approach, all area team leaders were given the responsibility to promote community development work in its widest sense, but in practice it was mainly limited to enabling people to help the team provide services or support to particular client groups. At any one time an average of three to four of the ten teams had a designated community worker, but only two consistently had one (though some teams also got additional funding for projects over and above their basic establishment). In the others community work and social work were viewed as interchangeable, or even the same thing. Some of them employed a community worker for a period, but did not continue with the work when the person left. Where community workers were appointed, they were selected by the social workers and thus shared their perspectives, and were subjected to pressure informally and in team meetings to do work which the rest of the team saw as valuable. In the early 1970s the vision of Seebohm was still fresh in social workers' minds, and the new teams had not become fully established in their areas, so some of them did become involved in other issues for a time. However, the increasing pressure of the case load, new statutory responsibilities, the establishment of the recreation department in 1974 which took away their involvement in adventure play, and other departments establishing their own links with the community, led to the social workers becoming more and more restricted in their outlook and field of activities.

Yet the department refused to recognise this, and argued that community work on all issues important to the neighbourhood was and should be undertaken by the area teams. Unfortunately, on the odd occasions that one of the community workers did support a group in conflict with another council department, the social services management refused to back them up.

Because community work and social work were seen as aspects of the same thing, it was never recognised that community work needed different skills and resources, and a different recruiting and support system within the department. It was thus even more difficult than usual to get a group of community workers to agree on what should be done. They had been selected to carry out different briefs by their teams and had different views and attitudes to community work and social work.

No information provision, training, management support or machinery for working on wider issues was ever considered, let alone developed. No encouragement was given to involving people in the management of the social services department either. In the whole period there was only one issue of this type - a 'management committee' for a new day centre was set up by one of the community workers, but the departmental management refused it any role other than an advisory one.

Many of the community workers had little to do with their area team. Shortly after starting work they thought it was an ideal base because no one took any notice of what they did, but after a while they felt the absence of information, resources, moral support and influence. They came to accept the argument that broad-based community work could not be based in the social services department, but left before doing anything about it. This process was repeated by three generations of social services community workers.

In November 1977 they did eventually agree to a report (19) arguing that community social work and community development work were not the same thing. The former was different from social work and required a specialist who should not be selected by an area team and left isolated within it, and the latter should not be based in the social services department at all. Thus all teams should have a community social worker, though they should be part of a team co-ordinated and supported from the department's headquarters.

Unfortunately, by the time they finally agreed to this approach the political climate had changed and there was no chance of getting such a proposal adopted. Even so, the social services department still maintained its stated commitment to broad-based community development work as advocated by Seebohm.

The effect of the wide divergence between the department's stated policy and its actual practice was to confuse the real issues of community work, to tie up resources in social work that should have been used for community development, and prevent the growth of the participation office as a central community development team.

The community workers employed by the department, who did not
contest the disparity between its stated policy and practical
performance for most of this period, themselves did the development of community work a disservice. Although most did accept
individually by the time they left that community work starting
from the priorities of the community could not be effectively
undertaken from the department, they never tried to establish
a working situation where they could do what they were employed
to do, or establish continuity from one worker to the next.

RECREATION

The recreation committee set out on a very ambitious programme
to increase the amount of public open space (Islington has less
open space per head than any other London borough), and promote
community-based playschemes.

The former was fraught with difficulty because it was usually
only possible if housing was demolished, and there were several
campaigns at different times by residents who wanted to keep
their homes. All plans were publicised and were the subject
of consultation (on both the land to be used, and the later
issue of the actual layout and facilities of the park) before
decisions were actually taken. Initial proposals were often
modified or dropped after residents' pressure. In some cases,
ad hoc council working parties were set up involving residents
to consider these issues in detail.

The early attempts to develop community-based playschemes
were fairly successful. Permanent and holiday schemes were
established by the Bus Co., the Play Association, social
workers, community projects and the council's play and recreation
officer. Unfortunately, the council's attempt to build on this
success - the creation of a recreation and play division in the
new parks and recreation department in 1974 - was a failure.
Many playgrounds got no support from the department and did
not know where they stood. Two community playgrounds were
taken over by the council after a row about their policy,
although there had been no advice or discussion beforehand on
what the department expected of them. The recreation committee
was inadequately advised on play issues and promises made to
playgrounds by the department were not kept. A running battle
developed between the department and the play association. In
the end the latter produced a detailed account of all the
department's broken promises, mistakes and failings and submitted
it to the council. An investigation by the chief executive led
to the resignation of one officer, although to some extent he
was made a scapegoat for the failings of the whole department.
Proper liaison procedures were then established, but the bitter
relationship between the department and IPA continued for some
time. Partly because of this, IPA's request for an additional
grant to increase the support they gave to playgrounds was not
approved.

Though IPA was highly critical of the department's performance, the real disagreement was a fundamental one over policy. Ever since the meeting to set up IPA in 1973 it stood for grassroots control of play. It engaged in a consistent campaign for this over the years, involving it in a real struggle with the department.

It encouraged groups to stick together, thus making it more difficult for officers and other opponents to pick groups off when they went through the inevitable difficult but transitional period, and increased the sharing of skills and responsibilities between groups and play workers. Their approach led to many local people becoming play workers, thus extending the involvement of people in play provision.

On the other hand, the council supported mixed provision, but with the council monitoring the community's efforts. The policy differences were also reflected in the argument about who should control the training support for the playschemes. The department secured an urban aid grant for two workers which IPA said should be employed by them, partly on policy grounds, and also because of the department's past incompetence. In the end a sub-committee of the recreation committee was set up to manage the project, which included representatives of IPA, the Bus Co., Islington Voluntary Action Council and the play workers.

Community controlled playschemes have been tolerated by council officers where they grew up of their own accord, or with the support of community projects, and provided they worked well by the council's criteria. But no attempt was made to encourage community groups to run permanent schemes or take over those managed by the council. While the recreation committee has been prepared to discuss any issue that groups raised, it did not have a consistent sense of direction of its own, and has thus endorsed the pluralistic approach. In all, nineteen community-controlled permanent playschemes and community centres were funded in 1979-80.

PLANNING

The most extensive and consistent attempts to involve the public in decision-making were made by the planning department. The Skeffington Report had recommended that planning departments should appoint community development officers, and some councillors proposed that three should join Islington. (20) It was eventually decided to appoint one planning liaison officer on an experimental basis in 1974, with responsibility for advising groups on how best to become involved in planning issues, and advising the department on ways of increasing participation. This post was filled until 1980, and for two years in 1976-8 there were two.

The department's main priority was establishing participation
in the preparation of the borough plan (originally envisaged as
both the statutory development plan and overall council policy).
However, in so far as people were interested in council matters,
they wanted action to solve their immediate problems, not an
invitation to help plan the future of the borough.   Initially,
the key staff recognised that developing participation in
planning would be a long, slow process which needed a flexible
and experimental approach based more on localised issues than
borough-wide ones.

Thus, in October 1973 it was decided to open up discussion
of the preparation of the plans so people could help shape the
issues and options, as well as the actual decision; and to work
through community groups rather than appeal to everyone and
interest no one. (21) Although there were obviously reservations
about the representivity of groups, it was felt that a series
of public meetings would be less representative. As groups
were being promoted by the participation office and several
community projects, and special efforts were being made to
involve people from all social backgrounds and walks of life,
a much wider range of views could be obtained.

The planning liaison officer went to groups' meetings to
explain the purpose of the plan and how groups could contribute,
and briefed other community workers so they could explain the
situation to the groups with whom they were working. Background
material was specifically produced for groups and mailed to
them. If requested, a planner went to their meetings to talk
about the plan and help them formulate their views. The group
could determine the level and extent of its own contribution,
and was not constrained by the planners' pre-determined view
of the nature or form of the contribution.

The first stage of preparing the borough plan - identifying
the issues - was based on a series of nine booklets ('Fact
packs'), one on each of the main topics the plan had to cover,
providing the necessary factual background, research and
statistical information. Every group was invited to one of
seven district forums to discuss the way in which the plan
should be prepared, what issues it should cover, and how the
groups should be involved. The late appearance of the 'Fact
packs' (they were not ready for the set of forums) gave the
impression that the council did not think the consultation was
important, and undermined the preparatory work done by the
planning liaison officers. It was hoped that each forum
would establish its own framework to contribute, but this was
over-optimistic as only one forum set up an ongoing group
(though it went on to produce a detailed report of proposals
for its own area - 'Highbury hopes'). The planning department
had to convene and lead the two further meetings in the other
districts to get any response.

Repeated requests were made at the forums for two additional

'Fact packs', one on council powers and duties and those of the
other tiers of government with responsibility in the borough,
so groups knew what could reasonably be expected; and one on
resources - what things cost, and how much money there would be
to pay for them - so they could discuss priorities. But this
essential background material was never produced, though the
planning department accepted the need for it.

A year after the conclusion of the district forums (and
several months after they were promised) the department issued
its 'Choices packs' - short papers setting out the options on
each policy issue - for the second stage.

The responses from groups and the general public, and
comments from council committees and departments, were then
incorporated into the draft plan which was again the subject
of discussion with groups. Yet again, it was late, but by now
(1978) the department was only interested in going through the
motions to satisfy the statutory requirements for consultation
and avoid objections at a public inquiry. They were disappointed
with the previous response, key people had been replaced with
others much less interested in participation, and the council
as a whole was attaching much less importance to the plan (and
the planning department).

However, the interest in Highbury generated by 'Highbury
hopes' led to co-operation between the Blackstock Advice Centre,
Highbury Manor Adult Education Institute, the Polytechnic of
North London and the Highbury Barn Neighbourhood Project, to
mount 'Planning for real' (based on Nottingham University's
'Neighbourhood action packs' (22)) in Gillespie Ward. The
final culminating event stimulated local people's ideas on
how their area could be regenerated. Aids to discussion
included a video film about the area, made by local people,
and a scale model of the area showing all the streets, houses,
open space and dereliction. A panel of experts was also formed
to provide information on the feasibility of ideas. Just under
100 people attended and 400 ideas were generated. This interest
and some detailed work by the Barnsbury forum in their area,
both helped maintain pressure for participation on the planning
department.

During the eight years the plan was in preparation (the
original timetable was three years), the planning liaison
officers were unable to persuade the department on a number of
key needs: to plan a realistic timetable so background papers
were circulated on time; to keep in touch with groups between
stages so the consultation process was continuous rather than
sporadic; to recognise that groups had different priorities
and commitments to those of the department, and limited
resources in terms of time, so they needed a lengthy period to
draw together their views on issues; to make better use of their
own time and money by not producing massive reports, self-
completion questionnaires, and exhibitions to promote consulta-

tion when the department's own previous experience (23, 24) had
shown they were virtually useless; and do groups the courtesy
of keeping them informed of progress, the reasons for delays
and the council's response to their previous submissions.

Thus, though the planning department put a great deal of
time and money into encouraging public involvement in the
planning process, they refused to take the steps that would
have given some chance of success. Basically, they tried to
add a more effective form of consultation to their other work.
They did not recognise the need to work in a different way with
different priorities if they were to achieve useful levels of
participation. The department did not plan realistically, or
establish a continuity of approach so everyone knew where they
stood. As time went on their unrealistic expectations were
not fulfilled and they became more cynical. The staff who had
worked on the plan from the beginning and had put a lot of time
into helping groups participate felt betrayed by the department's
changing attitude. The groups became more cynical too - promises
to them were not kept, their limited time and effort was wasted,
and they were not kept informed of developments. Whenever
there was a delay in the department's work the consultation
period was reduced to enable the overall timetable to be kept.
Planning liaison officers in the end refused to work on the
borough plan. It had always been low on their priorities, and
to work on it in these circumstances was a waste of their time
and reduced their credibility with groups.

The most important work of the planning liaison officers was
on local and action area plans.

It was here that the approach of opening up discussions on
the issues and options, rather than consulting on a draft plan,
was developed to its full extent. The local plans team held
open-ended discussions with residents usually through three
separate meetings over a period of months with informal
discussions in between. They could thus shape the planners'
perceptions of the issues and problems and get across what
they wanted done. This was followed by consultation on the
draft plan before its adoption.

In some of these areas there were no groups at all, and
here the planning liaison officers would undertake basic
community work, knocking on doors, finding out the issues and
starting informal groups around them.

In other areas, work was based on existing groups, or done
jointly with community projects and workers. The planning
liaison officers briefed groups on how the process worked and
how they could make the best of it, including how to get
information, lobby the various councillors and officers involved,
and how to make formal representations. Whereas the tenant
liaison officers had been used as a buffer between tenants and
the council, the planning liaison officers carefully avoided

this role - they facilitated dialogue between the community and the planners.

The planning department fully acknowledged that this procedure led to the production of a much better plan. (9) It was based on a clearer understanding of the area, and included proposals that improved the conditions of the people who lived there from their own point of view. Basically, the experience shows us that most people do have views on the improvements that should be made to their area, and a sensitive community-work approach integrated into an informal planning study can lead to a high level of participation.

It would have been a very successful approach to local planning if the council had the machinery to ensure the plan was actually implemented. It was only after the first plan was agreed that this major deficiency came to light. Other committees agreed with the recommendations but did not think they were sufficiently important to divert money from their own priorities. The ineffectual planning department management never got this issue resolved, and it meant that to some extent the community was being involved on false pretences. Further, groups were not kept informed of progress in implementing the plan, and were given little direct help in campaigning for results, because the liaison officers' work programme did not allow the time. These factors, and the need to provide further support to groups generated by the planning study interested in other issues, showed the need for a planned distribution of community workers in the borough, so work that was initiated could be supported to fruition.

The planning liaison officers' role thus had some successes and some failings. The biggest difficulty was sustaining the morale of one person in a department whose main role was entirely different. Many of the staff were sceptical about participation, and few of them understood the factors and lifestyle that motivated ordinary people and limited their involvement in planning and local government. The planning liaison officers talked a different language about a different world, and constantly felt as if they were banging their heads against a brick wall. Individual morale was much better during the time when there were two liaison officers working together.

The conclusion is obvious - reforming the way of work of a whole department is too big a task for one person with no management responsibility. A team of people with a political commitment from councillors and a departmental management willing to back them up and change the way the department works is needed.

COMMUNITY GROUPS AND VOLUNTARY ORGANISATIONS

Inevitably, encouraging community participation involved the

formation and development of community groups. In Islington
they were promoted by independent community projects moving
into the borough; Labour party members and councillors; and the
council itself.

Three separate projects came into the borough and made a
major impact: the Quakers established Friends Neighbourhood
House as a community centre in Barnsbury in 1967; a playgroup
was set up, and the informal network of contacts it created
rapidly led to the project worker becoming involved in the
other key issues in two distinct neighbourhoods.

Barnsbury is an area of continuous Georgian terraces and
garden squares. The large houses were mainly multi-occupied
tenancies, and in the mid-1960s the old Labour council wanted
to redevelop part of the area. At the same time, it was becoming
very fashionable. Estate agents and speculators were combining
to force out the tenants, modernise the houses and lease or sell
them to the young professional middle classes. This process of
'gentrification' grew rapidly and they set up an amenity society,
the Barnsbury Association, to oppose the redevelopment plans
and to 'improve' the area further. They persuaded the Conservative council to designate it as a conservation area and totally
eliminate through traffic. Pressure increased on both the
tenants and the people living on the perimeter roads which took
the diverted traffic. The Barnsbury Action Group was set up to
fight the traffic management scheme, and was based on Friends
Neighbourhood House. The scheme was the subject of endless
debate and bitterness, which largely divided on class lines.(27)
At first the relatively rich professional classes dominated the
consultation the council established, and exercised considerable
informal influence through their knowledge of the planning
process, even though they were only a tiny proportion of the
population. It took much longer for the Action Group to mobilise
the deep-rooted opposition to the scheme, which was partially
dismantled by the Labour council in 1973.

Because of the intense harassment of tenants during this
period, a neighbourhood law centre was established in 1971,
employing three full-time community workers on trust grants,
and a panel of volunteer solicitors to provide legal advice.
The community workers followed up cases, but also brought
individual tenants with similar problems together into community
groups and tenants' associations. Although only a small
proportion of people with a particular problem went to the law
centre for help or advice, they did indicate the issues and
problems to the workers and provided a nucleus group for a
campaign to rectify the issue.

Some of these tenants' associations joined with the action
group in 1972 to call a public meeting to discuss housing
issues, which elected a steering committee to set up the new
Barnsbury People's Forum, a federation of groups. However, the
Barnsbury Association was deliberately excluded, as many of the

issues were class-based, and a federation which encompassed all
groups would be unable to take action to defend tenants'
interests.

In late 1973 the forum applied to the council for a grant for
a worker, but were turned down by the Labour group as one of the
ward councillors argued that they did not represent the whole
neighbourhood. A subsequent application after the 1974 election
was successful (the councillor concerned had been forced to
stand in another ward).

Most of the combined work of the forum and law centre was
directed against the estate agents, developers and large-scale
landlords that controlled much of Barnsbury's housing. They
initiated associations of all the tenants of individual landlords,
and campaigned for housing improvements and compulsory purchase/
municipalisation as the best way of giving tenants security from
harassment and poor conditions. The first example, Stonefield
Street, (28) where the tenants were actively involved in
campaigning for a takeover, and were then involved in the
redesigning of their homes, was one of the key developments in
establishing municipalisation and rehabilitation as the main
instrument of housing improvements in the borough.

The campaign against harassment of tenants and against the
role of one particular notorious estate agent also led to
changes in the law. The chairman of the forum was the local MP
and he used their work to successfully amend the Housing Bill
in 1974 to give tenants the right to know who their landlord
is, and to require a notice to quit to be accompanied by an
explanatory note setting out the rights of the tenant.

Most of the forum's work for several years was with tenants'
associations on housing issues, until the back of the problem
had been broken. The forum then took up other issues, mainly
old people's welfare, and took over a building for a community
centre. The forum lost its grant when the council started
cutting community projects in 1979, but continued to run the
community centre on a voluntary basis.

The Barnsbury experience is only summarised here, because it
has been written up extensively elsewhere,(25-30) but it was of
crucial importance in influencing the attitudes of community workers
planners and councillors to participation and community action.
It led to the development of better consultation techniques
than public meetings, the avoidance of class divisions in
neighbourhood groups, and the policy of positive discrimination
within the community development programme.

Friends Neighbourhood House also became involved in the
housing issues of the adjacent neighbourhood, Lower Holloway,
through their early playgroup work. Although the conditions
were atrocious and it was heavily overcrowded, the old Labour
council did nothing about it (largely because it was a

predominantly black area). When the Conservatives gained power
in 1968 the area was one of their highest priorities, but
furnished tenants had no security of tenure and the council
refused to accept any responsibility for their rehousing.
Council intervention encouraged landlords to evict tenants so
they could sell with vacant possession. Estate agents encouraged
the evictions, and the process was compounded by the council
agreeing to buy houses only with vacant possession. Several
hundred families became homeless in a very short space of time.
The Westbourne Housing Action Group was formed to organise the
tenants in self-defence. After a vigorous campaign, (25) the
council backed down and agreed to accept rehousing responsibility
for furnished tenants, whose needs were dealt with more
sympathetically when the new Labour council stepped up the
redevelopment programme in 1971.

The experience also provided considerable ammunition for the
campaign at national level to increase tenants' rights,
particularly the security of tenure to furnished tenants
(finally achieved in 1974) and the rehousing of homeless families.

The Friends Neighbourhood House activity (25, 30) also left
other benefits - a permanent park from derelict land first used
as a play area by the project, an adventure playground, several
playgroups, and the House itself which is now a nursery.

The second community project which came into the borough was
a spin-off from the first. People who had previously worked
with the Friends Neighbourhood House worker in Notting Hill set
up the North East Islington Community Project with funding from
the British Council of Churches, with the objective of improving
the housing conditions of the thousands of tenants living in the
twilight areas. On the basis of its initial assessment, the
project obtained funding from 'Shelter' to establish the North
Islington Housing Rights Project in 1972. It had already
established the Holloway Housing Aid Centre in 1971, funded
initially by an Urban Aid Grant through the council, and
additional funding was subsequently provided by 'Shelter'.
Though it was mainly a casework agency, its experience formed
the basis of the strategy that the Housing Rights Project
adopted, and it also encouraged many tenants with the worst
housing problems to join the Holloway Tenants' Co-operative -
established by the Project in 1972 with a grant from Rowntrees
Trust as a community controlled response to bad housing
conditions. The plan was to work through a housing association
to buy houses on the open market, rehabilitate them and let
them to the co-op members in greatest housing need. Anyone
who lived in North Islington and was in housing need was able
to join the co-op, which was self-governing and developed
structures to ensure that all members could play an active
role in its decision-making. (31) In 1976 it became a housing
association in its own right, giving the co-op members direct
control of the houses bought and the way they were converted,
in addition to control of lettings and management of the improved
housing. (32, 33)

Having established the housing aid centre and the tenants' co-op, the Housing Rights Project set about developing a policy and strategy to achieve the rapid improvement of sub-standard housing without recourse to wholesale redevelopment. It did a detailed survey of half a dozen streets in 1973-4, demonstrating the appalling living conditions of many tenants, and failure of previous council action to persaude or force some landlords to improve them. On the basis of this report, (34, 36) and supported by the residents' association promoted by the project, it proposed that the council declare the area an improvement area, systematically and intensively persuade landlords to improve tenants' conditions to a minimum standard, and compulsorily purchase the houses that were not improved.

Although the council complained it had no powers of compulsory purchase in these circumstances, the project contested this view. Further, it was known that the government was drafting a White Paper on the systematic improvement of twilight zones, to become known as housing action areas, and the council was persuaded by the project successfully to approach the government to treat the area as a pilot for the new Act.

The project's research work also provided ammunition for the campaign at national level (involving 'Shelter') for support for such an Act.

Over the next few years the project made major contributions to three other areas of housing policy.

First, the council officers' report on the 1974 Housing Action Areas Act said it did not contain a viable strategy or sufficient powers to deal with the borough's sub-standard housing. The project contested this view (35) and persuaded the housing committee that the Act, in spite of its limitations, gave powers systematically to improve areas through vigorous use of compulsory purchase powers. HAAs were subsequently used by the council as the main instrument of housing renewal.

Second, the project helped the residents in Charteris Road campaign against council demolition of their homes. They argued that rehabilitation was preferable on both social and cost grounds. The Officers persuaded a majority of the housing committee to reject their proposals, as many councillors felt they had little choice but to accept the 'expert' view of their officers, who said rehabilitation would cost more. The project took the issue up with the Department of the Environment and the Minister of Housing summoned a meeting on the scheme, where the civil service tore to shreds the council officers' calculations on the relative costs of rehabilitation and redevelopment.

Using their original arguments, and this additional ammunition, a deputation from the residents persuaded the majority of the council to scrap their original plans and rehabilitate the houses.

This victory, (36) the previous work on HAAs, and the work of
the Barnsbury Forum in Stonefield Street, helped establish the
rehabilitation programme as the main instrument of the council's
housing policy.

Third, the project itself worked in several HAAs to promote
tenants' associations and tenants' co-operatives. The second
neighbourhood it surveyed resulted in a GLC housing action area.
The tenants' association was encouraged to become a housing co-
operative and, working through a housing association, they
rehabilitated to their own design the houses acquired by the
GLC, and then let and managed the improved houses themselves. (36)

Other work has led to the establishment of a further tenants'
co-op in a housing action area where the co-op lets and manages
houses owned and converted by the borough council, (37) and an
agreement with the GLC to manage part of a newly-built estate
by a tenants' co-op leading hopefully to tenants in other
blocks on the estate taking over the rest of it when they see
the evidence of the initial effort. (38) This co-op (on the
Elthorne Estate) has co-operated with the Holloway Tenants'
Co-operative to organise a training programme for co-op members
on the responsibilities of the co-op managing its own housing.

As the Housing Rights Project and Holloway Tenant Co-op have
written up their own work extensively, (31-38) it has only been
briefly summarised here in the context of its effect on public
participation and housing policy and provision. Many of the
difficulties they had - in mobilising demoralised private-
sector tenants (many of whom at the time had no security of
tenure); in persuading council officers, councillors and tenants
to take new ideas seriously; enabling tenants to relate to the
complex and mysterious bureaucratic machine; and maintaining
morale over the huge timescale from initial action to improved
houses being completed - are covered in their own publications.

The third major project that became established in the
borough was the Islington Bus Company. It was originally part
of 'Interaction', the community arts organisation, who
negotiated a contract with the new council in 1971-2 whereby
the council funded the Bus Co. (a converted double-decker bus
and six workers) to provide a mobile playcentre for a number
of council estates - partly as an end in itself, but more to
develop community involvement in play provision as a base for
permanent facilities.

In 1973 the Bus Co. took the initiative in calling a meeting
to set up an Islington play association, a federation of playgrounds and groups to co-ordinate work on play issues and
provision and represent their collective interest to the
council. The meeting rejected the Bus Co's detailed proposals,
as it was dominated by people running local playschemes who
insisted on grass roots control of IPA and an active commitment
to community controlled playschemes. However, the Bus Co.

continued to play an active and supportive part in the development
of IPA.

The Bus Co. broke away from Interaction in 1974, when it had
established a programme and identity of its own, and moved to
its own base in the borough. It extended its role, developing
as a resource centre for community recreation groups of all
types, as well as a community project in its own right. In
particular, it encouraged groups to produce attractive publicity
and newsletters and had the reprographic equipment to do so.
The facilities were also used in community action campaigns
and demonstrations as well as play and recreation activities.
Several hundred groups have used the Bus Co's resources to date.

Through their continued active involvement in the play
association, the extension of their resources to support pre-
school playgroups and their involvement in the under-fives
committee, their work to develop and support groups and tenants'
associations on particular estates and areas, the creative use
of their resources for community action, and their involvement
in wider issues and campaigns, the Bus Co. played a significant
part in enabling people to run their own activities and
participate in council decision-making. (39)

Most of the remaining rapid growth of community groups in
the borough in the early 1970s was promoted directly or indirectly
by sections of the Labour party and the council under their
control, in ways and for reasons described earlier.

The groundwork leading to the formation of these groups
and the continuing support which enabled them to function and
flourish came from individual community activists, established
voluntary organisations who were encouraged or chose to work
in the borough, community workers employed by both voluntary
organisations and the council, council officers employed to
promote particular programmes, federations of groups already
involved in that type of work, tenants' associations and other
community groups, and the area teams of social workers. It was
also a continually expanding process - new groups and projects
identified new needs and demanded more resources and created
new groups to meet them. The number of groups and the total
funding made available to them increased throughout the 1970s.
In 1979 the social services committee funded 170 groups for a
total of £1.1 million (including urban aid and partnership
money).

Other committees of the council encouraged and funded the
voluntary organisations and community groups that came within
their area of responsibility, and by the beginning of 1979-80
the council was funding about 220 groups at a total cost of
about £1.75 million (over 3 per cent of its total non-capital
expenditure).

The policy to fund voluntary organisations (a term which

covered all non-statutory organisations from a small tenants'
association to a large national welfare agency) developed in
an ad hoc way for the first few years and in March 1975 the
council adopted a policy statement which codified and extended
the policy, 'to encourage and assist voluntary organisations,
for reasons of flexibility, speed and sensitivity of service
provision; cost effectiveness; independence of action required
in some cases; and greater public participation in the management
of services'. The policy statement dealt with all aspects of
the council's relationship with voluntary organisations, based
on the principle that the relationship was one of partnership
and that the agreement between the partners should specify the
rights and obligations of both. It also recognised the need
for proper support and advice to be available to voluntary
organisations from both the council and independent bodies, and
that the council should encourage experimental and innovatory
initiatives by voluntary organisations.

All this is not to say that every voluntary organisation got
funded and had freedom of action to do what it wanted. The fact
that open procedures had been established to enable groups to
put proposals to councillors did not mean they would automatically
be supported. While the councillors responded favourably and
quickly to proposals that coincided with their own views, novel
proposals took a great deal of arguing through. The more
experimental projects had to produce lengthy reports for their
funding committees which prompted endless debate. However,
while this was time-consuming for the groups concerned it
contributed to the education of councillors and officers,
usually reinforced the earlier commitment to fund the project
and made it easier to get further proposals accepted later.

The projects that prompted most debate were the neighbourhood
forum projects initiated and funded by the participation
committee.

THE NEIGHBOURHOOD FORUM (MILDMAY AND THORNHILL) PROJECTS

The participation committee invited ICSS and the Islington
Committee for Community Relations (ICCR) to put forward proposals
for the creation of neighbourhood forums in 1972. The council
envisaged these bodies as having a similar role to neighbourhood
councils, but defined their functions rather than their structure:
to provide a framework for groups; to inform the council about
needs; and to obtain resources for new activities.

Both ICSS and ICCR believed that these bodies could not be
imposed from the outside, but needed a considerable amount of
basic community development work before any neighbourhood
organisation was possible. Both successfully applied for a
grant to employ a community worker as the first step in the
project, and both workers started work in 1973.

But the basic approach differed. ICSS believed that a forum could be established with one or two years' groundwork and then would require little further support. Thus the worker could move on and repeat the process in a different area while remaining an ICSS employee.

On the other hand, ICCR believed the project could only be successful if the people in the area had control over its development, and they outlined four phases it should go through:

1 contacting existing groups, identifying other needs and
  problems, and establishing a base in the area (estimated
  to take three-six months);
2 stimulating the formation of new groups, supporting new and
  existing groups with information, advice and encouragement,
  and fostering co-operation between the groups (at least
  one year);
3 when co-operation has developed sufficiently, encouraging
  groups to join a steering committee as the basis for a
  neighbourhood forum, to whom the worker would become
  accountable (another year);
4 the formal establishment and recognition of the neighbourhood forum. (40)

In the event, the project was able to carry out this plan more or less exactly.

The commitment to the base in the area and accountability to local people enabled the project to become established much more quickly than its counterpart in Mildmay and to obtain further funding for two additional workers to run the centre.

When it started there were three active groups in Thornhill, but within two years there were a dozen dealing with a wide range of issues. Initially, they had been mobilised around single issues but gradually the project worker encouraged them to take an interest in the wider issues of the neighbour-hood and the project itself.

In 1974 the management committee started to set up a parallel local management committee, consisting of one voting representa-tive of each community group in the area, to take over the project in its entirety.

By 1975 the project clearly achieved its initial aims. Local management was established and proving a success, there was a firm basis of local support, community organisations were functioning across two-thirds of the Ward and grant aid had been forthcoming beyond the initial three year trial period. In discussions about our work we began more and more often to summarise it in terms of two overall aims:

Politically: to increase the power ordinary people had to control and improve their homes and home environment.

Socially: to encourage the growth of natural communities to replace those which had been destroyed by redevelopment and the conditions of modern life.

Towards these aims, in addition to our individual casework and our group work strategy, we were now able to talk more and more of adopting a neighbourhood approach. Our political campaigns centred on area facilities like a new park, location of doctors' surgeries, traffic schemes, designs for a new estate and provision of pedestrian crossings, but we also became involved in a much broader range of activities. What we were aiming at was not something we thought the project would achieve by itself - we were just a small part in what would be a long process. But we did hope that we could catalyse the growth of a feeling that the people belonged to an area, and that the area belonged to them.

Most important in initiating all this was the local project Management Committee. This met monthly and was attended by representatives of twelve member groups. By autumn 1977 all three of the staff had been selected by the local committee. It was at the meetings that the directions for our work each month were decided. Issues on which we became active were those brought to or raised by our Management Committee. Additional to our monthly meetings we agreed to hold at least four larger scale public meetings per year to decide on matters of concern to the local community. Activities like a barn-dance or the neighbourhood festival were organised by a group of tenants who reported back to the Management Committee. It became, in fact, the most successful feature and the most distinctive character-istic of the Thornhill project. The meetings had a flavour of their own, a blend of aggression and humour, of enthusiasm and cynicism which arose from the varying persona-lities of those taking part, and our chairman, thank God, would always have us packed up and down to the pub before closing time where the antagonists of a few minutes earlier would generally buy each other drinks. It was also largely thanks to our successive chairpeople that we managed to maintain a semblance of order, combined with an informality that did not inhibit. (41)

The clearest example of the success of the local management committee was the campaign for a health centre in Thornhill. The local people themselves raised the difficulties of registering with GPs and calling them out at night (as many of them were approaching retirement age). Research by the project workers showed a very low level of primary health care, but the health authority was preventing new doctors setting up in the area. The project's report and subsequent campaign demanded a health centre, and as a first step the area health authority funded a research worker (on its own staff but based in the project's premises) and a community worker for the project to develop further local interest in health issues generally and the health centre idea specifically.

The Mildmay project also envisaged basing a forum on the federation of a variety of community associations. It identified four main issues in the neighbourhood: lack of recreational facilities, particularly for youth; lack of open spaces; the proposed inner-London motorway box which was to have gone through part of the area; and poor housing conditions.

The project successfully applied for an urban aid grant to convert a disused factory into a community recreation centre. 'The Factory' had its own local management committee which took formal responsibility for the running of the building and employing the staff in 1977. A cleared housing site was used for a temporary adventure playground which became permanent.

The campaign for more open space and the local demand for the housing site to be turned into a playground led the council to undertake a local planning study for the neighbourhood. The local groups, helped and co-ordinated by the forum, exercised considerable influence on the eventual content of the proposed plan. While it was successful in developing groups it relied much less than the Thornhill project on a base in the area. It did not get one until May 1974, fifteen months after starting, and provided only very limited 'drop-in' advice work.

By 1975 the project was assisting fifteen local groups (most of which it had helped start). At first there was little local representation on ICSS' project steering committee, but this was broadened during 1975 when ICSS concluded that the idea of withdrawing the worker from the area was not feasible and that the local groups should take over the project, as Thornhill had done. The forum was finally established in November 1975. The failure of another project in 1976 gave the forum a four-storey shop front building in the centre of the area, and money to employ two additional workers: one to maximise use of the building as a community resource and run an advice centre/ coffee bar with the help of volunteers; and a Turkish speaking community worker, the only one in London.

There were two housing action areas in the neighbourhood. In the first run by Islington Council the forum helped four local residents' groups deal with the council through the housing joint sub-committee and a tenants' co-operative was formed in 1977 to manage the improved dwellings. In the second, the GLC handed the responsibility for both conversion/improvement work and management to a co-op which was initiated by the forum. Funding for a worker was obtained by the forum from the GLC in 1976 and this was transferred to the co-op when it became established. Both co-ops used the forum building as an office.

From the community work viewpoint, the projects should be assessed by the extent to which they have been successful in:

(a) getting action from public authorities on issues that

local community groups or the project itself had identified
and campaigned on;

(b)   influencing council decision-making on issues the council
has identified;

(c)   increasing the extent to which the council consults local
groups on issues that affect them;

(d)   increasing facilities under direct community management;

(e)   enabling people to manage these facilities effectively
(including the project and its workers);

(f)   increasing people's knowledge of their rights and
opportunities;

(g)   maintaining a dynamism in the neighbourhood so new issues
are identified and tackled and new people are involved
all the time;

(h)   developing a neighbourhood consciousness.

Considerable success has been achieved on each count by one
or other of the projects, but their different approach, and the
widely different nature of their respective areas and key issues,
precludes close comparison.

One factor in their success was the council's requirement
that each project had to produce a report of their activities
and plans every six months. While this was a considerable chore
and very time-consuming, it also meant that the projects had to
be very clear on what they were trying to do and why.

Both projects demonstrated that the council was incapable of
developing a co-ordinated and consistent approach to a neighbourhood. While many council departments used both projects to
gather local intelligence and provide a framework for discussing
particular issues with local residents, other departments (and
even different staff in the same departments) ignored them. In
1974 the Thornhill project proposed that the council establish
an area committee to tackle the neighbourhood's problems as a
whole, but this recommendation was not adopted. The local
planning study was the only way for the council to look at a
neighbourhood as a whole, but there was no machinery for
ensuring other council departments actually implemented the
final plan. The forum thus had to campaign for the implementation of the Mildmay plan, on which they achieved mixed results
over several years.

The main impact of the projects has therefore been on the
neighbourhoods themselves and on influencing specific decisions
and programmes of the different public authorities. Other
early hopes - that they would help the council relate as a whole
to the neighbourhood and they would lead to changes in council
procedures and structures to facilitate participation - have
not been fulfilled. Neither project was successful in creating
a strong independent neighbourhood forum, because they continued
to develop and work through more local and specific organisations
to which people related more easily. Though participation in the
forum itself was relatively low (usually 5-15 people at each

meeting), the number of people each project supported in more local groups and campaigns was much greater.

Based on its experience of the neighbourhood forum projects the council argued against proposals set out in a government consultation paper to establish elected statutory neighbourhood councils: a federation of active groups enables much more participation than a formal neighbourhood council. (42, 43)

The council cut the grants to both these projects in September 1979. The local response in Mildmay was to protect the specific projects which had been built up though the forum itself was lost. The Thornhill project was able to continue, partly on the basis of its funding from the area health authority.

COMMUNITY WORK

Community work was extensive but grew in a haphazard way. Each council committee considered its own staffing requirements and grant applications from community groups without the development of any overall plan for participation and community work.

By 1979 the council employed two participation and two information officers in the participation office, two planning liaison officers, seven tenant liaison officers, a voluntary organisations liaison officer and seven community workers in the social services department, and two area officers in the recreation department. All of them had as their main task either support for or liaison with community groups.

Nine workers were employed by the four neighbourhood forums. Four community associations had their own centres with full-time workers (all with community work responsibility) and the largest of them had an additional neighbourhood worker. Four play projects and a neighbourhood group each had community workers and the family service unit employed a community worker. In addition, several co-ordinating bodies had full-time staff - Islington Voluntary Action Council (the successor to ICSS) had 2½, the Play Association 1½, Age Concern 1 and the Disablement Association 1. Several agencies and advice and information centres also adopted a community work approach, or had staff who saw themselves as community workers - the Housing Rights Project, two law centres, the Holloway Housing Aid Centre, Islington People's Rights, the Bus Co., the Citizens Advice Bureau, several tenants' co-ops and an employment project. All these jobs were funded by the council except for the co-ops and two workers at the Housing Rights Project and two on the employment project.

Most of these jobs became established through one of four main routes: the two independent community projects that came into the borough before the council changed in 1971; the Labour council's commitment to participation from 1971; the community

pproach to social work; and the community approach to play.
ost existed by 1974-5 (though a few of them were not funded
y the council until after that date), but there was an increase
ach year until 1979.

Many workers were in isolated situations; they were the only
ull-time workers in their organisation, or they were the only
ommunity workers employed by an organisation with a different
asic role (e.g. a social services team or a playground). Most
ere appointed without relevant qualifications or previous
xperience and learnt on the job. While on balance it would be
ore harmful to insist on community work qualifications
especially as there aren't any - only ones for social work
nd youth work), there is a need for workers to organise a
utual support system of some sort. Few community organisations
ave a management structure to ensure that when one person
eaves the person who replaces them knows what the job involves,
hat is expected of them and generally to provide support and
ncouragement. Most organisations in other sections of society
rovide this as a matter of course. This contributed to the
eneral demoralisation and high turnover of workers, which
urther compounded the lack of continuity and sense of direction
n community work. The development of participation suffered
articularly because it required a wider knowledge and range of
kills amongst workers to enable people to understand the forces
hat affect their neighbourhoods or estates and try to do
omething about them. Day-to-day pressures inevitably tended
o make workers focus on their immediate concerns in their own
rea and develop the knowledge and skills to deal with them.
 countervailing pressure, from the worker's own experience and
raining, or a management and support structure, is needed to
rovide the knowledge and skills to develop participation
utside the neighbourhood.

This role could be fulfilled by a community workers' group,
ut given the different objectives of the different jobs, and
he wide variety of employing bodies and selection committees,
t is not surprising that the personalities, values and
bjectives of the workers themselves varied so greatly. This
recluded the creation of a successful group, though several
ttempts were made. In each case, workers were not prepared
o surrender any of their independence to a wider collective
effort. All attempts to formalise a group were resisted by
ost workers, and the preparatory work was minimised and shared
ut. There was no secretariat to do the ground work to make
he meetings successful, or follow up issues between meetings.
ssues were verbally presented and ill-prepared, so there was
o focus for discussion, conclusion and action. Most meetings
were thus badly attended and the people coming changed from
onth to month. The two organisations with the inclination
nd resources to provide a secretariat - ICSS/IVAC and the
articipation office - were not acceptable to many workers
ecause they feared it would be the first stage in a take-over
id for management of all community work in the borough.

The only real attempt to provide any sort of training did not happen until 1978, when the community work lecturers at the Polytechnic of North London were prevailed upon to organise a formal course. About a dozen workers attended (mainly those in isolated situations), and the lecturers could draw them out without being seen as a threat. Most participants found them very useful and wanted the courses extended.

The lack of disciplined organisation and skills, and the varied working situation, also affected the relationship between workers and groups. One of the basic tasks of community workers is to transmit skills to group members to enable them to involve their own members, manage their own affairs and organise their own campaigns, but no proper arrangements existed for workers to learn skills to pass on and develop the proper relationship between workers and groups. While some workers were employed by, and responsible to, community group management committees, and could only act with their explicit or implicit support, other agencies had peer group management committees or provided community workers with no management support or direction. Workers in those situations often felt able to put forward their own views as those of 'the community' and often ended up in advocacy roles rather than the community work role of enabling people to organise and speak for themselves.

This had two harmful affects.

First, workers actually prevented people from developing leadership roles with widespread community support. Instead of making space for people and helping them grow into the leadership role, the workers occupied the space themselves (often on the grounds that there was no one around to say what they thought needed saying). This was a self-fulfilling prophecy. Although there were other factors as well, it was certainly a significant and contributory factor to the decline in the number of community leaders and activists over the decade. By 1978 the only people interested in the broad policy questions raised by the new Partnership were workers.

Second, workers infringed the role of elected councillors, without whose support the work could not be funded. While obviously community work is controversial, and some councillors opposed every aspect, in the main councillors opposed some things that workers did and supported others. But no concerted attempt was made to inform and involve councillors in the things they would approve, or consolidate their support, though the community-controlled projects had a much better record in this respect than the others.

When it was realised that the old guard had regained control after 1978, and community work was under threat, an attempt to canvass councillors was made, but it was too late. Prior to then, many workers had treated the old guard councillors with contempt, without recognising that whatever their shortcomings

they were people with whom many sections of the working-class
community identified. Many of the criticisms of community work
by right-wing councillors - that they spoke on behalf of people
without a mandate, prevented other people becoming involved,
and undermined the councillors' role - were justified by the
behaviour of some workers. The origins of such behaviour are
understandable - a personal conviction in one's own beliefs, a
genuine belief that other people are not acting in the
community's best interest, the fact that these criticisms
applied equally to the right-wing councillors themselves, the
effects of an elitist education system, or the acceptance of
a set of professional values which take higher priority than
democratic control. However, such behaviour was clearly
incompatible with the community work ethic - to enable ordinary
people to stand up for themselves.

The absence of a common set of values and sense of direction,
the high turnover of workers with limited continuity and
achievement, and the absence of support services, all reduced
the potential contribution that the extensive community work
input to the borough could have made. What lessons should be
drawn? Workers all wanted to maximise their own freedom of
action, even where that meant remaining in an isolated,
frustrated position. The absence of moral support and someone
to discuss issues and problems with, and the lack of continuity
from one worker to the next, means no project should employ
only one worker. But the obvious solution - that there should
have been fewer projects, each properly staffed and managed -
was unacceptable. With the small amount of contact and co-
operation that existed between workers, and each believing that
their own work was of paramount importance, there was no
possibility that a collective approach could be negotiated.
In some cases the workers recognised the need for this, but
left before doing anything about it, and were replaced by new
people who went through the whole process again.

The only body that had the power to impose a solution was
the council. The increasing tendency over the decade was for
new projects to be funded if they made a contribution to one of
the main department's programmes as seen from the department's
viewpoint. In practice, workers accepted these limitations on
their role by not organising to work in a different way. The
first projects to be cut in 1979 were those that worked from
the community's point of view rather than from the council's.
The community-based approach, supported by many councillors
early on, was not consolidated by community workers' own
efforts as councillors changed or developed other priorities.

In practice, the funding body is bound to impose a solution
in the long run, and if workers do not have a clear collective
position of their own, they will be powerless to influence the
council.

THE REASONS FOR THE DECLINE

From the beginning of 1975 interest in extending participation
steadily declined. There were many reasons for this, some
specific to Islington, some of more general origin.

   The political commitment of councillors was ebbing away. Those
elected on the 1971 programme had established many of their basic
objectives. They had also set the direction of the council and
thus increasingly had to defend it - they could not side with
critics against the previous council as they had done in their
early years of office. They were becoming more self-confident
in exercising their power as their knowledge and experience
increased, so they felt the need for public comment less. The
new councillors elected in 1974, although just as radical, did
not have the same opportunity to make an impact - they were
absorbed into the prevailing direction and power structure.

   A sophisticated set of sub-committees and working parties had
been established after 1971 for the councillors to manage and
monitor their policies and programmes. Many senior officers
could not stand the heat in the kitchen and others were forced
out. They were replaced (in the main) with more dynamic people
with some commitment to the council's objectives who put forward
ideas of their own. Meetings to discuss and develop programmes
became even more frequent. Coupled with the large number of
public meetings, pressures from constituents and the increasing
number of community groups, the time commitment needed from
councillors rose enormously. There was less time to think
about overall direction as they became more preoccupied with
immediate issues, and absorbed into managing the council
structure.

   This process was greatly reinforced by increasing financial
constraints. Councillors became even more introverted,
concentrating on minimising the harm of cuts to their programmes.
New demands for resources continued to come forward, mainly
from the big departments. Although there was real overall
growth in every council budget in the 1970s, increasingly there
was not enough money to pay for all the programmes and they
were funded by cuts elsewhere. This pressure - to make limited
resources go further - led to a substantial centralisation of
power. Performance Review and Finance and Expenditure sub-
committees of the Policy Committee were established in 1976,
budget reviews became annual events, every staff vacancy was
considered and many posts were left unfilled. As power became
more centralised in the hands of a few leading councillors, so
they required more support from the officers. Recognising that
their own workload was getting too big to cope with, the
councillors believed they would have a better chance of retaining
overall control if the officers' procedures were made more
formal. A centralised controlling body would ensure uniformity
of direction, and it would be easier to see the forces at work
and hold the officers accountable. The chief executive was

required to establish a policy planning office in 1977 to advise
the centre on the council's overall objectives and service the
policy and resources officers' working party (consisting of the
chief executive, the directors and heads of a few of the central
departments). This working party became increasingly powerful.
All major reports to any committee had to be approved by it, and
it became the arena where the deals on allocation of resources
between departments were cemented before presentation to
councillors.

To some extent the chief officers had to move into a political
leadership vacuum as well. A bitter row broke out in 1976 which
completely changed the power structure and working relationships
in the Labour group, leaving a situation of substantial personal
acrimony between the leading members, and an absence of political
direction. The council marked time for the eighteen months until
the 1978 elections. The bitterness and frustration of having to
put so much time into council work without being able to achieve
anything demoralised many councillors, over one quarter of whom
did not seek re-election in 1978.

The designation of Islington as a partnership area under the
government's inner-city programme in 1977 also had the effect
of centralising power. A new sub-committee of the Policy
Committee consisting of all the Committee chairmen was set up
to deal with all matters relating to partnership, including
the allocation of money. It was serviced by the head of the
policy planning team, who (with the chief executive) dealt
with the government at officer level. Reports on allocations
of money had to be approved by the policy and resources working
party. Perhaps most importantly the timetable imposed by the
government was incompatible with the council's own committee
timetable, so certainly in the early stages important decisions
were taken on programmes without reference to the appropriate
committee.

This process of centralisation happened gradually over
several years. The opportunity for back-bench councillors to
influence decisions declined. Though this topic was discussed
quite frequently, the usual solution was token back-bench
representation on the front-benchers' meetings. It did not
affect the basic trend that the structures through which
decisions were taken were becoming more centralised (i.e. were
controlled by fewer people), and this process inevitably
excluded more and more councillors from an effective role. In
the early 1970s, many of the councillors cultivated middle-tier
officers as a means of finding out what was going on in
departments and gaining an insight into disagreements between
officers that were glossed over in committee reports. As fewer
councillors had influence and as their advice came from an
increasingly centralised and hierarchical source, this informal
interaction lessened considerably.

Having established a management team that could give advice

on policy and programming, the councillors lost the initiative.
Debate was increasingly centred on marginal issues of organisation, particularly as financial constraints grew, and officers'
greater working knowledge gave them the edge here. While
councillors who had thought out their policies were setting the
scene for new officers in the early 1970s, the converse became
the norm.

These changes had a major effect on the development of
participation. The loss of a political base - the participation
committee - was not replaced by another. The councillor who
was the strongest advocate of participation, and had been the
first chairman of the committee, left the council in 1973.
Thus, while open government, participation and community groups
continued to be objectives the council supported, there was no
political pressure to develop them.

Links between councillors and community groups also became
more tenuous, as councillors became more absorbed in governing
the town hall; as groups learned to lobby the councillors who
would decide issues, rather than their local ward councillors;
and as debates on important issues increasingly revolved around
details of bureaucratic organisation, rather than the issues
themselves.

Emphasis changed in the relationship between the council and
groups too. The initial approach of providing groups with
financial support and independence to use their own initiative
was increasingly replaced by the council defining the terms
on which groups could operate. Although they were often
involved in the discussion that established the programmes,
the resources for groups to do their own research and analysis
were gradually withdrawn. Thus the council increasingly
defined the needs that the two sectors combined to meet.
Further, because of the council's increased emphasis on
programme planning and making the best use of scarce resources,
groups were increasingly caught in a web of financial rules,
value for money assessments, reviews and monitoring, which
limited their independence and increased the amount of time
and effort they had to use to satisfy the council's requirements.
Instead of resources being used to provide proper accounting
advice in a way which groups would find helpful and supportive,
the council started auditing the books of arbitrarily selected
ones. The relationship became one of paymaster and servant,
rather than either a partnership to achieve particular objectives
or the same sort of contractual arrangements that the council
has with other organisations that it pays to provide a service
(e.g. building contractors).

Many of the pressures for these changes came from officers
who started applying their own bureaucratic standards to
community groups.

The initial pressures for reform of the council, to make it

operate in a way and at a level that people could understand,
and thus influence it and hold it accountable, were reversed -
everyone had to operate on the council's terms. The same
process increasingly applied to public consultation arrangements,
and open government became a substitute for participation and
community development, rather than an aspect of it. The hostile
attitude of some officers to participation found earlier was
reinforced by the later recruitment of new people to key posts,
who were not sympathetic to the basic principles, and who were
not made to change by councillors enforcing their policy.

Thus, attempts from within the council systematically to
extend the opportunities of people to influence decision-making
and service provision disappeared with the participation
committee in 1976. In spite of this, the pressures from the
groups and projects to influence their own direct concerns, and
the precedents, policies and styles of work already established,
continued to a large extent. Although the opportunities for
groups to influence key decisions and their relationship with
the council were changing for the worse, the amount the council
spent on grants and its own liaison, consultation and participation activities continued to increase in real terms each year
up to and including 1978-9.

This was largely made possible by Islington's designation
as a partnership area, thus getting an injection of additional
government money. The partnership was supposed to develop
strategies and programmes to regenerate inner-city areas, but
attempts to involve people were largely unsuccessful. Issues
were presented in a very generalised and meaningless way. In
the main, groups had by then become cynical about the council's
willingness to consider policy questions, become preoccupied
with their own concerns and (like many parts of the council)
viewed the partnership as a source of funds for projects, but
little more than that. While some community workers were
prepared to take up partnership issues, groups were not. In
general, the partnership brought home the changes that gradually
evolved. The council was run from the centre; the powerful
councillors and officers concerned were not interested in
enabling groups to put forward alternative policies for
debate, though they went through the motions of consultation;
but they still believed groups had a contribution to make in
the actual provision of welfare services.

THE CUTS

In the borough elections in May 1978, Labour won all the seats
but two, but the composition of the Labour group itself was
very different from that in the previous council. Eighteen
councillors had not sought re-election and the usual bitter
battle between new and old guard had taken place at selection
meetings for candidates. The old guard made a comeback, and
had a small majority, although they did not organise straight
away.

The following year a major row broke out on the size of the
rate increase. The recommended level of nearly 40 per cent was
too high for the old guard, who united and mobilised at the last
minute to make cuts in the proposed budget. They won the vote
at the rate-making council meeting by a majority of one, and then
proceeded to win all the committee chairmanships in the Labour
group elections the following month.

Their violent opposition to many of the new guard's innovations
was reinforced by the election of the Tory government, committed
to massive public expenditure cuts. Early rate forecasts for
1980-1 showed another massive increase on the way, and the
majority on the council wanted to keep it as low as possible.
In the end a 40 per cent increase in the rates still meant an
8 per cent cut in services in real terms. In spite of opposition
by the new guard councillors, and major campaigns against the
cuts by community groups, the old guard forced the cuts through
in two stages. They included all the neighbourhood projects,
the participation office and the grants for a lot of specific
groups (about 10 per cent of all grants).

The organisations they cut were not those that provided a
specific voluntary service which supplemented the council's
own; they were the community organisations that gave people a
direct say in running a particular service, or the community-
based community development agencies that enabled people to
find out about the council's policies and services and develop
their own alternatives. Many of these organisations had
been constantly critical of the old guard and its policies,
and had supported the new guard in the local power struggles. Many
had actually been created by the new guard and the older councillor
resented the pressure they generated. They disagreed with their
values and objectives, and objected to the large amount of money
involved.

The reason the council gave for cutting these projects, and
the participation office, was that they had done their work.
Groups were well established and did not need help any more.
This obviously ignored the fact that new groups arise all the
time for many reasons, including council intervention in their
area; that many groups have a high membership turnover and
need constant support; that projects provide direct services
to groups, particularly to enable them to communicate and
publicise their activities; and that even well-established
groups do not have people with the time to ferret through the
bureaucracy for information, even if someone tells them what
is happening. Although the Code of Practice on Open Government
and Public Participation was not formally rescinded, the
closure of the participation office meant that many of the
rights it gave to groups and individuals no longer existed in
practice. There was no one to do the work involved.

But not all community work was cut. Workers who support
self-help projects, particularly in the fields of welfare,

community play and community centres have so far retained their
jobs. However, the inclination of the old guard to make cuts
anyway, their pathological hostility to welfare programmes,
community workers, groups, and rate increases, and the cuts in
government support, suggest a difficult future for even this
work.

In spite of the pressure from national government for cuts
in local authority expenditure, community work in Islington
was cut for political reasons rather than financial. A change
in the composition of the council gave the right-wingers control.
While it is likely that the new guard, had it remained in power,
would have made substantial cuts in expenditure in the face
of the council's financial position, they would not have made
so many and it is unlikely that they would have wiped out the
community development organisations and the participation
office. They still saw some value in public involvement in the
council's work, and community projects with advice and information support to promote it. Nevertheless, there is no doubt
that the importance to them of increasing participation in
decision-making declined steadily from the mid-1970s and there
is no evidence to suggest that the decline would have been
reversed by the present new guard councillors.

If participation is to become a main platform of the council's
policy again, a new initiative is needed to establish it in the
manifestos for the next local election in 1982.

CONCLUSION

The key to the achievements in Islington was the investment of
resources in community groups through encouraging their information and grant-aiding their activities, coupled with changes
to the way the council itself worked. They were made possible
by a group of professional, highly competent, and energetic
councillors who were partially freed from the usual pressures
for continuity in government provided by political party and
full-time bureaucracy.

The participatory structures enabled groups and projects to
gain background information on the council's policy and objectives, and the reasons for them; develop informal contact with
councillors and officers to exchange information and ideas,
or lobby them; and table reports and present their own case
on many issues through membership of sub-committees, or
deputations to committees and full council. Without these
opportunities they would have had much greater difficulty in
influencing decisions, while councillors would have been
limited to their officers' advice, which obviously reflected
their own points of view, and on some occasions was obstructive
and on others just plain wrong.

Although the council's powers were severely limited by

central government's control of both money and legislation, the
achievements in Islington were substantial in terms of physical
improvement of housing, open space and community facilities, and
the range and quality of services. Further, the constraints
imposed by central government were successfully challenged to
alter legislation and increase the money available.

Community groups played a substantial part, by their own
efforts and their pressure on the council. Many improvements
were only made by hard work and extensive campaigning to overcome
bureaucratic delay, or to defeat scepticism or opposition from
some sections of the council. When the council's own efforts
to extend participation faded, the groups and projects that had
been established continued to make gains. With about 220 groups
receiving grants, and 800 groups on the 'Info' mailing list, the
number of people active in them numbered several thousand; and
the quality of life of many thousands more was improved by the
services the groups initiated and ran themselves, and the
council's policies and programmes which they influenced. While
some gains were vulnerable to later cuts, many of them were
permanent physical improvements.

Many of the groups were promoted by community projects, but
their benefit was uneven. There was no overall plan for the
distribution or role of community workers. If the need had been
recognised in the early 1970s, when money was less tight, before
other projects had been set up, and while the old guard
councillors were still in disarray, it may have been possible
to establish one. Without it the old guard councillors were
largely able to prevent community projects being established
in their wards, and avoid the consequent pressure to be more
active and effective representatives. If one of the roles of
community projects is to develop this pressure (and in Islington
it was) then an overall plan is necessary to establish projects
in hostile territory.

The absence of an overall policy also meant that other areas
with equal need were without community projects, though there
they wouldn't have been opposed by local councillors. It
wouldn't even have been necessary to increase expenditure on
community work to have had a neighbourhood project with two
workers in each ward, but by the time the issue of a planned
distribution was identified there were several projects already
in operation that wouldn't fit into an overall plan, so there
was considerable opposition within community work itself, as
well as from many councillors and service departments.

The absence of projects from many areas also limited the
scope of liaison workers within the council, who could work
much more effectively with and through neighbourhood projects.

An overall plan could have provided for the necessary support
and training of workers too, and focused more attention on the
way the council actually worked to make participation easier.

The loss of the participation committee, demise of the
participation office, centralisation of power, transfer of power
from councillors to officers, and the basic structure of the
council were never challenged by community workers.

   Participation also posed another dilemma for workers: should
they try to encourage groups to take up key local issues before
the groups had the confidence, knowledge and resources to do so,
or let the council resolve the issue without any input from the
group. The answer was an individual one, depending on the
relative importance of the group process or the council decision
to the worker.

   The structure of council departments, and the grading system
and career structure for local government officers, tends to
prevent them identifying with the local community and becoming
accountable to it. One of the results of increased participation
was a partial breaking down of departmental hierarchies, and
increased direct access to officers by groups. However, this
became less significant as the power of middle tier officers
steadily declined as departments re-established their hierarchical
pattern. This crystallises an important dilemma - how to
structure the council so political control of overall planning
and resource allocation is possible, whilst still allowing
effective participation on the issues groups feel to be
important, and the necessary corollary of a highly decentralised
power structure. As councillors became more absorbed in running
the town hall, some hoped that groups would help them deal with
the management problems posed by scarce resources, but few
groups became concerned with issues outside their own immediate
interests. The council itself encouraged this limitation, as
it largely kept control of policy issues, and never accepted
the case for strong independent federations of groups with the
resources to do their own policy development work, and thus they
were never adequately funded.

   The opposition of old guard councillors to community projects
was symptomatic of a wider problem. The new guard councillors,
many officers and most community workers, were well-educated
professional people, and tended to look down on both the old
guard councillors and their main political base - the tenants
of the big council estates. The participation programme
established and encouraged associations of these tenants so
the old guard councillors had mixed attitudes to it to start
with, but no real framework was provided for the tenants
associations to have a positive influence, and they felt the
quality of life on their estate was going down due to the
council's neglect and lettings policy. They started vehemently
attacking the council, but on some issues the community workers
did not support the right-wing views of the tenants' associations.
If the community workers had made the effort to work with the
old guard councillors and the tenants' associations in the
early/mid 1970s there was a chance that the great cultural
divide could have been overcome, and at least some of the

working-class councillors could have been encouraged to support community projects. While it is likely that the problems posed by the mutual reinforcement of the class and political divisions within the power struggle would have defeated any such attempts, they weren't made, and so it was not surprising that the old guard started cutting community projects as soon as it could.

The most important lesson of the case study is that participation is political - it is trying to involve people in decision-making by elected representatives, or contesting or sharing the power of those representatives. It increased in Islington for as long as the councillors encouraged it and were prepared to respond to public demand. Though many community groups successfully argued for improvements and changes to council policies and services, they did not recognise the importance of the political change in the control of the council that enabled them to do so, and thus they did not attempt to permanently secure it. Although the effect of the council as an institution promoting participation (and using public money for it) was to involve many more people than would otherwise have been the case, it also made it 'non-political'. So while more people increased their knowledge and self-confidence, and learnt political skills of organisation and tactics, they were able to influence public policy from outside the normal political framework. Some of these people joined political parties, but many did not; and many joined the Labour party to oppose what the council was doing. The new guard councillors got too bogged down in running the council and in their internal conflict to extend their base. Councillors have both a political and a management role, but the pressures of the latter led to the neglect of the former. Thus the old guard were able to win back several wards in 1978, and proceeded to cut the programmes and community projects that had facilitated participation. While large numbers of people actively opposed cuts to projects and services with which they identified, the right-wing councillors were bitterly determined to cut the main advances made by the left, although some groups were able to use the skills and confidence they had built up over the years to successfully defend themselves by skilful lobbying and community action.

But, more significantly, many people have realised how powerless community action is if the council is not at all sympathetic to their needs and aspirations. The struggle for control of the Labour party has intensified and recruitment is increasing as many people have reacted against the cuts to services in which they were involved, and they have recognised the importance of the political framework which made their involvement possible. Many of the 1971 councillors joined the Labour party to improve the local situation without having much regard for the Party's wider performance. It looks as though this may happen again.

The real test of the participation programme will be the extent to which community groups relate to the political process

to regroup after their political defeat, and re-establish the
services and projects in the way they want them, and at the
same time learn the lessons of the last decade.

NOTES AND REFERENCES

1 Many of the references in the article refer to council
   committee papers or publications of community projects. All
   of these papers are deposited with the Islington Central
   Reference Library, the Library of the Polytechnic of North
   London and the Islington Bus Company, along with other
   papers of interest.

       'SAC' refers to reports submitted to, and approved by,
   the Special Advisory Committee on Public Consultation and
   Participation. They would then be referred to the appropriate
   committee (and sometimes to the full council) within the
   following two months. Annual progress reports were also
   published.
2 The full report, compiled independently by Richard Kirkby,
   is at the Central Reference Library. A synopsis was presented
   to the SAC in September 1974.
3 'Criteria for Funding Community Newsletters', SAC, April 1975.
4 This is now held by the Islington Bus Co., Palmer Place,
   London, N7.
5 Included in the 'Code of Practice on Public Participation
   and Open Government' approved by the Council in October,
   1976.
6 SAC, September, 1974.
7 'Review of Participation in the Work of the Recreation
   Committee', SAC, September, 1975.
8 'Review of Participation in the Work of the Housing
   Committee', SAC, December, 1975.
9 'Review of Participation in the Work of the Planning
   Committee', SAC, January, 1976.
10 'Review of Participation in the Work of the Social Services
   Committee', SAC, March, 1976.
11 'Review of Participation in the Work of the Public Services
   Committee', SAC, March, 1976.
12 'Review of Participation in the Work of the Policy
   Committee', SAC, March 1976.
13 SAC, September 1975.
14 'Islington's Multinationals and Small Firms - Magic or Myth?',
   Islington Economy Group (c/o Peter Brimson, 56, Cowley Road,
   London, E11).
15 SAC, October 1975
16 Partnership sub-committee, October 1978.
17 'Tenant Participation in Estate Management', SAC, September
   1974.
18 Report of the Royal Commission on the Personal Social
   Services, HMSO, 1968, Cmnd 3703.
19 'Community Work and Social Services' - report of council
   community workers group to an officers working party reviewing

community development (it never reported due to the change in control of the council).

20 Participation in Planning, HMSO, 1968.

21 Report to the planning committee, 'Public Participation in the Borough Development Programme', October 1973.

22 Dr Tony Gibson, Nottingham University Institute of Adult Education.

23 'Islington Borough Plan and Public Consultation - A review of the Issues Stage', R. le B. Williams, Open University, May 1976.

24 'Whose Choice? Islington - a study of an exercise in Participation', Keith Cook and Liz Dawtry, Urban Planning Research Unit, Polytechnic of North London, May 1978.

25 'I Woke Up This Morning', Anne Power, Community and Race Relations Unit of the British Council of Churches, 1972.

26 'A Battle Lost: Barnsbury 1972', Holloway Neighbourhood Law Centre, 1972.

27 'Participation in Urban Planning: the Barnsbury Case', John Ferris, Occasional Paper 48, Social Administration Research Trust, 1972.

28 Anne Power, 'David and Goliath: Barnsbury 1973', Barnsbury Forum, 1973.

29 'Gentrification in Islington', James Pitt, Barnsbury Forum, 1977.

30 'Friends Neighbourhood House 1967-78', S. Clarke and Paul Henderson, Friends Community Relations Committee, 1978.

31 'A Better Place', Shelter, 1974.

32 'Holloway Tenant Co-operative - 5 years on', Anne Power, North Islington Housing Rights Project, 1978.

33 Anne Power, 'Helping Tenants to Help Themselves', 'The Times' (Guest Column), 13 September, 1978.

34 Chris Holmes, 'A Better Tomorrow', NIHRP, 1974.

35 Roger Hamilton, 'The Case for Housing Action Areas in Islington', NIHRP, 1975.

36 Roger Hamilton, Anne Power and Chris Holmes, 'Street by Street - Improvement and Tenant Control in Islington', NIHRP, 1977.

37 A Case Study by Maggie Hindley on Regina Road HAA in 'Collective Action', ed. Michaela Dungate, Paul Henderson and Leo Smith, Association of Community Workers and Community Projects Foundation, 1978 (c/o Community Centre, Colombo Street, London, SE1.

38 The NIHRP Annual Report for 1979/80 describes the Elthorne Project.

39 See the Bus Co's Annual Report.

40 SAC, September 1972.

41 An unpublished article by Bob Gilbert, one of the project workers, in 1977.

42 'Neighbourhood Councils in England - Response from the London Borough of Islington', SAC, September 1974.

43 See also 'The Promotion of Neighbourhood Projects in Islington', by Leo Smith in 'Towards Neighbourhood Democracy', Ed. Stephen Hatch and Stephen Humble, ARVAC Pamphlet No.2 (c/o 2 Alma St., Wivenhoe, Essex).

3 Area management: Newcastle's Priority Areas Programme

Chris Miller

INTRODUCTION

Newcastle's Priority Area Programme (otherwise known as 'Stress Area Project') announced in June 1976 is one of the eight area management schemes monitored by INLOGOV for the Department of Environment's area management trials. (1)

Area management has been described by the Department of Environment as 'a natural development of the new approach to local government organisation ... extending the corporate approach down to an area level.' (2) The trials have been to 'analyse problems, formulate policies and monitor their effects in a corporate way at an area level; operate services more sensitively to local needs by better evaluating their performance; provide a convenient channel of communication between the council and neighbourhood councils, residents associations and other groups and individuals; (and) provide a framework in which elected members can relate Council policies to local case-work and vice versa.' (3)

Newcastle's approach, however, is markedly different from many of the other schemes being established explicitly to tackle deprivation (labelled 'stress' by the city) within the inner area. Indeed the authority had already rejected an area management project styled after the Liverpool 8 scheme. (4) The key feature of the programme has been the command over resources by local priority area teams (PATs), and a strong centre has been favoured in the belief that this provides greater flexibility at the periphery than that of traditional area management systems. This emphasis on alleviating stress rather than devolving broad local government functions is crucial in an assessment of the scheme and the response to it by local organisations and community workers.

Although the council created structures at a ward level which they hoped would facilitate the active participation of local groups, the response to this invitation should be judged against

the likelihood of the scheme successfully combating the problems
it identified, i.e. inner-city deprivation. It was not an
invitation to 'participate' in the broad responsibilities of
the city authority. Whilst a minority did see it as an
opportunity to widen the debate into a demand for 'open
government', most political activists in the community saw it as
an offer to participate in, and thereby condone, a programme
that could never realistically make a substantial impact on the
problems of the inner city. For the majority of local groups,
their cynicism born of experience was however tempered by a
desire to make financial gain by their involvement. 'Participation' amounted to a very functional and opportunistic assessment
of how much might be gained in hard financial terms. There is
nothing unusual about this. 'Participation' should not be seen
as something intrinsically 'good', rather the question should
always be posed of participation for what and by whom. Whether
or not community organisations respond to area management
schemes, or other similar offers from above, will ultimately
depend on factors such as the specific origins of each programme,
the strength and direction of the groups concerned, an analysis
of the potential scope and dangers embodied in the proposals
and how these all relate to the needs and priorities of local
groups. Demands for participation per se tend to have a hollow
sound. The word is meant to describe a 'process' utilised to
achieve specific ends. To participate or not must necessarily
be a tactical decision to be made on the basis of what can be
gained, and at what cost. For socialists, the questions to be
answered are ultimately whether it provides opportunities for
a shift in power and resources in favour of working-class
organisations, whether it offers the possibility of politicisation and if it will assist in the process of building working-
class organisations aimed at socialist programmes, structures
and practice.

THE PROGRAMME

The Labour party was returned to office in Newcastle in 1974
with a manifesto that talked of devolution to local areas.
Very little emerged until the public expenditure cuts of
September 1975 when the authority's budget review adopted a
strategy of giving 'priority to the people in greatest need'.
This, with the planning department's interest in area management
and the revival of interest in the 'inner city', resulted in
the publication in April 1976 of the city's Green Paper, 'Top
Priority'. The paper outlined the authority's approach to
combating 'stress' in the priority areas, predominately the
riverside wards formerly dominated by heavy industry. The
paper asked for comments and was distributed amongst voluntary
and community organisations. A one-day conference was held in
June to which local representatives were invited. Final
approval was given by full council in October and the city
moved to implement it the following month.

Yet the origins of the programme are located in a wider
context. Positive discrimination, area-based approaches to
tackling deprivation and area management were all well known
in the vocabulary of urban managers. Newcastle's approach was
in one sense simply in keeping with central government strategy
for combating poverty and managing conflict. For ten years the
state has been experimenting in similar programmes with £80m
being poured into the urban programme, educational priority
areas, community development projects (CDPs), inner area
studies, quality of life studies and now area management trials
and comprehensive community programmes. Yet perhaps more
significant was the Newcastle Labour party's need to strengthen
its fragile power base at a time of cuts in public expenditure.
(5) The programme was an opportunity to demonstrate that the
council cared; it was a symbol of the party's political
commitment to working-class interests and its answer to the
crisis faced by many Labour groups, namely re-energising its
local base and the relationship between its members and the
local electorate. Pressures at the centre, city-wide responsibilities, the party line, not to mention the broader constraints
imposed by central government, have seriously weakened the
ward-specific role of the councillors, resulting in them often
being out of touch with their constituents, and therefore out
of control. When power is marginal this is crucial since
councillors face growing scepticism, a refusal to legitimate
their authority by a low turnout at the polls and the development
of alternative forms of political action. Hence a combination
of fringe spending and member involvement in the wards was
particularly important at a time of economic stringency and
Labour's marginal power in the city.

The priority area programme, based on the 1971 census and a
1975 5 per cent household social characteristics survey, had
three key features, none unfamiliar to earlier poverty
programmes. The first was an attempt to identify the socially
deprived areas in the city, with twelve of the city's political
wards being highlighted as 'areas with the greatest concentration of social and environmental disadvantage'. Public participation in the programme, the second feature, was not initially an
intrinsic part of the package, but was elevated in emphasis
following discussions with voluntary and community organisations.
(6) The third key element was the enhanced status of the ward
councillors, the Green Paper arguing that their combined skills
and local knowledge would be invaluable to the programme.
Beecham, the council leader, was more explicit, stating 'wards,
rather than wider areas, were chosen in order to provide a
political focus and maximise the role of the local representatives', (7) and not because they were the most appropriate
boundary for tackling the identified issues. Finally, the
Green Paper recognised the city's limitations, noting that they
were intent on alleviating the symptoms of stress rather than
the root causes. The programme's main features included a
review of the authority's existing work to ensure that positive
discrimination both to individuals and geographical areas under

stress became a reality for all departments. A team was
appointed to attract more job opportunities for the unemployed
and the authority established ward-based priority area teams
consisting of officers, the local ward and county councillors.
A policy and resources sub-committee was created as the ultimate
authority on the programme, in charge of the centrally allocated
budget, authorising and monitoring team expenditure and impact,
and co-ordinating the council's priority areas activities.
Two other wards, both Tory controlled, were added to the
programme, the first in April 1977 and the second in 1978. (8)

During the scheme's first financial year (1976-7) the
authority allocated £500,000 drawn from its accumulated reserve
fund. With only five months to spend there was considerable
urgency to find projects, yet by the end of the year £90,000
remained unspent. Each local team was allocated £10,000, the
remaining sum being distributed centrally to proposals submitted
by the mainline departments. There was little that was new or
exciting amongst the centrally funded projects but included
were such items as environmental improvements in HAA and GIAs,
acquisition of a voluntarily run community centre, funding for
additional playleaders and an adventure playground, the
provision of residential accommodation for the elderly,
additional nursery classes, landscaping and industrial training
courses, all of which were quite clearly the normal responsibility of the mainline departments. Beecham had to admit
that the 'Central Fund proposals had been cobbled together
rather hurriedly', (9) and included projects that 'could hardly
be justified as coming within area-based stress'. (10)

The local PATs managed to account for £93,000 on such items
as grants to youth clubs, purchase of play equipment, support
to local jazzbands, a food co-operative, recreational facilities,
minibuses for community transport and support for an urban
farm. Grants varied from £20 to £13,000 and between wards from
£5,000 to £16,000. The largest proportion of the funds went to
youth provision (£328,125) followed by environmental improvements
(£154,945), community meeting-places (£148,940) and the elderly
(£120,000). During that first year voluntary and community
organisations received £43,000 from the central fund (8 per cent
of total) and £88,000 from the area teams (25 per cent of the
total).

The 1977-8 programme was increased to £1,000,000, £10,000
coming from the Department of Environment, £500,000 being
allocated to local teams (£45,000 each). Of the centre's £½m,
£250,000 was earmarked for assistance to the employment
programme, £60,000 to establishing a new nursery, £60,000 for
residential care for adolescents and the £40,000 worth of urban
aid applications rejected by the Department of Environment were
also taken on. Area teams were now able to allocate a maximum
of £500 on any item, with a £5,000 per annum ceiling, without
ratification by the central sub-committee. The £1m budget was
retained for 1978-9 with supposedly more emphasis on the local

teams and less on central spending, whilst £60,000 was also set
aside for projects in non-priority areas.

AN ATTACK ON STRESS?

As a scheme designed to tackle 'stress', Newcastle's programme
was always intended to be something more than a different
approach to local government management. Yet, measuring the
scheme against its original outline is difficult since the
language and emphasis have changed considerably as the project
developed. Indeed it is sometimes difficult to gauge how much
importance the authority really attaches to it, for, although
described by Beecham as 'the instrument for breaking free from
the shadow of deprivation and disadvantage', (11) with the aim
of building 'a just city', it has also been described as 'mere
entertainment value' by another leading and active councillor.
Beecham's aspirations have indeed grown since the early days
when the authority was admitting its inability to attack 'root
causes' and confining its hopes to 'alleviating the worst
symptoms'. Further, the authority has never appeared clear
about what it meant by 'stress' and has often viewed it, not as
a symptom but as an objective 'thing'. Everything from poverty
to mental illness to inadequate housing is labelled as 'stress',
a practice which allows the city to ignore the structural
causes of social problems and the leverage points for political
pressure, confining itself to the already redundant social or
individual pathology model.

During the public deliberations, community organisations
were not slow to point to the contradiction of an authority
introducing a programme to combat 'stress' at the same time
as reducing basic public services. The city's tenants'
federation pointed out that £1½m allocated to the priority
area programme (1976-8) was the equivalent of £12 per head
of population in the stress areas. (12) This compared with
rent increases averaging 0.50p per week in September 1976 and
amother 30p in October 1977, making a total increase of £40
per year. Both the housing capital and modernisation budgets
were cut by £7.6m and £3 respectively during 1976-8, as were
proposals for new housing by £5m. Similarly, whilst £20,000
from the stress fund for alleviating conditions in clearance
areas was announced, this amounted to an actual loss of £30,000
compared to the original sum proposed. More recently, in
December 1978 the authority proposed further cuts including
£1½m from the education budget and a further £1 per week rent
increase. Similarly a desire to improve the take-up of social
security and local-welfare benefits cannot compensate for the
demand for wage restraint, the withdrawal of food and fuel
subsidies, and the real cuts in social security levels.

Against such a background the programme is at best an attempt
to maintain a very basic level of services, services normally
provided by the mainline departments. Projects that are

supplementary in character can obviously offer benefits but do require the authority to recognise the political realities and act, where necessary, against external forces such as central government.

The amount invested by the authority is also woefully inadequate £250,000 to develop employment opportunities through 'starter' factories, workshops, training/retraining facilities, whilst useful and possibly innovative , cannot affect the redundancies and closures within local industry, nor the high levels of unemployment (average male unemployment was 9.6 per cent in 1976 with peaks of 13.6 per cent and as high as 30 per cent in some wards) nor industry's ability to act in a socially irresponsible manner. In terms of the authority's total allocation the programme represents 0.9 per cent of its 1977-8 expenditure and only 10 per cent of its 'flexible' budget. Beecham maintains that over a five-year period 'the sums of money involved become significant ... in relation to the prevailing level of growth of the Authority as a whole', but this does not meet the charge that the amount is simply inadequate. Indeed many of the projects undertaken cannot be justified in terms of alleviating stress, e.g. repairing/ renovating churches, Jubilee celebrations, grants to jazzbands, scouting organisations and hobby groups, tree planting and other environmental cosmetics. Yet projects such as these have taken more than an insubstantial amount of the funds.

The extent to which an area-based policy is an appropriate framework for tackling concentrations of urban deprivation ... remains debatable. (13)

Newcastle has adopted the view that people suffer because they live where they do. Yet although people suffer, in relation to housing, jobs, schools, etc., because they happen to live in a particular area, this is not a function of their living there but is rather a consequence of certain historical developments combined with the particular values and power relationships within society. The city has learnt little from ten years of poverty programmes including Liverpool's inner area study which noted 'this poverty [in the inner area] is a reflection of inequalities in society as a whole. Clearly the scale and character of the problem is too great for policies concerned solely and specifically with inner areas to be effective. Any fundamental change must come through policies concerned with the distribution of wealth and allocation of resources'. (14)   Unequal access to environmental and recreational provision, and discrimination in service provision are not primarily a consequence of where you live but are rather determined by one's economic and social position, race, sex, family characteristics and beyond to the dominant economic interests and ruling ideas in society. What might be important about working in small areas would be to identify those situations where localised solutions could be appropriate and how action in a local area can ensure change in national policies.

Further, in Newcastle, the way in which the areas were chosen
was somewhat crude, the indices used being superficial and limited
in scope. The use of ward boundaries was an explicitly political
decision bearing no relation to the issues. The limited money
available was allocated equally to each local team rather than
on the basis of need, size of area, population, levels of
deprivation, incidence of deprived or 'at risk' groups, or
differential levels of existing services. Quite clearly, this
would have been politically unacceptable given the variations in
councillors' power and status. Additionally, councillors have
different levels of experience, commitment and interest in either
the whole question of resource allocation or their particular
ward and therefore local teams and the residents they represent
suffer accordingly.

A key variable in assessing schemes like Newcastle's is the
extent it can affect mainline committee policy. Local teams do
appear to be able to perform a catalytic role in that projects,
successfully established after initial pump-priming, become the
direct responsibility of the mainline service committee and the
central sub-committee is responsible to policy and resources.
However, to be truly influential the programme would require
far greater political unity than currently exists in the city.
Whilst INLOGOV could detect 'no readily identifiable clique
actively manoeuvring against the programme', (15) there is a
split into broadly two camps over the party leadership which
affects behaviour and decision-making. Team leaders have also
complained of a lack of commitment from departmental chiefs
and senior management who must, in part, see the programme as
a criticism of past practice. There is a degree of resentment
at the newly acquired prestige of back-benchers and junior
officers, who have moved into areas of information and influence
previously closed to them, and who are felt to be unqualified
to deal with matters normally reserved for specialised
committees. The community development aspect is also a
challenge to both social services and education, already in
conflict over who should hold responsibility for community work
in the authority. Consequently, there is a level of tension
and disharmony between both the local teams and mainline
departments and within the ruling Labour group. Naturally,
officers and members are aware of the conflicts and no doubt
exploit this should they think it necessary. In this context
local organisations have little chance of influencing major
policies if they confine their strategies to the authority's
structures.

Finally, the principal of positive discrimination - unequally
generous treatment for those who start with the greatest
disadvantage - looks somewhat shaky in the wider context. For
such an approach to be effective there must first exist a
minimally agreed standard of what is desirable and an equal
share of that minimum going to different groups and areas.
Yet, quite clearly this has never been the case and in a
situation of economic cutback positive discrimination becomes a

rather feeble attempt to maintain the pre-cut level of already
inadequate services. Since the public sector in the normal
course of service provision tends to reinforce rather than
redress inequalities, and inner areas do not normally receive
an equal share of services, it is misleading to speak of
positive discrimination. Concentration upon priority areas
cannot be an alternative to extra resources but rather assumes
their existence. In practice positive discrimination has meant
an increasing emphasis on how decreasing resource can be better
managed and reshuffled, energy being put into fine technical
decisions over the advantages or otherwise of marginal policies.
Inevitably too, in such circumstances, departments will exploit
these schemes to develop their normal activities.

The city is very proud of the participatory components to
their programme. Beecham saw it as a way both of influencing
decision-making and making local councillors and officials more
accountable. Participation offers, according to the authority,
'a unique opportunity', with 'local people identifying the
problems of their own community and formulating proposals for
tackling them....'. (16)   This view is reflected at least
amongst some of the councillors, for in a survey of twenty-two
Labour members involved in the programme, INLOGOV found 70 per
cent in favour of public participation (although in a situation
where the political influence of particular personalities is
often crucial, it would perhaps be as important to know who
was not in favour). The authority points out that between
October 1976 and March 1977 alone there were 62 public team
meetings at which approximately 124 groups or organisations
were represented. It has further expressed a wish to improve
this level for despite feeling that 'by all known yardsticks
the level of public participation appears encouraging (compared
with, for example, attendance at council committee meetings
and attendance at public meetings in other cities as reported
by INLOGOV), nevertheless 30 to 60 people per meeting represents
only 1% to 2% of the total ward population'. (17)   Consequently,
it agreed to commission a survey to explore the public
participation element of priority area team work. This was to
establish whether additional resources should be used to
promote public meetings, to measure the level of public
awareness, and receive feedback on the team's effectiveness
with and emphasis on any reported difficulties in trying to
influence the decision-making process. However, the results
showed that the percentage of households who had even basic
information was at best 34 per cent within a ward, and at the
lowest 11 per cent - a piece of information which generated
virtually nil response.

WHAT RESPONSE FROM COMMUNITY ORGANISATIONS?

The dilemma facing community workers committed to a socialist
perspective is how to respond to a programme that is so
confusing and contradictory. On the one hand it offers very

little relative to the scale of the problem and there are costs
and dangers to being involved. Participatory schemes initiated
from the top down are often concerned with the management of
conflict through the ability to anticipate events, the absorption
of oppositional forces and the imposition of a consensus ideology.
Yet the programme does offer badly needed resources, controls
the access to most state funding, and has provided support to a
number of worthwhile community projects. Since the authority
not only took the initiative but successfully involved local
groups in the process, workers with an alternative perspective
need to be involved in order to change the definition of reality.
Quite clearly there is a need for political education. An
alternative explanation, both for the causes and solutions to
problems facing inner-city residents, needs to be accepted by
those same residents. There is a need too to highlight the
ineffectiveness and contradictions of the authority's policy.

Workers need to warn groups of the dangers of parochialism
and fragmentation between groups and areas in the misplaced
belief that they are securing crucial resources. However, just
where this kind of work is carried out, either from within the
authority's programme as a participant or from the outside,
having rejected it as an irrelevance, is the crucial point.
The dilemma, though, is often resolved by the real needs of
local groups for money and resources which the programme provides.

To date, a concerted and critical opposition to the programme
based on a socialist analysis has been sporadic, limited in
scope and badly organised. Most of the initial criticism came
from three public meetings sponsored by the city's CVS and
subsequently via the inner city forum. A number of weaknesses
in the programme's structure were brought to the authority's
attention quite early with, so far, little response. At that
point city-wide opposition petered out and the forum became
more of an information exchange. At the public meeting, groups
pointed out that the system lacked any central direction or
guidelines, each team being left to establish for itself both
the level of participation and how that should be expressed.
Yet the idea of having minimum criteria to be followed by each
team was explicitly rejected by Beecham. Consequently, many
neither have regular public meetings at a fixed time and place,
nor do they necessarily meet in the local areas, choosing
instead the comfort of the civic centre. Many also meet during
the day, making it additionally difficult for working people
to attend. No attempt has been made to have local representatives elected on to the team through say, a street representative system, nor has there been an examination of the relationship between representatives of local groups, other agencies
and individual citizens. The public's right to participate
is undefined, some holding 'open' meetings, others inviting
selected representatives,and others offering no encouragement
whatsoever. Since there is no regularity of meeting, and no
requirement to meet in public, 'sensitive' matters are
resolved in camera, often between chairperson and team leader.

The whole question too of the public's ability to influence
decisions remains unresolved. What is clear, however, is that
councillors retain the right to make the ultimate decision.
Representatives of voluntary organisations are not voting members
and the authority has not taken up the option (under the 1972
Local Government Act) to co-opt representatives either to the
local teams or the central sub-committee. Indeed the latter
behaves like any other major committee with certain matters
being defined as private business and the local teams requiring
sub-committee approval for any item of expenditure above £500.
At the local level the situation is such that decisions made on
the basis of patronage, favouritism, social network, or vote
catching are not unusual. Pet schemes, personal prejudices
and ill-conceived ideas are all likely to succeed, providing
your relationship with significant team members is satisfactory.
Most meetings tend to view proposals in isolation from other
developments and many local groups attend meetings only when
seeking grant support. Consequently it is the members who are
left to devise any long-term strategy and there is no direct
and immediate public accountability as to how they spend their
allocation.

The authority has failed to take an active role in
encouraging and facilitating the public, both individually and
through local groups, to participate. Publicity - about
forthcoming team meetings, decisions made at earlier meetings,
projects undertaken, or ideas for the future - is at best
sporadic and often non-existent. The city has adopted the
traditional and passive role of creating structures and leaving
it up to the public as to whether or not they participate.
Given the widespread degree of mistrust and cynicism toward
the political system held by working people, (18) the lack of
faith in elected members and the tendency to dismiss 'politics'
(by which is meant party politics) as opportunism rather than
legitimate debate, (19) this is clearly inadequate. An
authority claiming a commitment to public participation or
open government must recognise that 'participation' has not
been seen as a worthwhile experience relative to the tangible
benefits or changed decisions brought about as a consequence
of the efforts of local people. More often than not it has
been a public relations exercise designed to legitimate
decisions already taken, 'cool-out' any likely opposition,
persuade people of their 'real' needs, or act as an electioneer-
ing tactic. Additionally, problems often arise for local
groups from the high level of sophistication, confidence,
ability and responsibility demanded by the authority, skills
which are often lacking in communities systematically deprived.
Paradoxically, it is in those areas where people may have had
the least opportunity or incentive to learn the skills of
citizenship that active involvement in local government decision-
making is now being sought. At the very least a policy of
positive discrimination must be paralleled by a commensurate
emphasis on community education if groups are to be called to
strengthen their capacities and take a more active role. It is

too easy for the authority to interpret non-attendance as a sign
of apathy, or validation to do whatever they wish, without
critically examining their own role in the continuing process
of facilitating involvement.

It is hard to determine how influential a group has been as
a direct consequence of their participation in the programme.
Increases in the level of skill, knowledge and political
consciousness are often either intangible or unmeasurable.
In Newcastle, groups have tended, perhaps realistically, to
measure the worth of their efforts by the amount of resources
that accrue to them. Yet groups also need to be aware of what
cost is involved in gaining such benefits. They often need to
acquire skills and confidence, they must initially learn the
rules of the game as defined by the authority, and given its
nebulous nature and informality this can be especially
frustrating and unproductive relative to any benefits obtained.
Their very presence may do no more than provide legitimation
for the authority's definition of the problem and method of
resolution and as a consequence they may forfeit their right to
independent criticism. They must develop personal contacts
with councillors which might involve them in a set of relationships from which it is difficult both to withdraw and to be
critical, and which councillors may attempt to exploit for
their own personal glorification. Groups may also be expected
to modify their behaviour if they are to receive continuing
support. A personalised approach at the fringes where marginal
issues are tackled in a very earnest manner can result in
attention being deflected from both the more significant areas
of decision-making and the more significant concerns.

Yet such schemes also provide possibilities. They can act as
a vehicle for a campaign for open government. They can expose
councillors to both a greater volume of pressure and a pressure
of a different nature. They can make councillors more
responsive to local needs and accountable to local groups.
They can provide a local forum in which groups can challenge
both the authority's definition of reality and its ideas for
problem resolution within that reality. Similarly there is an
opportunity for political education and consciousness raising
and an opening through which demands can be articulated. They
might also provide the basis for joint action between tenants
and workers within an area and for alliances with councillors
committed to radical change. They provide for the possibility
of immediate feedback on service delivery acting as an easily
locatable focus of attention in increasingly centralised
bureaucracies. Finally, they can provide a rationale for
funding for a range of innovative and valuable projects that
might otherwise be blocked or rejected. Groups must be
constantly aware of the pros and cons, their participation or
not being a tactical decision based on the potential of what
is offered for community control against how this might be
threatened.

Yet there is often a gap between such theoretical decisions and what actually happens in practice. In Newcastle, the city clearly took the initiative in establishing the programme and has maintained that position ever since. Thus, although some groups have attempted to offer alternative definitions and proposals, their influence has been insufficient to affect the 'hierarchy of credibility' used by large sections of the population. The authority has retained its ability to control the terms, the forms and the content of local political debate and action, thereby removing important issues about unequal distribution of scarce resources from local politics and redefining public issues as private troubles and political issues as technical concerns. It has been assisted in this both by its own flexibility in the kind of projects sponsored, its ability to place all the major resources relevant to community organisations under the programme's authority, and by the weakness of those most likely to pose an alternative construction of reality.

The city has funded or initiated a whole range of schemes many of which have been innovative and exciting and are likely to receive support from community workers. This would include such things as the trades council's centre for the unemployed, a resource centre, an urban farm, a workers' co-operative, a food co-operative, a variety of community meeting places for tenants' organisations, community transport projects, local theatre groups, a community press, a women's aid refuge, adult education projects, and play equipment and resources. Although much of this might have happened without the programme and not all are new or innovatory, none the less it is difficult for those concerned to make such distinctions when their prime interest is in getting resources. Second, and significantly, many community work posts within the city depend directly on either the Manpower Services Commission or the priority area programme. It is hard for workers not to give undue credibility to a programme that provides their livelihood. Third, the city has gradually centralised funding for community projects so that the priority sub-committee controls not only its own budget (£1m) but also the partnership programme (approximately £2.5m, of which £125,000 went to voluntary agencies in the first year) and urban aid. Similarly other departments are re-directing groups to the sub-committee if approached for funding.

Newcastle does not have a proliferation of community workers engaged in working with grass-roots organisations, and those groups most likely to provide an oppositional base have been unable to do so. Benwell CDP was for some time in a state of flux awaiting its official closure, and the establishment of its successor. Although it did supply some opposition, in the form of a critique (20) and in its support for the Campaign Against the Cuts, its main priorities have been elsewhere. Newcastle neighbourhoods project, originally funded by Community Projects Foundation, was closed in April 1978 when

the city refused to take over the funding. Byker CDP was too
closely tied to and compromised by the local councillors to
offer much of a critique. Indeed, there are strong links
between many workers and the local Labour party which possibly
inhibits a radical challenge especially when Labour's control
is still marginal. Many community activists would be out
canvassing on behalf of the party and having to defend the
priority area programme. The local tenants' federation has
had to concentrate its energies on its own organisational
development and has suffered through a lack of funding and
full-time workers. The sections of community organisers with
perhaps the closest links with the authority are those providing
a 'service' to others, largely staffed by 'professionals', and
not area-based but functional in nature. These have been quite
willing and capable of utilising the authority's structures
and have used their skills and influence to enhance their own
position, their relationships with local groups in the priority
areas being somewhat marginal or, if existing, then unequal.
These have provided the authority with considerable support
through their legitimation of the programme.

   In Newcastle, then, the response from local groups has been
uncoordinated and piecemeal, with the majority using the
programme as a means of obtaining funds. Very little in the
way of a critique has been developed, no alternative programme
prescribed and little attempt has been made to exploit the
opportunities. It is difficult to detect any significant
policy change within the authority as a result of community
participation.

   Certainly the authority has not been faced with any organised
opposition when introducing the February 1979 cuts. Groups
have apparently decided either to take what they can in hard
cash forgetting anything else, or that the programme is so
ineffective both in its structures and philosophy as to
become impotent. As always, the situation in which we practise
is a set of contradictions. Fine judgments rather than
grandiose actions are more likely, as workers tread their way
down that fine divide of co-option and socialist progress.
It is impossible to legislate for community activists faced
with area management schemes initiated by the local authority.
They must assess whether and how to use them. However, whether
activists should themselves campaign for such a system as a
means of resolving local issues and encouraging public
participation is another question. An examination of Newcastle
would indicate that the programme has done neither of these
and may well have hindered the development of other political
approaches. Other strategies, such as linking local groups
and trade unions, developing the political strength and
consciousness of local groups, building federations, rebuilding
local political structures etc., may all in the long term
prove more effective in changing local power structures and
resolving structural issues than programmes similar to that
operating in Newcastle. The extent of the public expenditure

cuts and the policies of the Thatcher government bear this out. The priority areas programme within the city has now lost virtually all of its publicity and significance not only because its limitations have been truly exposed or because the urgency and importance of other issues is there for everyone to see and experience, but also because with a right-wing Tory government the local Labour group no longer need it to bolster their own flagging support or act as a cover for the poverty of their own ideas. So long as community workers and community organisations allow themselves to be continuously defined by the terms and politics of the Labour party they are unlikely to contribute much to a socialist alternative.

NOTES

1 The others being, Dudley, Haringay, Kirkless, all of which were initiated in 1976, Liverpool and Stockport, set up in 1974 and 1970 respectively, and Islington and Middlesborough, added to the programme in mid-1977.
2 Department of the Environment discussion document to Local Authorities, 4 September 1974.
3 Ibid.
4 The proposed Walker neighbourhood management scheme was rejected, October 1974, by the city's policy and resources committee on the grounds that it was a solo exercise, was too bureaucratic, and it implied a third tier of government.
5 In the April 1974 local elections Labour had an overall majority of 24. In the following year this was reduced to 16 and in 1976 it was down to 10.
6 In fact this was the only significant change in the proposals. 'As a result of the public discussion greater emphasis was placed in the final document approved by the Council on the role of the local community and the possible widening of the scheme to include one or two areas not in the initial list was envisaged', Beecham, 'Breaking Free from Poverty in the Inner City', INLOGOV Seminar, July 1977.
7 Ibid.
8 INLOGOV, 'Area Management: Objectives and Structures', First Interim Report, University of Birmingham 1977.
9 Beecham, op.cit.
10 Ibid.
11 Ibid.
12 Newcastle tenants' federation, 'Federation Special', no.2, February 1978.
13 INLOGOV, 'Area Management: Objectives and Structures', Second Interim Report.
14 'Inner Areas Studies', HMSO, 1977, summaries of consultants; final reports; Liverpool's third review.
15 INLOGOV, Second Interim Report.
16 Newcastle City Council, 'Urban Trends', 1976.
17 Report of priority areas co-ordinator to priority areas sub-committee, 22 September 1977.

18   R. Batley, An Explanation of Non-Participation in Planning',
     'Policy and Politics', vol.1, 1972. P. Malpasa, Rebuilding
     Byker, DOE, unpublished. M. Zutshi, 'Speaking for Myself',
     Newcastle Council for Voluntary Service, 1978.
19   M. Zutshi, op.cit. Based on in-depth interviews with
     tenant activists; noted that they strongly denied the idea
     of community development work as 'political'.
20   'West Newcastle in Growth and Decline', Benwell CDP.

4 Lambeth and neighbourhood councils

Charles Allwright, Mark Brangwyn, Fiona Crosskill, Jo Osorio, Mary Turle

The London Borough of Lambeth, formed in 1965, covers an area from the Thames between Waterloo and Vauxhall, through Stockwell and Brixton to Clapham, Norwood and Streatham in the south. The borough councils have traditionally been Labour controlled with the exception of 1968-71 when even this stronghold fell to the Conservative party.

The borough now has a population of some 260,000 of which over half is accommodated on large Greater London Council and Lambeth Council housing estates; it has a housing waiting list which has risen from 10,000 in 1970 to 17,000 in 1979 and many of the problems which characterise Inner London. It has a small and declining industrial base with a handful of large employers which includes the local and health authorities.

During the late 1960s Lambeth Council earned itself a reputation of being a 'progressive' local authority with the creation of a corporate management structure, the first comprehensive housing advice centre, and major development proposals all seen as pioneering the kind of new-style local authority appropriate to the creation of a borough fit for the twenty-first century.

In 1968 the Labour party lost its majority on the council - possibly a reflection of dissatisfaction with its grand design for the borough but more probably resulting from the national swing to the right. The redevelopment programme, with its associated massive compulsory purchase orders, continued unabated and one of the results was a greater demand from residents for a voice in local affairs to try to influence the course of events.

WHY NEIGHBOURHOOD COUNCILS (NCs)

The period in opposition, 1968-71, coincided with the emergence of younger and professional members of local Labour parties,

particularly in the Norwood constituency. Doubtless influenced
by the trend towards greater public participation elsewhere in
the country (see Chapter 1), several were elected to key posts
in the 1971 council on a platform of more open local government.
But the 'Young Turks', as the 'New Statesman' called them, were
also committed to a seven-year rolling housing programme of
redevelopment and rehabilitation, a policy set out in 'Lambeth
into the seventies'. (1)   As each new compulsory purchase
order reached the ears of the public, so the council set up
large-scale public meetings to try to explain what it was doing.
At the same time, the Norwood party's manifesto had committed
the Labour council to the establishment of neighbourhood councils
as a new forum to allow participation in its work. According to
the council

> the aim of the establishment of neighbourhood councils in
> 1971, which would be non-statutory bodies, was to provide
> a vehicle for the development of a community spirit, for the
> gauging and drawing together of public opinion relating to
> the Council's present and future activities and for the
> encouragement of greater community participation in local
> government within the borough. It was not intended, however,
> that such NCs would duplicate or usurp the functions of the
> Borough Council, though they might initiate voluntary projects
> to meet local needs with the encouragement and assistance of
> the Council. It was contemplated that the Council would
> give assistance to meet the secretarial and administrative
> needs of NCs. (2)

The council's community plan (1974) records that the aim was
to 'increase communications in both directions between the
council and local communities in order that the people of
Lambeth may contribute more fully to the formulation of council
policies and be able through their own intervention to overcome
local problems'. (3)

WORK INVOLVED

There were no explicit guidelines nor any more defined strategy
than the paragraphs quoted above. The council began to carry
out its manifesto pledge by organising public meetings in wards
where councillors requested them. As was usual practice, the
meetings were arranged by the public relations division of the
directorate of administration and legal services. Initially
one NC assistant was employed to develop new NCs and to deal
with arrangements common to all; subsequently four neighbourhood
development assistants (NDAs) were appointed to

> be responsible for the servicing of the meetings of the
> neighbourhood councils and their committees, and for
> ensuring the transmission of appropriate references,
> requests for information, etc. between them and the Council,
> its committees and directorates as well as other authorities ...
> the Neighbourhood Development Assistant will be expected to
> undertake certain community development work in the area of
> those neighbourhood councils allotted to him which will

involve close liaison not only with members of the neighbourhood council but with statutory and voluntary associations
working within the particular community. (4)

The first public meetings called by the council were intended
to result in the formation of steering committees which would
consider the area to be covered by the new neighbourhood
council, draw up a constitution, and make recommendations to a
further meeting about possible projects or matters requiring
action in the neighbourhood. A policy document produced by
the council and quoted by a councillor at a public meeting in
November 1971 stated

> first there would be a meeting where members of the public
> in a roughly defined area which appears to the Council to
> represent the neighbourhood community will be invited to
> attend. At the same time, letters of invitation will be
> sent out to organizations who appear to have some link
> with the community. The meeting will be chaired by a member
> of the Labour Group and he or another member of the Majority
> Party will open the meeting by explaining the purpose of
> the meeting. At the end a steering committee will be formed.
> Now it is not proposed to have a rigid agenda for the
> meeting but it would probably fall into three basic sections,
> a) opening and explanation of intent by the Council, b) public
> discussion, c) formation of a steering committee. It should
> be emphasized at the first meeting that the neighbourhood
> councils will not be associated with any political party
> whilst at the same time indicating that individual party
> members could be equal members within the NCs. Further,
> a strong attempt should be made to involve local inhabitants
> in the establishment of the NC to ensure that it does not
> simply become a federation of existing community organiza-
> tions. (5)

The initial publicity was produced by the town hall and
said very little about the purpose of the meeting except that
it was intended to 'talk about local affairs and decide what
we want from Lambeth Council. What we can offer them to make
our locality lively. Find out what the chances are on setting
up our own neighbourhood council.' Follow-up publicity was
again produced from the town hall on behalf of the steering
committee. That tended to make statements about the lack of
local facilities and ways in which the neighbourhood council
might be able to solve local problems.

The neighbourhood councils which emerged from the first
pilot meetings were 'elected' from volunteers at the follow-up
public meeting in each area and the constitutions which were
adopted generally included an opportunity for the co-option
of others. None of the steering committees were encouraged
to hold ballot elections although Stockwell and Vauxhall,
North Lambeth and South Lambeth neighbourhood councils tried
an 'area representative' style of election with North and
South Lambeth holding meetings in each part of their large area.

By 1979 there were fourteen groups recognised by Lambeth Council
as neighbourhood councils; only five had not been formed as a
result of council intervention. The council had been publicly
committed, until 1974, to establishing about thirty neighbourhood
councils but subsequently modified its policy; in two areas its
initiative was thwarted: in one case this was by angry residents
protesting over the council's failure to consult over planning
proposals - why have a neighbourhood council if you are going
to demolish the neighbourhood - and in the other by a politically
motivated response which rejected the idea. By 1975 the policy
was altered in the light of experience and the council would
thereafter 'consider the demand from the residents of any
neighbourhood in Lambeth for a neighbourhood council in their
area'.

ROLE AND ACTIVITIES OF NEIGHBOURHOOD COUNCILS 1971-4 AND
CHANGES IN COUNCIL ATTITUDE

During 1972 the first neighbourhood councils drew up estimates
of expenditure and the first ideas for projects emerged. There
were requests for information and applications were made for
grants to establish local centres. Following Angell NCs
example, some neighbourhood councils started to establish groups
around a particular issue or on individual housing estates or
in a group of streets. At the same time the neighbourhood
development assistants were quickly aware that a thriving
neighbourhood council would require constant community work
support to enable it to relate to all the different clusters
of communities and interests within its area and to tackle a
range of issues. Considerable efforts were made to draw in
new people and encourage neighbourhood council members to
focus on local problems, start door-knocking, seek methods of
campaigning like making video films, acquire premises and
expand their local base. The NDAs actively supported neighbourhood councils in establishing local centres which were accepted
as a way of making contact with people who were less likely to
attend monthly meetings or whose individual problems could not
be dealt with in such a context. Once established, the centres
provided an excellent contact point for local people and
individuals seeking advice often had problems linked to wider
issues which led to action on a group basis; for example, poor
housing conditions or the absence of a tenants' association or
play facilities in a particular area could be brought to the
neighbourhood council's attention and action taken to improve
conditions. The NDAs continued to take an active part in NC
centres to develop their use and help with advice sessions,
supporting part-time workers and volunteers.

    By May 1972, in order to deal with the requests for grant-
aid and to implement the council's policy and to keep it under
review, Lambeth Council established a neighbourhood councils
sub-committee (of finance and management services) and in
June 1972 neighbourhood councils were each invited to send a

representative to its meetings. The sub-committee was chaired
by the deputy leader of the council but usually attended by few
other councillors. In 1972 council committees still met in
closed session and there was a general lack of information about
council policy. The neighbourhood councils started to use the
sub-committee to try to obtain information and to make
recommendations concerning developments in their areas; they
made proposals for council action and promoted their ideas
for projects in addition to making forceful comments on, for
example, the use of short-life housing, the establishment of
a hostel for the single homeless, squatting, the effects of
the new Covent Garden Market and to seek support for a campaign
to oppose the 1972 Housing Finance Act.

The neighbourhood development assistants were given
instructions by the chief public relations officer, to whom
they were managerially responsible, not to 'initiate' activity
or to provide information unless specifically requested to do so
by the neighbourhood council. They were expected to wait for
the NC to ask and to attend meetings and take minutes; and
when requests for information were made, to refer them to
officers in other directorates of the council for an answer.
The chief public relations officer took an active interest in
their work, signing all correspondence and requiring all
activity to be recorded on a daily basis. When the inevitable
leaks occurred, senior officers complained of a 'fifth column'.
They also resented neighbourhood councils questioning the
council's actions or trying to help local residents with
housing problems by, for example, accompanying them to
interviews at the housing advice centre. Charges were made
that NCs were unrepresentative or not responsible. Although
neighbourhood council projects were frequently approved by the
neighbourhood councils sub-committee, the council's corporate
management structure seemed unable, or unwilling, to give
effect to most of the suggestions made.

In retrospect, demands for information were modest.
Frequently, however, the council hid behind statements about
lack of time to produce answers or the shortage of staff, and
confidentiality in the public interest. Neighbourhood councils
found their ideas lost in the machine of council committees
and a growing list of 'reports outstanding' was appended to
each committee agenda. Even though the later Local Government
Act provided for meetings to be held in public from 1974, the
volume of business discussed in closed session was still
considerable. Councillors consented to the adoption of a code
of practice drawn up by the board of directors for officers
dealing with requests for information. This effectively
resulted in any request being refused by the director responsible
for the production of an answer if it would have cost more
than £20 in staff time to provide. Such requests were referred
to the chairman of the appropriate committee.

As a result of their growing frustration with the council and

the neighbourhood councils sub-committee, neighbourhood councils
began to meet together during 1972 and 1973 in attempts to
formulate a policy towards the sub-committee and to support
each other at its meetings. They continued to meet to discuss
the council's attitude towards them and to take action on
borough-wide issues, e.g. an empty houses campaign. Several
also became involved in direct action, squatting, militancy over
playspace provision, occupation of council offices, demanding
information rather than simply asking, an alleged libel of the
chief planning officer and friction with councillors who failed
to support local issues. Whoever was responsible, the neighbourhood councils collectively seemed to be blamed. Their activities
and those of the neighbourhood councils sub-committee were given
considerable local press publicity which added to the pressure
felt by councillors and officers alike. In addition, the
neighbourhood councils' militancy was given an effective voice
through the regular distribution of their own newspapers which
were financed by grants from the council.

The chief public relations officer retired. A younger man,
appointed from the private sector, took a less active interest
in the neighbourhood councils and the work of the NDAs. In
August 1973 the neighbourhood councils sub-committee was
disbanded. NCs were informed that, in the interest of
efficiency, their proposals should be submitted directly to
the main council committees 'which would expedite their
consideration'. Henceforth the council's policy in connection
with neighbourhood councils would be the prerogative of the
policy committee. To deal with requests for grants which were
now an accepted part of the policy, in 1974 and 1975 an ad hoc
group of councillors drawn from the new community liaison sub-
committee met to make recommendations.

Despite growing doubts amongst councillors on the development of their brainchild, neighbourhood councils survived and
managed to expand their range of activities.

ROLE AND ACTIVITIES OF NEIGHBOURHOOD COUNCILS 1974-9

After the disbandment of the neighbourhood councils sub-committee
the NDAs began to take a more positive community development
role with their neighbourhood councils; the neighbourhood
councils themselves set to developing stronger links in their
areas. The NDAs' developing role was outlined in a job
description approved by the community liaison sub-committee
and the changing needs of the neighbourhood councils were
reflected in the NDAs' activities. Community groups within
the neighbourhood councils' areas were encouraged to relate
to the NCs and helped to build their own organisation and
undertake their own projects. NDAs became involved in helping
tenants' groups to tackle housing and other problems on their
estates, residents' associations to form in housing action
areas and general improvement areas, playschemes and youth

activities to develop, and advice centres to flourish. Neighbourhood councils made annual applications for grant aid to
Lambeth Council committees for their general administrative
needs and activities in addition to applications for specific
projects to the ILEA, Greater London Arts Association, trusts
and charities. Local groups would be encouraged to approach
the neighbourhood council for funding for projects and assisted
in making their applications to other sources of finance. There
was no apparent consistency in the council's overall attitude
to the neighbourhood councils, however, and although the grants
continued to grow, scant regard was given to the fact that a
substantial proportion was actually returned to the council in
the form of rent and rates for the premises used for advice
centres and meeting places. Whilst NCs were able to operate
free from day-to-day interference in their activities, some
councillors would complain that they did not represent value
for money, few regularly attended NCs meetings, while others
approved urban aid applications to fund additional projects and
congratulated themselves for doing so.

The NDAs consistently worked towards the broadest possible
involvement in the neighbourhood councils from community groups
and individuals; this approach helped to counter-balance the
representation from more middle-class enclaves often attracted
to the neighbourhood council through an interest in local
planning or amenity issues, the declaration of a conservation
area, a traffic management scheme or general dissatisfaction
with council services. The neighbourhood council structure
with its regular meetings, minutes, letter-writing and dealing
with officialdom was immediately accessible and attractive to
the more middle-class and educated residents of an area. Aware
of the lack of representation of residents from generally run-
down and depressed council housing estates, NCs were anxious
to draw new members in, and with the encouragement of the NDAs
would develop links with active tenants' groups or form new
action groups or working parties around issues affecting a
particular area. The neighbourhood council would discuss
the desirability of forming a street group to fight a
compulsory purchase order, or to encourage one to tackle
poor housing conditions created through the neglect of private
or municipal landlords, campaign for action on traffic
conditions, urge the provision of additional playspace, fight
the closure of a school, and consider action on the whole
range of similar problems affecting the inner city. The NDA
would help in the initial stages of door-knocking, contacting
residents concerned, producing leaflets and organising meetings,
surveys or lobbies. An emerging group would have the support
of the neighbourhood council, but not necessarily any formal
link to it, and would be able to look to the NC for finance,
publicity and community work support from the NDA.

The ideas and input to a flourishing neighbourhood council
would come from many sources but the NDA would often be crucial
in initiating action and in co-ordinating response to it. The

role of the neighbourhood development assistant could be
summarised thus: encouraging wide participation in the
neighbourhood council and undertaking community development
work throughout the NC area; providing the main link between the
various community groups within the neighbourhood council area,
the groups working under the auspices of the NC and the
neighbourhood council itself; keeping the neighbourhood council
and other groups informed about developments and issues in the
locality; through information and active support, encouraging
response to those issues and helping to establish groups of
residents to tackle them; providing practical assistance in
all aspects of the neighbourhood council activity including
the production of newspapers and other publicity material,
book-keeping, organisation of meetings, etc. and active
support of other groups in the community as well; providing
continuity in a situation where officers of the neighbourhood
council changed annually, and linking from year to year on
longer-term issues.

The council's policy of responding to demand from residents
of any area for a neighbourhood council led to the establishment
of new groups and more community activity. The NDAs had a brief
to work with two neighbourhood councils but the suggestion that
more staff should be employed led to the establishment of a
council working party, in August 1975, to carry out a 'major
reappraisal' of the support services and funds to neighbourhood
councils while 'in no way wishing to direct NCs development'.
The final report of the working party (prepared by the chief
public relations officer) was considerably watered down after
protests from the NDAs but, nevertheless, discussed the
withdrawal of their services from 'well established neighbourhood councils'. Although the working party's conclusion was
that a further NDA should be appointed, the policy committee
was able to use the restrictions by central government on
expenditure, 'the cuts', as the reason for not increasing its
establishment. The result was that the original neighbourhood
council assistant was redesignated an NDA since his task of
developing new neighbourhood councils was no longer relevant
or in accordance with the council's policy which did not
promise staff support to any new NCs.

The activity of existing neighbourhood councils continued
to develop and in late 1976 five applied for grants to employ
part-time workers, mainly to service their well-established
advice centres. These applications prompted yet another
review, this time of the neighbourhood councils as well as
the NDAs. The senior officers were forthright in their
opinions and the chief public relations officer prepared a
report arguing that a senior neighbourhood development assistant
should be appointed to ensure proper 'management' of the NDAs
who, by this time, were established away from the town hall in
an office which was being developed as a useful resource
centre. The report went on to say that the NDAs had 'frequently
adopted the stance of NC spokesman at public meetings, possibly

putting Councillors and senior officers in a difficult position'.
It continued, 'some Ward Councillors are also unhappy at the
failure of the NDAs to keep them informed and consult them on
local issues.' Other comments, relating to unspecified
complaints from councillors, were withdrawn only after NALGO
had been asked by the NDAs to intervene. This attempt to
impose a management structure was seen by NCs and the NDAs to
be a waste of scarce resources and an alternative proposal,
that the NCs should become the employers, was regarded as
inoperable since the NDAs would still have been working with
two neighbourhood councils; it was also felt that access to
council information would suffer. By the end of 1977 the
neighbourhood councils had won their case for more workers and
were given additional grants but on an experimental basis and
there was to be a further review after one year; in addition,
the situation was to be reconsidered if and when any of the
NDAs left.

PARTNERSHIP AND THE 1978 ELECTIONS - A NEW ERA FOR PUBLIC
CONSULTATION

The announcement of the 'Policy for the Inner Cities' (6) and
the creation of a partnership area for the northern half of
Lambeth in August 1977 were seen by many local groups, including
neighbourhood councils, as an opportunity for direct participation in the development of new policies and programmes for
action. There seemed to be greater potential with the
involvement of the other local authorities as well as government
departments, and the availability of grant aid on a much larger
scale than before attracted a wealth of new ideas and projects.
The neighbourhood councils falling within the partnership area
contributed significantly to the formation of the Lambeth inner
city consultative group which was established by community and
trade union groups to ensure they had a full role in the
enhanced urban programme allocation to the Lambeth partnership.

    The 1978 elections, resulting in a 'marxist' council (7)
under the leadership of Ted Knight, then moved Lambeth into a
new era of community involvement. Making a series of commitments to improve public access to councillors and the work of
the council which were strangely reminiscent of the 'Young
Turks' of 1971, a special review committee was established to
consider ways of restructuring the council's directorates and
committees; and to improve public participation the council
embarked on a series of 'ward-based consultation' public
meetings. Whilst the new structure of the committees was to
include a community affairs committee which would draw up
and implement a community development policy the ward-based
consultation scheme was introduced by Ted Knight thus:
    One of the first acts of my administration was to set in
    motion a new approach to public consultation based on
    electoral wards. The Council is fully committed to more
    open and responsive local government and we feel the public

should have every opportunity to meet and question their councillors, together with the officials paid to provide local services.

Some of the Council's attempts at public consultation have failed because meetings have tended to be about long-term issues or have not been local enough in character. We recognize that the public is concerned to discuss present services and what is likely to happen in their area in the immediate future. That is the main objective of our ward consultation programme.

We are determined that this will not be an empty exercise generating nothing but hot air. Special arrangements have been made to feed ideas or criticisms into Council committees and the Inner City Partnership machinery. Some money is being set aside to enable good, low-cost ideas to be taken up quickly with the minimum of red-tape.

This is the most ambitious public consultation programme ever undertaken in Lambeth - and possibly by any local authority. It is something of an experiment and we hope you will bear with us if everything is not perfect from the word go. I can say that it is something we plan to improve and develop into a major plank of our future policy of increased public involvement in Lambeth. (8)

Three staff to run the consultation were employed in the public relations division and £46,000 set aside for staff, administration and small projects. Compare this figure with Table 4.1.

TABLE 4.1   Lambeth revenue estimates (published annually) Neighbourhood councils grants and council administrative costs (£)

Year	Grants to NCs	NDAs Admin., etc.	Total	Less * Urban Aid
1971-2	–	2,000	2,000	–
1972-3	3,500	5,000	8,500	–
1973-4	8,770	n.a.	n.a.	8,250
1974-5	11,102	26,166	37,268	10,207
1975-6	19,141	33,786	52,927	10,207
1976-7	27,049	54,110	81,159	15,750
1977-8	37,200	51,140	88,340	15,750
1978-9	40,180	53,180	93,360	15,750
1979-80	43,520**	57,360	100,880	16,800

Notes: *   75% contribution made by Home Office Department of the Environment; 25% contribution made by Lambeth Council
      ** Estimate

HAVE NEIGHBOURHOOD COUNCILS SUCCEEDED AS A FORUM FOR PUBLIC PARTICIPATION?

Lambeth Council's attitude to public participation through neighbourhood councils has been very mixed, as the previous pages demonstrate. Despite the formation of these new vehicles for consultation, the council continued its own programme of meetings on redevelopment plans, planning proposals, management committees for council playcentres, housing action areas and on any other issue the council wanted a public meeting about: for example, there were fourteen in the six months from October 1976 to April 1977. Subsequently, the new era with its ward-based consultation has generated a series of up to twenty meetings with their associated publicity and expenditure. Neighbourhood councils were often not consulted on specific issues and, if they were, it was usually as just another community group. The neighbourhood development assistants had little part to play in the council's corporate management or in influencing an increase in participation procedures because the council was not anxious to encourage it and the NDAs chose to concentrate in community work in the neighbourhood council areas: neighbourhood councils continued to develop links on estates or in streets, on playgrounds or in housing action areas, etc. at an informal level whilst using the council structures where appropriate. Simultaneously Lambeth's housing committee was encouraging the formation of district housing committees and considering similar district committees for consultations in housing action areas and general improvement areas; the planning committee established a conservation areas advisory committee; and others such as a sports council, safety council and arts and recreation association have an 'official' status and are serviced by council officers but have no powers and small grants.

There can be no doubt that councillors had good intentions when they embarked in 1971 on establishing neighbourhood councils as one method of developing public consultation; nor that they became increasingly concerned at the behaviour of their offspring. While some councillors remained committed to open government others clearly did not; and the evidence confirms that more than good intentions are required to make such an exercise succeed. As Cynthia Cockburn rightly pointed out, (9) attempts to really improve consultation and participation were often frustrated by the conservative attitude of directors and other council officials who saw their responsibility to the council solely through the corporate management system.

Nevertheless, the merits of neighbourhood councils have not rested entirely on their capacity to influence the decision-making processes and corporate management structure of the local authority. The development of participation in the borough as a whole *has* evolved during the years from 1971 and neighbourhood councils have played a crucial role in that

process;   there *has* been continuous pressure from a growing
number of groups through new projects, issue-orientated meetings,
the development of local centres and the publication of newspapers.

Neighbourhood councils have created good local networks,
increased regular community activity, developed methods of
information exchange, and the projects they have undertaken and
the experience gained have all increased the politicisation of
members of the community. Instead of confronting overall
policies and joining with neighbourhood councils and other
groups in the search for alternative solutions to problems,
many councillors adopted a managerial role and tried to
accommodate both their own officials and community groups.
Still committed to major redevelopment, often the legacy of
previous administrations, the council tried to keep opposition
at arm's length; houses would be given to one squatting group
whilst others were evicted or moved on; individual councillors
or officers would leak a plan, but a majority would refuse
demands for publication; whilst questioning of housing policy
was not allowed, approval would be given to advice centres
and a law centre whose existence would encourage such policy
strutiny. (10)

The accusation that neighbourhood councils were unrepresentative could also be levelled at other community groups, and
councillors; not all neighbourhood councils have been equally
successful in broadening their bases or tackling local issues.
None the less, most have developed into a local resource
providing a forum for the exchange of ideas and information
and have received sufficient community work support and grants
to aid substantially the development of community action in
Lambeth. The existence of the central office and the neighbourhood development assistants has enabled good contacts to be
developed between neighbourhood councils and other groups as
illustrated by the rapid establishment of new organisations
to respond to changing circumstances, e.g. the Lambeth inner
city consultative group.

As a result of Lambeth Council's initiative, groups are now
better equipped for effective involvement in council business,
though it would be unrealistic to expect participation to work
unless the council, which holds power, is willing to allow it to
succeed. It could be argued that the lack of an effective
challenge to the council's policies represents a lack of
political consciousness within neighbourhood councils and that
they never presented a real challenge to the council's
prerogative to do as it wishes. Such an analysis ignores the
reality of the formidable forces pitted against neighbourhood
councils so soon after they started.

REFERENCES

1 Lambeth Council, 1969. A short description of the origins

of Lambeth Council's redevelopment programme is also contained
in David Donnison et al., 'London: Urban Patterns, Problems
and Policies', Heinemann for the Centre for Environmental
Studies (CES), 1973. For a fuller description see Michael
Harloe et al., 'The Organization of Housing', Heinemann for
CES, 1974.

2 Lambeth Council's reply to the department of environment
consultation paper on statutory neighbourhood councils, 1974.
For a DOE attitude to NCs see 'A Voice for Your Neighbourhood',
HMSO, 1977.

3 Lambeth Community Plan, 1974.

4 Neighbourhood development assistant, letter of appointment,
1972.

5 Minutes of a meeting of South Lambeth neighbourhood council,
November 1971.

6 'Policy for the Inner Cities', HMSO, 1977, Cmnd 6845. See
also 'New Society', 21 December 1978 for a description of
the first phase of the partnership programmes.

7 A phrase used several times by the London 'Evening Standard'.

8 Councillor Ted Knight, Leader of Lambeth Council, Introduction
to 'Ward Profiles', Lambeth Public Relations, 1979.

9 Cynthia Cockburn, 'The Local State', Pluto Press, 1977.

10 For a full description of neighbourhood councils activities
see 'Lambeth Interface' written and published by Cedric
Jackson, 1975 and Lambeth neighbourhood councils office
unpublished report, Lambeth neighbourhood councils 1971-4.
'Lambeth Interface' accurately conveys the atmosphere of
the times.

5 Organising in three neighbourhoods

Marilyn Taylor

If decisions, and the ways in which decisions are made, are to
be challenged or influenced by the people who feel their effects,
it is important that these people are able to organise themselves
effectively, whatever action they then decide to take.
Effective organisation does not stop at the immediate neighbourhood, the single campaign, the isolated issue. People are
increasingly coming to appreciate the value of meeting with
other groups with similar interests, in order to combine
experience, pool ideas, and pursue common issues.

Joining together in this way can take a number of forms, and
has received encouragement from various quarters. There are
neighbourhood or community councils in many parts of the
British Isles, indeed in Scotland they are statutory, and an
association for neighbourhood councils promotes their existence
in England. There is also an association of community
associations with a less formal emphasis. It is clearly in
government's interests to relate to one body expressing the
views of the 'community' rather than to a number of disparate
groups. A report on the voluntary sector, for example, (1)
and the resulting consultative documents from government (2)
give some prominence to the support of 'local intermediary
functions' such as co-ordinating voluntary organisations,
giving them a forum, spotting gaps in provision, and representing
their views. From a different point of view, recent publications
in the community-development field have stressed the limitations
of action in isolation, given the way that local problems stem
from wider economic and social factors and the increasing
centralisation of decision-making. (3) This analysis has
encouraged work with federations, and the development of links
between local action groups and those with allied interests,
e.g. the women's movement, trade unions, etc.

This chapter describes a relatively elementary stage in the
development of joint action in three different areas. In each,
a community association was formed covering a fairly small
constituency (in the first two a neighbourhood, in the third a

small town) to bring local groups together under one umbrella, and to create one group which had within its purview all the issues of concern to the community. They illustrate some of the strengths and weaknesses of building organisations beyond the single group or issue that are also experienced by many more widespread or complex federations.

The three examples are taken from areas where the community projects foundation (CPF) had set up a community development agency. They were set up on the invitation of the local social services department which contributed to their funding and in two cases (A and C) was represented on the project's management committee.

THE THREE GROUPS

Group A

Group A was set up in a town within commuting distance of London. The neighbourhood it covers is disadvantaged relative to other parts of the town, but it is not deprived or stigmatised to the extent of other areas where CPF has worked, e.g. inner city areas, isolated council estates.

  Property in this neighbourhood has been relatively cheap for this part of the country - small terraced housing in transition from the private sector to owner-occupation. Its population consists of people on the first rung of the housing ladder, ethnic minorities, transient single people and a large proportion of elderly people who have lived in A since the turn of the century and reared families there. While it is a mixed community, however, it is predominantly working class.

The neighbourhood is sandwiched between major traffic routes out of town and an industrial estate, and also has a number of small industries built in the gaps left by the housing. The major problems, as far as residents are concerned, are traffic, lack of space - especially for play and garage facilities - the welfare of the elderly, housing improvement, and the presence of small industries. The local community project was set up in 1970. After working with individual groups on specific issues for three years, it decided to test out the support for the idea of a community association in order to build a more comprehensive approach to the area and involve more people. The association was set up at a meeting attended by over 100 people and developed the following set of aims:
      The Association seeks to improve the quality of life in
      [the area]. In particular, to make the area a better place
      to live in and to encourage local residents to take a greater
      and more effective part in what is happening to the area.
An executive committee was selected. Despite the level of support, the role of the community association was not very clear. The individual groups in the area liked the idea of a

discussion forum and central focus, but wanted to preserve
their independence regarding their own activities. There was
some suggestion of an initiatory role - identifying needs which
were not covered, developing new work - but the association
was wary of becoming too closely identified with one or two
activities, especially in view of the uneasy relationship in
the area between service provision and campaigns on environmental
issues. The executive committee found this situation frustrating:

> No one ever defined what the job of the Executive Committee
> was to be - the actual management tasks performed by the
> committee were financial, organisational (e.g. setting up
> general meetings) and the appointment of representatives
> to the Management Committee of the project. These tasks
> are not highly time consuming.

However, it did develop some work which was new to the area,
providing a focus and legitimation for new ideas. It set up a
meeting on the county structure plan, from which there emerged
a committed group who eventually produced a detailed response
to the local authority. It also ran a bus survey at the request
of residents who were dissatisfied with the service, set up a
lunch club for the elderly and put on social events.

As the association moved into its second year, the project
was preparing to withdraw from the area. This removed the
executive committee's anxieties about whether the association
had a job to do. But it raised questions instead about which
aspects of the project's role the association was best placed
to take on, and exposed the weaknesses of its structure.

The committee consisted of representatives from several of
the groups in the area, but the project worker felt that they
were involved much more as individuals than as representatives
of anyone else. They were, he felt, too remote from the people
in the area and accountable to them only at annual general
meetings (AGMs) or any other public meetings that were held.
He recommended the development of sub-committees with
responsibility for particular areas of work, so that people
could at least get to know parts of their constituency better,
but these proved difficult to operate. People did not have
time to devote to them, unless they were to reduce their
commitment to their own individual groups. Even the main
committee had to cut down the number of meetings it had, to
reduce the pressure on members.

While questions of structure remained unresolved, the
association was developing another method of establishing
contact with its constituency - through producing a community
newspaper, both to inform residents about what was going on
in the area, and to highlight problem issues.   Every household
in the area was given a copy free and costs were met by
advertising, and when necessary, by the association. The
editorial group gradually emerged as a successful sub-committee
of the executive. At first, the project worker took on a
large part of the paper's production, but by the time he left,

the group was independent of him and had ceased to use the project
address as a contact point.

The question of how far the association should take over the
project's various roles, as it withdrew, was difficult to
resolve, especially when it came to initiating work or working
with individual groups. Whereas the project had been able to
develop a breadth of involvement in a number of different issues,
there were doubts about the ability of an association which was
under the control of local groups to cope with new initiatives
which might upset the current balance of interests in the area.
Direct service groups, for example, were suspicious of pressure
groups and the newspaper group, whose activities might prejudice
their own more comfortable relationship with the local authority,
and whose values they did not share. The co-ordinative focus
of the association might well be rendered sterile if the
association was felt to show preferences in its development
work. Alternatively, its hands would be tied when advising one
particular group, by its concern for overall harmony on the
estate.

It was at this point, with the future still under debate
(1976), that the study from which this information is drawn
was completed. (4) The group is still very much alive, however,
and still has premises, although they are not secure in the
long term. If the premises go, the role of the association
will be undermined and its future prejudiced. The departure
of the community worker has left two main gaps. The first is
that the part-time administrator is isolated and has very
little support, the second is that fewer new initiatives are
being taken, both for the reasons outlined in the previous
paragraph and because of lack of time and people.

Group B

Group B emerged in a post-war council estate (population
c.6,000) on the edge of a northern city. Social services
concern about the number of cases referred from this area led
to a community project being set up in 1973. The estate had a
bad reputation, there was little history of local action, and
general apathy towards local politics.

The workers started by getting two or three small groups
organised on immediate issues such as play, damp, etc., in
the hope that once they had generated interest and involvement
through specific actions, people could be brought together in
a more broadly-based umbrella group. But events turned out
differently. A booklet produced by the project brought
publicity to conditions in the area, publicity which stirred
some local tenants into action. They wanted to challenge the
bad reputation attached to the area, and to improve the
provision of services locally. Against the project's advice,
they called a public meeting to explore the issues which

concerned local tenants and set up a community association. They felt that working initially with street groups might well be divisive.

The public meeting - the first of its kind on the estate - was well attended and lively. Some thirty people volunteered to join a steering committee. However, the issues that were raised - bad tenants; problem families; transfers out of B being difficult to come by - were not a promising basis for a community association. B was clearly not a united community. None the less, the first meeting of the steering committee went well. Officers were elected and three sub-groups - on housing, old people, and children - were proposed, with a vice-chairperson elected to each one.

Unfortunately, this opening flourish of activity was not sustained. There were conflicts between people on what needed to be done, personalities clashed and resignations followed. The group was meeting once a week - far too often for people trying to set up individual pieces of action, such as visits to old people, casework on housing, a community newspaper, a campaign to improve poor housing conditions in one street. As the group continued, both attendance and action gradually diminished, and much of the business at meetings centred around debates on function and procedures. The action that did take place grew up separately, e.g. a claimants' union was set up as a result of some of the centre's advice work; an adventure playground was set up by a group of new contacts in the area; a community newspaper was launched as a fairly independent initiative (there were some links with the association). As the strength of these separate initiatives grew, the community association became less and less central to action in the area and finally disappeared altogether. The project re-orientated its work to reflect this and focused on the building (now known as the advice and social centre) and on transferring this work to local people.

As it prepared to withdraw, after five years' work, the project drew together a group of local people from the individual groups it was working with to form a management group for the building and the work connected with it. Thus, a new broad-based group emerged on the estate, but this time growing out of current action, and with clear responsibilities. At the time of writing, this group is fairly new and has its hands full with the launching of an independent agency funded by the local authority and a charitable trust. It will be interesting to see how far this group and the advice centre workers it manages act as an umbrella for the separate activities on the estate, support groups who no longer have a development worker, and develop new initiatives on the estate, i.e. perform the job, at a different stage, that was expected in the initial community association.

Group C

Group C was set up, like Group A, on the basis of several years
of development work with individual groups. It was a federation
of a number of groups in a small town in the south-east
(population c.50,000). Two people in local residents' associations
which had not had much contact with the CPF project approached the
worker to discuss their ideas for getting the various groups in
the town together. They wanted to combine the experience and
resources of tenants' groups in pre-war council estates who had
organised successfully around repairs and modernisation, with
those of groups in post-war council estates whose main concerns
tended to be managing or acquiring community centres. The town
had had two previous experiences of joint action - a flourishing
play council, which involved all local groups interested in play,
and an attempt to get groups together to campaign against the
Housing Finance Act, which had failed to attract enough support.

A general meeting to float the new idea attracted interest
from ten groups in the town, and set up a working party to
develop a constitution. Once this was accepted, a committee
representing all the interested groups and elected from the
general meeting decided on a work programme. Its priority was
to build up a formal relationship with the local authority.
Over time it was successful in this, gained formal representation
on the council's public relations committee, and had formal
meetings with local officers. A second task was to produce a
newsletter for groups in the town. Unfortunately, however, the
issues that were produced were rather dry and concentrated on
federation business, rather than identifying and investigating
issues in the area, as Group A and indeed the newspaper in
area B had done, and can have had little immediate impact on
those not immediately involved.

A third task was to build commitment from individual local
groups and links between them. However, given limited time
and the other priorities mentioned above, this received a low
priority. One of the most active groups in the area, for
example, was overlooked in the round of initial explanatory
visits before the federation was formally set up. Since the
project worker who was servicing the federation had close
links with some groups, their contact with the federation was,
it seems, taken for granted. However, before the end of the
federations' first year, the project worker left. His replacement was briefed to work mainly with the federation by the
project's management committee and did not pick up the
individual group work. Neither the newsletter nor the priority
of establishing a relationship with the council attracted the
interest of people involved in action at the neighbourhood
level and, increasingly, the people on the committee came to
represent only themselves rather than local activists throughout
the area.

Perhaps it is not surprising that Group C did not last, in

contrast to the town-wide play council which still flourishes. The latter has a clear active focus in helping to organise and resource playschemes each year, and tangible benefits to members: (a) in the experience it has built up, e.g. in appointing playleaders, training them, applying for grants and (b) in the resources it can offer.

DISCUSSION

The sketches presented above demonstrate that, although it might be a good idea to set up groups which combine interests and share experience, in practice a good deal of hard thinking is needed if an organisation is to evolve which is to be useful to its members and maintain their interest. The second half of this chapter, therefore, questions again the whole concept of broad-based community associations on the basis of these experiences and puts forward some suggestions as to the kind of role that can be useful in supporting and developing community action.

Why form an umbrella group?

After the initial bout of enthusiasm for a new idea has passed, a community association has to offer something tangible to its membership if interest is to be maintained. Vague ideas about common interests, more power, a common voice, pooling resources, getting together, have to be translated into programmes and pieces of work which will persuade local activists to add another commitment to those they already have. Each of the groups studied had difficulties with this, although Group A overcame them.

   Umbrella groups which cover a wide variety of interests have a particular problem. A federation evolving around a single issue has a more obvious point to it in terms of common interests, sharing specific expertise and developing a common approach to specific policies. An organisation with a wider brief is going to have to look further to justify its existence. Because of this, it is probably important that such an organisation arises out of the work of individual and different interest groups rather than precedes them (as it did in B). When some of the immediate concerns have been worked on for a time, people begin to see their wider needs, and the potential usefulness of a wider resource and forum. They are also more likely to have the energy for it at this stage.

What can a community association do?

It seems, both from these examples and from literature elsewhere that two main types of function can be identified for community associations. One is enabling, and includes such functions as

servicing, providing a communication vehicle within the
neighbourhood, identifying unmet needs, providing a discussion
forum. The other is representing, and includes often similar
functions but with a view to identifying and communicating a
community view and acting as spokesman for the neighbourhood.
Group A undertook the first and rejected the second. Group B
never really defined its position clearly, and Group C tended
towards the second function.

There are dangers in assuming that because a community is
defined as existing, either that it has any significance to
those within it, or even if it has, that consensus exists
within it. There is not the space here to question the
assumptions and beliefs attached to the word 'community', but
it is clear that in areas A and B there were different interests
within the area, even among those who were active. Even within
small areas, tensions arise between the employed and the
unemployed (in area B, the claimants union was held to give the
project a bad image); between the different interests of
owner-occupiers, council tenants, and private or housing
association tenants; between those involved in direct servicing/
self help, and those whose activity criticises the local
authority. Tensions also arise due to personality differences
and competition for leadership, although these are by no means
confined to this type of organisation. All these are reflected
in debates on strategy and between priorities. This may lead
to taking on the lowest denominator of activities, or to people
getting disappointed and opting out, leaving behind a group
which no longer reflects the balance of interests of the
constituents.

This brings into question the validity of such a group
taking on a representative function. Group A eschewed this,
leaving individual groups to represent themselves and retain
their autonomy. Except in the one case where the umbrella group
was asked to represent individuals in one corner of the estate
over their housing conditions, direct negotiations with the
council occurred at the level of individual groups.

It is possible for an umbrella group to enable representation by bringing together smaller clusters of groups within
its constituency when they have a common issue to address.
Experience suggests that federations founded upon issues are
more able to work towards a common view than broader-based
groups, e.g. the play council in C. One of the member groups
of A was itself a federation of traffic groups which held
together very well and represented its members' views to the
council. Even so, a lot of ground work is needed, especially
as the constituency covered grows larger. The evidence of
these three groups alone demonstrates that people in the
leadership of an umbrella group can become divorced from the
membership, both because of the type of people they are, and
the difficulty of keeping communications flowing. Inevitably,
the leadership of such an organisation will be atypical. The

number of people who can spare the time, who are interested
in this type of activity, or even who have the confidence, will
be few. It may attract people on the fringes of the community
who aren't on the informal networks that already exist. What is
therefore important is that the flow of information to and from
member groups is as good as possible, and that priority is given
to servicing member groups and ensuring that communications and
interest go further than the individual representative. Group A
did this eventually through the newspaper, and through the
project worker's contact with individual groups. However, it
was precisely the lack of supportive work of this kind which
cost Group C its credibility, especially after the project
worker left.

    Given these reservations about representation, especially for
broad-based groups, is there any role for such groups to play
vis-a-vis the local authority? Group C was the only one to give
priority to a formal relationship with the local authority.
This group succeeded in getting representation on the public
relations committee of the council, 'so that matters relating
to particular estates can be highlighted at an early enough
stage for us to be involved before the matter goes to council'.
Presumably, this committee was chosen because it was inter-
departmental, reflecting the variety of issues local groups
were concerned with. But by the same token, it is not a
committee with any real power or resources, and public relations
is a concept more often used to smooth over discontent than to
deal with it.

    Groups A and B were less clear about their role with respect
to the council. Group A worked with councillors, and its
chairman at the end of the research study was a recently retired
councillor, but the group saw itself as something quite apart
from the local state. 'If you have community groups replacing
councillors as such, you will still have the same problem,
only at a lower level - I don't think it would help a lot in
the near future just to lower it a little and say that those
are now the people you have got to make sure do what you want
to do.' There was also some distrust of councillors, who the
group felt only represented its interests when it suited them.
Indeed, the councillors said they felt in no way bound by the
group, although they found it useful. 'I find it easier to
push for things as being right for the area if I know the
Community Association agrees. Many of the people in the
Community Association would not be in a political party anyway.
Group B only had contact with the council in that individual
activities involved contact with officers. The new group
managing the independent project is still resistant to the
idea of councillors on their group, although it may be
inevitable, given local authority funding.

    Undoubtedly there is a role to be played in relation to
government policy affecting the area. An umbrella group can
act as a focus for communications, channelling information to

the appropriate group, or putting the local authority in touch
with the group or consortium of groups in the area, relevant
to the issue in hand. In acting as a central focus for informatio
it can identify issues which need local attention and bring
together those groups which are appropriate (as Group A did in
order to develop a response to the structure plan). If local
groups are to be able to respond to policies affecting their
area, the most important ingredients are a good background of
information and discussion and a strong tradition of local
action and political awareness. It is in this arena that an
umbrella group has an important role to play.

This indeed was the role Group A settled for. It was a
resource group, a discussion forum, a focus for information with
occasional forays into developing new initiatives:
The groups are the association. It's managed by the Executive
Committee and encompasses all the activities. It's essential
in that it gives the more militant groups an air of respecta-
bility, but it encompasses different points of view. In
effect, it has very little power, but power by consent works
quite well. It's a communications vehicle. Most of the
active groups are jealous of their independence. We feed in
and out and share problems.
This sort of role does not lessen the need to keep member groups
informed and serviced. The group has to be relevant to its
constituency to have its existence justified.

The functions mentioned bear some resemblance to those
outlined in the Wolfenden Report as being local 'intermediary'
functions (with the exception of representation) but are based
on an organisation rooted in the community rather than brought
in from outside. It is not surprising, therefore, that such a
group needs resources to perform its role adequately. All the
groups discussed had resources from the local project. Group
A, for example, reflects a community work involvement of some
six years - nearly half of this prior to setting up the
association. It has in addition premises and administrative
resources. The amount of resources required to develop such
associations and their member groups will vary according to
the area and the current levels and traditions of group
organisation, the issues of concern etc. None the less it
is difficult to see how an association can operate effectively
without being able to call on someone with time and skills
to supplement theirs.

If resources are to be provided the question of control
arises. In all three cases discussed, the project which
resourced the association was set up first, but only in one
(Group A), was there formal representation of the association's
executive on the project's management committee (three out of
nine). Project B had no management committee, although, as we
have seen, one has now been set up, composed of members of
local groups. Project C had a largely professional management
committee with one member of a local group only.

It is not uncommon now for local community associations to
employ their own worker(s) but, as employers, many of the
pitfalls indicated above may still apply - who represents whom,
who is in control. Yet again a structure which involves people
as fully as possible, is open and communicative, is absolutely
essential. Also, it would probably be helpful if some form of
training was available for groups having this responsibility.
So many are dependent on the worker they manage to teach them
how to manage, or on professionals in the group. Some opportunity
to get information and possibly discuss their experience with
others in a similar position would surely be invaluable.

SUMMARY

These three examples of broad-based community organisations
begin to identify some of the special features of this kind of
group and the circumstances in which they are likely to be most
effective. Their experience suggests that if an active,
committed group is to be built, which will span the interests of
different localities and interests, then such a group needs to
be built on the basis of existing action and organisation;
that if it is to be sustained, a lot of energy needs to go
into servicing the links between the central organisation
and its member groups. Such a group has to offer something
to its members. The abstract idea of common action may fire
people for a while but, given the level of commitment to their
own local group or interest, they need a clear idea of what the
organisation offers if a wider commitment is to be maintained.
Further, the group needs the constant interest of its member
groups and a pool of committed individuals from those groups
if it is to develop rather than remain abstract or turn into a
small and separate elite. The group is rare that is not in
some measure limited in its leadership - few people can afford
this level of commitment, and in our experience genuine feedback
to groups beyond their individual representatives has certainly
been the most difficult thing to achieve in federations.
However, the sustained interest and support of member groups
guards against dangers of separation, and acts as a monitor on
the activities of the leadership.

Servicing an organisation in the way that these conclusions
suggest, however, requires resources and time, at the least
premises and administrative staff, but preferably, community
work resources as well. Given an active federation, it is
important that it has as much control over these resources as
possible, with a measure of independence from the local
authority so that it can pursue its objectives without prejudice.

The question of how far these organisations can achieve
consensus, act as a sounding body for outsiders (e.g. the local
authority), represent the interests of their constituents, is
a complex one, and is not easily answered from these three
experiences alone. To some extent the answer depends on the

aims of the organisation and the interests that it represents.
If it is predominantly servicing, as Group A was, then it can
span a wide range of interests. The more it seeks to reach a
common view, however, the more commitment it requires for a
particular line of action or campaigning, then the more likely
it is to do this if its member groups have similar backgrounds,
or are working on similar issues. For example, the interests
of owner-occupiers and council tenants may converge over such
an issue as building a motorway through the area, but are
unlikely to coincide when it comes to housing issues. Group A
recognised this in allowing its member groups to represent
themselves. This pattern, where groups settle into the networks
which are most meaningful to them is not likely to be a tidy
one and may at times be conflictual, but it is likely to give
a more accurate picture of actual views and interests than
attempts to bring too wide a selection of groups into apparent
consensus.

NOTES

1   'The Future of Voluntary Organisations - Report of the
     Wolfenden Committee', Croom Helm, London, 1978.
2   'The Government and the Voluntary Sector: A Consultative
     Document', HMSO, 1978.
3   There is no one list of all CDP publications, but most of
     those published centrally can be obtained from the Home
     Office, 50 Queen Anne's Gate, London SW1H 9AT. These
     include, for example: 'Gilding the Ghetto', 'The Costs
     of Industrial Change'. Individual project publications
     can also be obtained from: The West End Resource Centre,
     87 Adelaide Terrace, Newcastle-upon-Tyne NE4 8BB, and
     CDP Unit, Department of Social Administration and Social
     Work, University of York, Heslington, York YO1 5DD.
4   'The West Watford Community Project: A Research Report',
     Jolyon Flowers and Marilyn Taylor, June 1976. Published
     by the West Watford Community Project, 15 Harwoods Road,
     Watford, Herts.

6 Promoting participation in planning: a case study of Planning Aid, Dundee Area

Laurie Bidwell and Bill Edgar

An ad hoc planning aid group was first formed in Dundee in April 1976 and was forerunner of Planning Aid, Dundee Area, which was constituted on 31 January 1978. This case study examines the work of the group in promoting participation in planning during 1978 and suggests how this might be more widely applied.

PLANNING AID

In January 1973 the Town and Country Planning Association (TCPA) set up the world's first planning aid service. This is a national, London-based service with a nucleus of full-time staff, which has not yet developed its own local or regional groups. By contrast in Scotland, since 1976, a loose-knit federation of volunteer-run independent groups has evolved and there are now planning aid groups in Aberdeen, Dundee, Edinburgh, Glasgow and Inverness.

On the basis of the very limited research to date on planning aid in Britian, (1) we suggest that there are at least four different models of providing planning aid and these are set out in Table 6.1.

The models in Table 6.1 are clearly not mutually exclusive but the distinctions are considered to be useful ones. As well as offering potentially different modes of participation and learning and relating to long- and short-term goals, the models have implications for the role of the professional planner. Inevitably, the planner involved in advocacy or advice is not promoting demystification and citizen learning, and retains the role of the expert urban manager. The alternative models not only have implications for the role of the planner but require a multidisciplinary approach if they are to be successful.

Table 6.1   Models of providing planning aid

		Short-term goals
Least effective modes of promoting citizen participation in planning	A Advice Model A group of qualified planners, either autonomously or as part of a network provide, in a voluntary capacity, free access to information and advice on planning matters. This typically operates through surgeries at, or referral from, CABx or advice centres. The advice model was originally adopted by the TCPA and Scottish planning aid groups and is favoured by the Royal Town Planning Institute in general and in particular by RTPI local branches, where they have entered into planning aid. This model is a derivative of the legal aid model. B Advocacy Model A professional planner represents an individual or group who cannot afford to pay the fees of a consultant planner (planner in private practice). This service runs rather like the legal aid scheme, but generally does not include an overt means-test. The planner works as an advocate to protect or promote the planning interests of his clients. Central government has consistently refused to fund a legal aid type of provision for planning representation, even though it has also generally refused to award costs to objectors who have incurred great expense to be represented at a public inquiry. Consequently, this model has been more extensively developed in the USA and Canada but has been favoured by some community-based consultancies, who work for expenses or reduced fees.	

C Adult environmental education model

The model emphasises promoting learning about local government and environmental issues through the provision of short courses, workshops, publications
and exhibitions to make good this general deficit in most adults' earlier
education. This model has been developed by environmental education resource
centres, WEA and other adult education providers.

D Community development model

A planning issue provides a vehicle for learning by doing, with an emphasis
on both the outcome of the participation in planning, and the learning by
both individuals and groups from the process of participation. This approach
is favoured by the TCPA planning aid service and some community planners and
community workers.

Long-
term
goals

Most effective
modes of
promoting
citizen
participation
in planning

Originally, both in England and Scotland, planning aid was
conceived as a safety-net advice service offering a free service
similar in function and form to legal aid, which would assist
those who had fallen foul of the planning machinery. It is our
impression that all planning aid groups in Scotland quickly came
to realise the limitations of operating within this quasi-
professional model. In particular, the groups were concerned
that those who failed to identify and articulate their planning
grievances were unlikely to be precipitated into participative
action merely by the provision of a relatively obscure, free
planning advice service. This concern was reinforced by the
limited nature, number and type of cases encountered by the
Scottish groups in general and the Dundee group in particular
over the period June 1976 to October 1977. (2) The effect of
this in Dundee led to a deliberate decision to reform and
formally constitute the group. The new approach, which was
recorded in the Dundee group's recent report, (3) emphasised
the twin aims of promoting participation in planning at all
levels and encouraging, through informal adult education, a
high level of awareness of rights of participation and of the
political context of decision-making in the planning process
(adult environmental education/community development models).
In our opinion this approach is consistent with the central
principles of community work. (4) These latter aims were
enshrined in the organisational structure and work of the
group, where three overlapping functions were identified: (5)

(a) Liaison - to liaise with local community groups in
    order to forge links, which could be used when these
    groups encounter a problem with a planning dimension.
(b) Education/community development - to assist community
    groups to learn by doing, when they are motivated to
    participate. To this end, a dialogue model of adult
    education is encouraged. In parallel with this, the
    group is committed to prepare and disseminate informal
    education programmes and materials to assist individuals,
    community groups and local community workers to identify
    planning problems and to know how and when to take up
    rights of participation in the planning process.
(c) Advice - to provide assistance to enquirers to enable
    them to understand the planning dimension of the
    problem raised, to clarify the courses of action
    available and ways of making their views effectively
    known.

The formulation and fulfilling of these aims and functions
depended on a membership drawn from a wide variety of backgrounds. Dundee, in this respect, is probably more diversified
than other planning aid groups, with a volunteer membership
(which fluctuated in 1978 between twenty-five and thirty),
including planners in local government housing and planning
departments, planners and architects in higher education,
community workers, social workers, and other social service
personnel. The orientation of the group was also influenced
by its assessment of the main operational area, Dundee.

DUNDEE

Dundee is the third city of Scotland and is the administrative
centre of Tayside Region (equivalent functions to a non-
metropolitan English county). Its population of approximately
200,000 is predominantly housed by the district council or the
Scottish special housing association, who together provide 62
per cent of the total housing stock, (6) which is concentrated
in a crescent of peripheral estates.

The economy of the city has not benefited yet from the oil
boom and is in serious recession. Traditional industries like
ship building and jute are in decline, while more recent multi-
national based industries such as National Cash Register and
Timex seem well past their post-war prime and are shedding
labour. Furthermore, development grants and advance factories,
though available from the Scottish development agency, are not
in demand. Since the 1920s, the labour movement has not been
very cohesive or militant and a lack of organisation and
political awareness is also evident outside the work place in
the housing estates where there are few active tenants' groups
and little history of community action. It is ironic that even
when Dundee became known, in the early 1970s, as the 'Chicago
of the North', because of the alleged corruption of some Labour
party councillors, even this did not stimulate the growth of
an alternative community politics.

Despite the fact that parts of the inner area of the city
could be identified as multiply deprived in the small area
studies of the 1971 census, very little has been initiated
under the urban programme. Of the spate of government-backed
poverty experiments which were nominally represented in
Scotland (7) only the EPA experiment was located in Dundee.
This and the other initiatives appear to have had only a very
marginal impact on the establishment and practice of neighbourhood community development work, and until recently this style
of local authority intervention has been virtually non-existent
in Dundee. For example, in Dundee there are only three
independent advice agencies: one full-time CAB run by volunteers
with a full-time organiser; one neighbourhood advice centre
with one full-time and one half-time worker; and one part-time
legal advice centre run by law faculty staff and students at
the University. Of necessity then, the work we have been
involved in here has been part of the opening moves of
community development in the area and may well, we suggest,
have much in common with community work in some non-metropolitan
parts of England.

COMMUNITY WORK AND PARTICIPATION IN PLANNING

The idea that securing and developing participation in planning
is central to the role of the community worker, has a relatively
long pedigree in Britain. More participation has been generally

perceived by government and people as a desirable end and this
has been given statutory expression in the recent parallel
English and Scottish planning legislation. However, in our
opinion, the honeymoon in participation in planning appears to
be over, as mounting criticism and scepticism of participation
is voiced. From within government and the planning profession,
criticism has been levelled at the costs to entrepreneurs of
delays incurred in the development process, about the value of
participation schemes in the face of low and unrepresentative
levels of response and concern about the unlikelihood of planners
being able adequately to include the diversity of public response
into the plans under preparation. Those outside planning have
ridiculed the often poor attempts made by 'the planners' to
involve the public and their failure to contact or elicit
responses from many minority groups. Peter and Suzie Beresford
of Battersea Community Action have recently added an action-
research study in North Wandsworth to the already extensive
literature on this subject. (8) On the basis of their research,
only 1¼ per cent of the population took part in a Wandsworth
borough participation exercise and those groups with the greatest
needs were least likely to be represented. In more theoretical
debates criticisms have included the difficulties of fostering
participation within a representative democracy, the implicit
consensus assumptions which underpin participation in planning
and the relative powerlessness of planning to grapple with
structural economic causes of problems.

In our opinion these pitfalls and difficulties do not
justify a policy of non-intervention by community workers.
First, planning is a political process because, as Fujishin
observes, 'planning practice invariably results in the
allocation of an amenity (or disamenity) to one group instead
of another and because it entails value judgements about the
desirable end result of the planning process. These value
judgements are about the nature of a new distribution of
wealth, amenity and political power.' (9) However marginal
the potential for redistribution through planning, it should
be noted that this redistribution could be progressive or
regressive; the underprivileged could be worse off if they
opt out of the process. The privileged interest groups who
already have inroads into the corridors of local authority
power have, through the planning legislation, another channel
of influence on local planning policy. A local instance of
this may be culled from the list of organisations making
comments on the recent Dundee Inner City Local Plan. This
list includes Delta Capillary Products, Dundee and Tayside
Chamber of Commerce, Scottish Gas and the University of Dundee,
but not tenants' associations.

Second, it cannot be assumed, as some would argue, that
representative democracy is sufficient to secure the interests
of the disadvantaged. Since development plans are longer
term than the life span of elected representatives, councillors
may have only a marginal influence on their formulation and

implementation. The back-bencher, as Cockburn observ
study of Lambeth, (10) tends to be excluded from deci
as decisions in a corporately managed authority are i
taken by senior officers and the political leadership
also doubtful whether the new development plans will
flexible as was originally intended. It may therefor
foolish to expect many local councillors to have the political
leverage to engineer a substantial departure from a development
plan. This would be rather like trying to shut the stable door
after the horse had bolted.

Third, for those doubtful of securing any beneficial outcome
from participation, it is worth noting that skilled participation
can contribute to non-decision-making or delay considerably the
implementation of undesirable proposals. A change of government
or public spending cuts have put paid to many products of local
government vacillation.

Fourth, we believe that an increase in take-up of the
opportunities to participate will help secure those rights and
extend their scope to the limits of the current legislation.
It is at least arguable that the law relating to planning will
remain vague, ill defined and subject to local policy unless
it is put to the test more frequently and systematically. For
example, how many community groups have exercised their right to
write to the Secretary of State (Secretary of State for the
Environment in England) to object to the adoption of a development plan (structure plan or local plan) on the grounds of
inadequate public participation?

Participation in planning can therefore have an important,
if marginal, extrinsic benefit, even if at times that participation supports the status quo by warding off disbenefits. We
have also claimed earlier that participation can lead to
important intrinsic benefits through the process of community
development.

It is not surprising that in a society increasingly dominated
by the values of freedom of the individual and the virtues of
private enterprise, collective participation tends to be
spasmodic, occuring only at times of crisis when group interests
are obviously and immediately threatened. It is through the
exploitation of this reactive collective action that we suggest
the community worker or planning aider, committed to raising
levels of participation in planning, must begin to work.

PLANNING AID IN DUNDEE DURING 1978

As we have indicated previously, the work of the group in 1978
was influenced by reflections on the previous low levels of
demand for planning aid in Dundee (when an advice model had been
operated), the experience and background of our membership and
the lack of a clearly identifiable local history of collective
action. These influences not only shaped the three functions of

ıe group, liaison, education/community development and advice,
but also the relative weighting to each of these in our initial
year of operation. Although these functions overlap, reference
to Table 6.2 shows clearly how our group managed to prioritise
its initiatives away from casework/advice to liaison, education
and community development, even though a greater number of cases
involved advice-giving. Table 6.2 also gives some measure of
the collective commitment of our planning aid group and our
overall performance in 1978.

TABLE 6.2 Summary of the work of the group in 1978

Function	Volunteer hours
(a) Liaison	
20 community councils in Dundee were visited by pairs of volunteers from the group.	120
Representatives from approximately 100 Community Councils outside Dundee (Tayside and Fife Regions) were contacted at five one-day seminars for community councillors (see education below).	
23 community workers were contacted through a one-day conference on planning aid for community workers (see education below).	
(b) Education/community development	
Members contributed to five-day seminars on participation in planning for a total of 130 community councillors. These seminars were organised by the Perth office of the Scottish Council of Social Service.	100
Members devised and arranged a one-day conference on planning aid for 23 community workers.	60
Development of educational and learning materials for seminars, conferences and trial usage of a planning education pack.	60
7 (approximately 25% of the annual total) involved the adoption of a community development approach.	270
(c) Advice	
23 cases (not including the 7 above) involved advice and assistance giving to individuals and groups.	75
Total hours	685

Note: This figure represents almost 20 full working weeks (at
35 hours per week) and was contributed by a membership
of approximately 25. The figures do not include any
time allowances for attendance at general, committee and
sub-committee meetings, and therefore tend to under-
estimate the overall level of commitment of group members.

CASE EXAMPLES

The following five cases give a clearer insight into the work
of the group and raise some of the problems of promoting
participation in planning.

Case 1: Housing association

Tenants of a housing association approached us after the
association's annual general meeting.   They had a variety of
complaints about development on sites adjoining their homes.
In working on this case with the tenants, further difficulties
were raised with our volunteers about the association's
constitution and how tenant representation might be secured
on the management committee. At our suggestion, this group
of tenants encouraged other tenants to become members of the
association and at the next annual general meeting there was
sufficient voting strength for the tenants to take over control
of the association.

     This illustrates the gains that can be made from implementing
a community development rather than an advice model of planning
aid. Wherever possible we try not to dispense planning aid
on the telephone but establish face-to-face contact with
individuals and groups. In this way a simple query can be
thoroughly assessed and clarified and in several instances,
as above, this has paid dividends, since a follow-up to the
presenting problem has established more serious and long-term
issues. This approach is obviously more demanding in time and
skills but this investment has ultimately been justified by
our experience.

     The housing association case arose through the contact
established by one of our members and illustrates the advantages
to be derived from developing networks of contacts and links
within the community. In our opinion, this network approach
is more conducive to bringing us in contact with planning
issues and cases, than formal and impersonal publicity. The
case also illustrates the importance of a broadly based group
of volunteers who are willing and capable of working with
groups on planning-related problems, which are often strictly
outside the parameters of what might be defined as town and
country planning matters.

Case 2: Hilltown residents

Several neighbours from a decaying inner-city area approached
a local community worker, who is also a member of our group.
The neighbours, all mothers, wanted to object to a proposed
housing development by a local housing association on the
grounds that this would remove a traditional local play space.
When volunteers followed up this request, it became clear that

lack of local play facilities was a more general local issue.
The volunteers were able to inform the mothers about the
development of the inner-city local plan, (11) which in the
report of our survey had identified a low level of all
community facilities in the Hilltown area. The mothers'
knowledge of the area and their willingness to suggest suitable
play sites, produced a short list of sites which were checked
on the planning register and subsequently the residents made a
submission to the local plan, which was accepted in toto.

This case illustrates the positive results which may emanate
from learning situations where both planning aid volunteers and
local residents involve themselves in dialogue. Local people
will often know an area much better than a planner or community
worker who works in that patch. On the other hand, volunteers
who know the time schedule for the rolling programme of
producing development plans for the area can encourage
participation by structuring this around concrete issues and
making full use of the residents' expertise. At the same time
the volunteer is also learning more about the locality for
future action.

One problem characterised by this case is that of the
representativeness of groups. This case involved a small group
of mothers but the issue eventually involved a much wider
social and geographical area and would normally have been
taken up by a tenants' or residents' association had one
existed.

Finally, this case illustrates by default the importance of
continuity of contact and follow-up. In this case, although
the local plan adopted the suggested play areas, subsequent
emasculation of the plan by the ruling progressive party has
made it extremely unlikely that the designated play areas will
be provided. The run up to the district council elections in
spring 1980 will probably provide the next opportunity to
press on with this issue.

Case 3: West End Roads Concern (WERC)

The regional council proposed to build a university bypass and
had to apply to the city district council for planning
permission. At a public meeting, called by a small cohort of
local concerned individuals, a pressure group was formed to
fight the proposals. After a refusal of planning permission,
the region marginally revised their proposals and initiated
a further round of public consultation with WERC and three
local community councils. As a result of WERC's well reasoned
objections, well-directed pressure and lobbying, the proposals
have once again been refused by the district and an appeal is
almost certainly pending after at least twelve months' delay.

The most important problem raised by this sort of case is

the issue of time. Primarily, there is the question of our
involvement with one case for over sixteen months. It is not
easy to maintain continuity of volunteers (up to three years
including an appeal) and in this case two of the original
volunteers moved out of the area and had to be replaced at a
critical stage in the development of the struggle. Now that we
have been involved for so long and an appeal is imminent we
also forsee some conflict between seeing the case through and
avoiding advocacy at a public inquiry.

There is also the community development problem of helping
maintain an issue-based group for a relatively long period of
time. This was exacerbated by the see-saws in local political
opinion and the erroneous assumption made by peripherally
involved individuals that one refusal by the district council
constituted a victory. As well as assisting WERC with forming
sound planning objections, we spent a lot of time helping the
group hold together and retain credibility in the face of
criticism from local community councils and other elected
representatives. This raises the wider question of how
realistic it may be for planning departments to expect active
citizen participation over a period of two to three years,
through the successive stages of development plan-making.

Case 4: Inner city community council

This newly formed community council homed in on the lack of
recreational and community facilities in its constituency.
The council contacted planning aid to request help with
identifying suitable local sites for a community centre and
securing any necessary planning permission. The site eventually
favoured was a disused factory and required 'change of use'
planning permission. Since the district council's published
policy had zoned the area concerned for future industrial
development, in addition to submitting a well-argued case,
local political pressure was necessary in order to overturn
the likely policy-related recommendation of the chief planning
officer to the planning committee.

Tactics rather than technical advice have often proved more
valuable to groups. This was a case where it is worth noting
the rule that where an application for planning permission
coincides with local authority policy in regional reports
(Scotland only), structure plans and local plans, a well-
argued case should ensure that the council implement their own
policy. Where the application is contrary to local policy, to
stand any chance of success, it is necessary to influence the
policy of the ruling political groups, which is invariably
decided at pre-council caucus meetings.

This case also illustrates the advantages of a well-
connected network or a diversified planning aid group. In this
case we were not only able to facilitate the services of an

architect from our group, but also to advise on a project
steering group and capital and revenue financing of the project.

Case 5: Objection to a development proposal

A group of neighbours wished to object to a proposed amusement
arcade in their road. The residents first approached the CAB
who referred the case by letter. By the time the case had been
received, only one working day was left to act. We were able
to reassure the group that on the basis of our understanding
of local planning policy and recent precedents, the application
concerned was unlikely to be approved. The residents were
advised of the decision and warned to look out in the regular
planning advertisements for a further application, or a notice
of appeal.

This case raises the dilemma of how styles of intervention
may be compromised when rigid planning deadlines have to be
met. This also points to the problems of relying on generalist
advice agencies for referrals, especially those like CABx who
appear not to attract collective problems. On the basis of
this and other referred cases, we are naturally disturbed to
learn that the Scottish Office favour using CABx for contact
points for planning aid rather than fund planning aid workers.
We consider our fears are confirmed by the fact that many of
our cases would not have arisen had we diverted our resources
into manning a planning aid surgery at the Dundee CAB.

PERMANENT STRUCTURES FOR PARTICIPATION

It is now increasingly argued that some form of permanent
structure (e.g. neighbourhood councils) is necessary if
participation is to be effective. Our experience in working
with community councils in Tayside and Fife suggests some
important difficulties with this type of solution.

Community councils have been established in most areas of
Scotland during the last two years under the provisions of
Part IV of the Local Government (Scotland) Act 1973. Although
introduced by statute, community councils were not seen as a
third tier of local government but according to the act, 'the
general purpose of a community council shall be to ascertain,
co-ordinate and express to the local authorities for its area,
and to public authorities, the views of the community....' (12)
In other words community councils represent a permanent
Scottish structure for participation rather like the department
of the environment proposals for neighbourhood councils in
England. (13)

Although we have been involved with a large number of
community councils in a variety of situations, our doubts about
their role as permanent structures for participation can best

be discussed by reference to the West End Roads Concern (WERC)
case. (The details of this case are described in Case 3, p.146.)
We can now highlight the role played by the two main community
councils involved.

   The regional council called a meeting of the leaders of the
two community councils together with other local bodies to
describe their revised proposal after their original planning
application had been refused by the district council. The roads'
convenor (chairman of the regional roads committee) obtained
the agreement of the community councillors present that he could
attend the next general meeting of each council. All community
council meetings are open to the public but these subsequent
meetings were not specially advertised locally. Despite this
about twenty members of the public turned up to each meeting.

   The chairman of the community councils on each occasion would
only accept questions concerning that part of the road in their
area. Questions concerning the road in totality, the need for
the road, alternative options, its place on the road strategy
and so on were ruled out of order.

   The councils on each occasion acceded to the roads' convenor's
pressure that the councillors should take a vote and reached a
majority decision in favour of the revised proposal. Although
some councillors expressed reservations on details only, a
minority opposed the revised proposal. This tactic enabled
the regional council to get good press. The local daily paper,
the 'Dundee Courier and Advertiser', featured articles with
headlines like (14) 'Bypass gets west end approval' and
'University bypass gains support' which attempted to discredit
the substantial local opposition which had created West End
Roads Concern, and also left the district council in a
vulnerable and potentially untenable position.

   Several interesting points arise from this concerning the
role of the community council. First, there is the role of
the chairmen concerned and their influence over other
councillors. Masterson (15) has shown that in Tayside and
Fife 9 per cent of community councillors have been former local
government councillors and a further 8 per cent had stood
unsuccessfully for local office. It is our understanding that
both chairmen were active members of the same political party
as the regional roads' convenor. Thus there is the suspicion
that community councils are in danger of becoming the bottom
rung of the political ladder with all that that implies.

   Second, there is the fact that the community councillors
acceded to the demand for a vote to be taken. They thus failed
to ascertain, co-ordinate and express the variety of opinions
of people in their area. There was clear evidence of a
substantial body of opinion opposed to any bypass proposal and
of opposition to the region's revised plans (a majority of the
members of the public attending opposed the plans as did a

minority of councillors). The community councils in this
instance took up a representative role rather than a participative one as the legislation intended. This is clearly
undesirable especially since, as Cosgrove points out, (16)
community councils are dominated by the elderly and higher socio-
economic groups relative to an area.

Third, even on this major local issue, the councils made no
attempt to publicise the meetings or to call street-level
meetings to seek the opinion of those directly affected. This
is understandable since the effort and resources required to do
so are considerable. However, there is evidence that planning
departments may be content to carry out their public participation exercises by merely consulting the community councils
(relying on them to publicise the meetings). Thus permanent
structures may deprive people of the opportunity to participate
rather than improve take-up of rights or participation. There
is also some evidence from people who have approached planning
aid, that community councils act as a filter mechanism, since
only issues going forward to the local authority with their
support receive serious consideration.

Silk has argued that the statutory requirement to 'ascertain,
co-ordinate and express the views of the community, does not
suggest a representative role whereby representatives are
validated by election to speak on behalf of a community' (17)
but is indicative of a move towards a participatory model of
democracy. However, this particular case tends to indicate
that it is perhaps inevitable that such bodies will act in a
representative capacity and indeed it is perhaps unrealistic
to expect more of them. Certainly, if a major local issue
such as this can elicit only a perfunctory attempt to ascertain
the views of residents or community groups in the area, the
hope that permanent structures such as community councils would
be able to stimulate greater public discussion is unrealistic
and possibly detrimental in the long term to the life chances
of the poor and underprivileged.

CONCLUSIONS

The year's work examined in this case study has in our opinion
provided sufficient positive pointers to validate the core
aims and objectives of the group. On reflection, we have
recently decided to deploy our limited manpower resources on
the basis of further positive discrimination to areas of need
in Dundee inner city. We anticipate that as well as continuing
to fulfil our previous functions in these geographical areas
(as specified below) we could also attempt to establish a
physical presence in shop-front premises. Additionally, where
we discover any important issues and an absence of community
groups of the appropriate constituency, we will be prepared to
help establish issue-based groups. Furthermore, we have
agreed to act as whistle-blowers on current environmental issues

and to expose the hidden agenda of the development plans for an area (regional report, structure plan, local plans, housing plan and transport policies and programmes).

For the rank-and-file community worker, we feel our case suggests three main things. Planning aid is a rather ad hoc, uneven kind of provision, which might be able to provide independent free back-up advice to a community worker with a problem, which has a planning dimension. It might also be capable of contributing to or promoting learning about planning for activists. Community workers would therefore be well advised to explore the scope of the potential planning aid service in their area (for contacts see n.18).

We would also suggest that planning issues have the potential to be at least as effective a motor of issue-based community development as more conventional housing issues. Development control issues in particular are remarkable in the way they can stimulate collective action, which can precipitate participation and, in addition to the planning outcome will promote learning opportunities for political education.

Finally, as government spending enters a period of decline or at best no growth, it will be even more crucial for people to participate in planning to protect their life chances. Planning is only part of the terrain where the struggle for scarce resources takes place, but one part that we suggest should be contested more often and more thoroughly.

NOTES

1 J. Ferier, F. Hutchinson and R. Johnson, 'Planning Aid: A Report on Scottish Experience', Glasgow, The Planning Exchange, 1978.
2 Ibid., pp.28-41.
3 L. Bidwell, B. Downes and B. Edgar, 'Report on Progress in 1978: Planning Aid, Dundee Area', Dundee, Planning Aid Dundee Area, 1978, pp.8-14.
4 D. Spence, 'Towards a definition of Community Work', London, Association of Community Workers, 1978, pp.13-14. See also The Community Work Study Group, 'Current Issues in Community Work', London, Routledge & Kegan Paul, 1973, pp.9-21.
5 Bidwell, Downes and Edgar, op. cit., pp.9-11.
6 Tayside Regional Council, 'Regional Report 1976', Dundee, Tayside Regional Council, 1976, paragraph 4.2.
7 EPA, Dundee 1968-71, CDP Ferguslie Park, Paisley, 1972-7; CCP, Craigneuk, Motherwell, 1976-8; and Quality of Life Experiment, Dumbarton, 1976-8.
8 P. Beresford and S. Beresford, 'A Say in the Future', London, Battersea Community Action, 1978, pp.9-12.
9 B.S. Fujishin, 'Styles of Advocacy: The Roles of Voluntary Organisations in the Birmingham Planning Process',

University of Birmingham Centre for Urban and Regional
Studies, 1975, pp.3-10.

10   C. Cockburn, 'The Local State, Management of Cities and
People', London, Pluto Press, 1977, pp.5-40.

11   A local plan is usually prepared by a district council
(the borough council in London) and concerns the policy
and proposals for the future use of land over a period of
approximately 5-10 years. The preparation of a local plan
must, by law, involve public consultation. If objections
to a local plan are lodged timeously, a public enquiry
must be arranged.

12   H.M. Government, 'The Local Government (Scotland) Act 1973',
Edinburgh, HMSO, 1973, part IV, paragraph 51 (2).

13   Department of the Environment, 'A Voice for Your Neighbourhood', London, HMSO, 1977.

14   The 'Dundee Courier and Advertiser', 25th November and
30 November 1978, Dundee, D.C. Thomson & Co.

15   M.P. Masterson and E.M. Masterson, 'Community Councils
Research Projects Interim Reports (October 1976-March 1978),
Edinburgh, Central Research Unit Scottish Office, 1978, p.8,
paragraph 33, and p.9, paragraph 38.

16. D.F. Cosgrove and H.N. Sheldon, 'Community Councils
Research Projects Interim Reports (October 1976-March 1978),
Edinburgh, Central Research Unit Scottish Office, 1978,
p.55.

17   P. Silk, 'Community Councils as Instruments of Democracy',
Glasgow, Strathclyde Area Survey, University of Strathclyde,
1978, pp.10-11.

18   To enquire about local planning aid resources contact:
(in England) The Town and Country Planning Association,
Planning Aid Service, 17 Carlton House Terrace, London,
SW1, Tel. 01 930 8903 and (in Scotland) The Planning
Exchange, 186 Bath Street, Glasgow, G2 4HG, Tel.041 221 9600.

7 Resource centres and participation

Nick Bailey and Marilyn Taylor *

1 PROBLEMS OF DEFINING PARTICIPATION

It may be no coincidence that participation, as a form of interaction with government, first appeared on the agenda for community groups during the period of relative economic prosperity in the late 1960s. The economy was relatively stable and local authority expenditure was increasing. Participation, especially in the field of town planning, became a means by which local groups could influence the distribution of public and private investment, although, as writers such as Cynthia Cockburn have shown, in many cases this was an elaborate form of co-option whereby new policies and plans were legitimated. In these circumstances, participation may or may not be worthwhile depending on the particular characteristics of the locality and a realistic assessment of the benefits to be gained.

Within the last five years economic conditions have changed, public expenditure has been cut in real terms and in many cases this decline in local authority involvement has been linked with a rapid decrease of investment in industry - both public and private. In this situation, the benefits of any form of participation with central or local government, where basic needs such as unemployment are not being met and where a decline in public services is being experienced, are often dubious. In areas where these changes are most acute, community groups may well consider it more advantageous to mobilise on a political level to change investment patterns and government policy to meet their assessment of social need, as well as fighting a rearguard action to hold on to benefits won in the past. Developing the means of setting up locally based groups and creating stronger links with the labour movement, where jobs and public expenditure are under pressure, is part of the purpose of community work and a particular function of resource centres.

Despite economic fluctuations, a number of collective needs

have been established which must be met through collective
consumption or the social wage and which over the years have
become essential to the smooth running of the economy. Similarly
in the political sphere, collective consumption is of considerable
importance and all political parties recognise the need for some
state involvement in it. Its size, range, distribution and
method of allocation are, however, open to question and therefore
have a profound political significance for community work
practice. As Lambert notes:

> The State has responsibility for these more collective
> needs.... Their provision is essential not only to satisfy
> the demands and expectations of the people but also for the
> continuation of profitable private business - workers must
> be housed and educated adequately, they and the goods they
> produce must be able to move easily in the market place.
> It is precisely because their provision is at one and the
> same time essential to the maintenance of the social order,
> an unprofitable part of the ordinary capitalist investment
> and the focus of demands, that their management, provision
> and allocation is problematical. So it is in relation to
> managerial efforts related to these kinds of facilities
> that the growth of participatory community work has been so
> marked in recent years. (1)

A clear distinction therefore exists between participation as
the term is often used by central government and local
authorities, which (at best) implies a dialogue between the
community and the state in order to determine priorities and
to plan action. The broader use of the term suggests a much
longer-term process in which people take a more active role in
the determination of the future of their living and working
environments, whereby a radical change is brought about in the
way in which problems are defined, needs voiced and solutions
explored. Bearing in mind recent political and economic trends,
this objective would appear to be far more allusive now than
for some time in the past.

The experience of many groups of participating with local
authorities from a position of weakness, is that 'participation'
is often a sham, an excuse for inaction or a form of co-option
which results in the community group being further weakened.
The desire for a greater level of participatory democracy is
founded on the principle that community decision-making should
be based as far as possible at the grass roots level. To those
working in resource centres, participation is more relevant as
part of a larger process designed to increase community self-
determination, whereby the resource centres enable and
facilitate the community itself to organise, articulate needs
and evolve appropriate organisations to meet them. The aim
is therefore to encourage the development of effective
community organisations and to ensure that they have sufficient
resources to pursue their chosen strategy.

This may involve participation with central or local
government over particular issues of collective consumption,

but where questions of production arise, developing links with
trade unions and trades councils will be more effective, for
example, in preventing industrial closures and redundancies.
Equally, community groups may decide in the circumstances that
their objective should be to become relatively autonomous and
to increase local self-determination. In this case, resource
centres will assist in fund-raising and mobilising latent local
resources and skills, for example, in setting up industrial
co-operatives.

Resource centres are often located in or serve areas where
community organisation is undeveloped and where local authorities
are able to ignore or divide local interests. Often these areas
are what are normally referred to as 'inner city' areas of the
larger metropolitan regions. Increasingly, however, resource
centres cover both urban and rural areas, the inner city and
the suburbs, and it is in areas such as South Wales, Greater
Manchester and Tyne and Wear that it is becoming evident that
the occurrence of poverty, deprivation and industrial disinvestment is by no means limited to what the government has very
closely defined as Partnership Areas.

Resource centres, therefore, exist to support community and
other interest groups which are concerned with reversing trends
towards greater deprivation, discrimination and inequality
through the use of a wide range of tactics. The remainder of
this chapter will explore in more detail how resource centres
relate to the community, the services they offer and some of
the strategies they adopt. Case studies will be used, drawn
from a number of existing centres, to show how they operate in
practice. First, brief mention will be made of the report,
'Current Issues in Community Work', which led to the experimental funding of six centres by the Home Office and EEC.

2   THE ORIGINS OF THE RESOURCE CENTRE CONCEPT

Although the development of the concept of the resource centre
can be traced back through the long history of British community
and social work - both the settlements and CDPs have experimented
with the idea - much of the collective experience of this field
was crystallised in the report of the Gulbenkian Foundation-
sponsored Community Work Group, 'Current Issues in Community
Work'. (2) Over a period of three years the Group examined
both broad trends in community work, such as the rise of
community action, and detailed aspects of the needs of groups,
sources of employment and training. Their conclusion was that
community work was an essential part of modern democratic
society and they defined it as follows:
   Community work is essentially about social change; about the
   redistribution of power and scarce resources; about the
   inertia of large institutions; about conflicts of interest
   between different groups in a community; about how the
   activists and the inarticulate may both have a proper say

in decision-making processes that affect them; and about
the extent and kinds of decisions that people wish to make,
or contribute to making, themselves. (3)

The report considered that 'many of the failures of community
action groups seem related to a lack of resources in terms of
money, influence and expertise' and put forward the proposal
that:

> Area centres should be set up within existing organisations,
> not necessarily within the same kind of organisation in
> each area. They should be in regular contact not only with
> the local groups but also with the national centre ... the
> functions of these area centres would vary according to
> the local needs and the services already available. (4)

The functions of these centres would include the collection
and dissemination of information, the provision of supporting
services in the form of professional and technical expertise,
making available a pool of typing and duplicating equipment to
local groups and providing facilities for discussion, training,
meetings and the exchange of information. With regard to
management and funding, the Group proposed:

> The form of management of these area centres will depend to
> some extent on the type of organisation within which the
> centre is established. It is important that members of
> community groups should participate in the management of
> each centre, and that all those concerned with the centre
> should share in decision making. Funding should normally
> be a matter for the local authorities and voluntary
> organisations in the area.... But in order to establish the
> practical value of these centres, it might well be necessary
> to obtain from central government and trusts sufficient
> funds to promote experimental centres, preferably in, say,
> two very different areas, and to publish reports on their
> work. (5)

After lengthy negotiations, the Voluntary Services Unit
(VSU) of the Home Office agreed to part-fund on an experimental
basis six centres, in conjunction with the EEC's Social Fund,
and in the case of Govan, the Gulbenkian Foundation. The six
centres are:

> British Council of Churches Community Work Resource Unit (BCC)
> Govan Area Resource Centre (GARC)
> London Voluntary Service Council Community Work Service (LVSC)
> Manchester Area Resource Centre (MARC)
> South Wales Anti-Poverty Action Centre (SWAPAC)
> Tyne and Wear Resource Centre (Tyne and Wear) (6)

These six were established between 1975 and 1977, initially
for three years, and since then a number of others have been
set up throughout the country, funded from a variety of
different sources.

The original concept of resource centres in the Gulbenkian
Report was deliberately designed to be flexible and adaptable
to local circumstances and this intention has been reflected in

the subsequent development of these centres. In making compari-
sons between the strategies of the centres a number of factors
can be identified which explain their different styles of
operation.

An important difference between the centres is the nature of
the parent body which established it. In two cases, SWAPAC and
GARC, totally new organisations evolved out of discussions between
community groups, voluntary organisations and in the case of
GARC, the local authorities. In these cases it was decided at
a very early stage to set up the centres based on principles of
local self-management and direct participation by members of
groups the centre is designed to serve. The other centres
largely evolved out of and remain attached to larger organisations, such as the BCC, LVSC and in the case of MARC and Tyne
and Wear, the Community Projects Foundation (CPF). For these
last two, local management groups have been formed while they
remain ultimately responsible to CPF. The centres therefore
display various degrees of local control and management over
their own resources and the way they operate.

A second factor comprises the size of the area served, the
types of deprivation which predominate and the relative
effectiveness of the various levels of government in ameliorating
major social and economic problems. Differences exist between
centres in large metropolitan areas, such as London, Manchester
and Tyne and Wear, and those in the 'regions', such as GARC and
SWAPAC, where the level of government resource input is lower
in relation to the extent of disinvestment and deprivation
found in those areas. Those centres covering metropolitan
areas also tend to operate differently in that they can usually
rely on a relatively large number of experienced groups already
in existence upon which community work can be built. The recent
growth in the number of specialist resource centres, such as law
centres, Women's Aid centres and trade union research units,
have also provided a valuable additional source of advice and
expertise to community groups and the generalist resource
centres, particularly in the metropolitan areas.

In the end, each resource centre evolves its own strategy
in the light of local circumstances and by using the inevitably
limited number of workers and resources where they can have
the greatest impact. In the early days, strategies tended to
evolve pragmatically partly in response to requests for
assistance and partly as a result of initiatives to fill gaps
where groups are non-existent, relatively weak or under
resourced. More recently, as a result of experience and with
discussion with others working in the field, centres have been
able to develop relatively sophisticated and long-term
strategies to increase the effectiveness of their work.
According to the original concept of resource centres and from
the experience of the six listed above, centres offer support
in four main directions:

1 a service function to extend a group's ability to articulate
   needs and to communicate them;
2 a linkage function to provide information, to develop
   information networks and to support and co-ordinate area-
   wide groups and campaigns;
3 a redevelopment function to encourage increased local self-
   management and control of resources;
4 a research feedback function to channel experience of needs
   and the effects of particular policies to groups, trade
   unions, officials and politicians, particularly where there
   are blockages in the system or where structural factors make
   particular policies ineffective.

In the following section these four functions will be looked at
more closely to see how resource centres carry them out in
practice.

3 THE FUNCTIONS OF RESOURCE CENTRES

Service

The service function to a community group is perhaps the most
basic and essential of all and at the heart of the thinking
behind the original proposal. There are a number of different
levels at which this function can be carried out, depending
on the particular needs of the group concerned. One of the
most essential services is to make available the basic hardware -
typewriters, duplicators, and photocopiers - so that groups
are able to serve their own members effectively and to gain
access to situations and institutions where the printed word
and visual image have the greatest impact. In providing this
basic service and in encouraging groups to operate the
equipment themselves, the groups are able to develop skills of
communication at their own pace, as well as having access to a
central point of reference should further help or advice be
needed. This role is particularly supportive to new groups
trying to attract and organise new members and new contacts are
often made, as in the case of MARC, when small grants are given
to enable new groups to organise and communicate their presence
effectively.

    In some cases this role can be developed further in providing
information about a particular issue, such as housing improvement
or how to apply for urban aid funding. In other cases it may
involve longer term assistance on, for example, how to set up a
representative management committee or draw up a constitution.
All resource centres are involved in this kind of work on a
day-to-day basis and where long-term assistance is called for,
a resource centre worker may devote a large proportion of his
or her time to one or two groups for several months. At least
two centres, LVSC and SWAPAC, have produced training packs on
funding, management and constitutions, where there is a
consistent demand for this kind of advice. SWAPAC has also
prepared a series of leaflets on employment issues, such as

unfiar dismissal, lay-offs and short-time and unemployment
entitlements. The BCC, which is concerned to see greater community
use of church buildings has produced a leaflet called 'Building a
Better Community', which explains ways of achieving this multi-
use role.

Both GARC and MARC have annual budgets from which small grants
can be made to local groups. In the case of GARC, £4000 is
available annually for this purpose and in 1977-8 19 grants were
made to assist groups, often for producing leaflets or newsletters,
or when embarking on a new area of activity. Larger sums have
been given to employment creation projects and the West Drymoyne
Modernisation Action Group, which fought an extended battle with
the City Council over housing improvement procedures. (7)   A
further sum of £500 was given to an independent community
newspaper, 'The Govan People', where the resource centre also
trained the editorial group in the technical skills of putting
a newspaper together. In the last nine months of 1977 MARC gave
out 33 grants totalling almost £900 to community groups.

Thus the provision of information, hardware, professional
skills, training as well as making small grants, are all
integral parts of the service function to local groups. Great
care is taken not to interfere with the independence of the
group or to decide for it how it should develop or what
particular course of action it should take.

Linkage

The linkage function offered by resource centres is also of
great importance since they are often the only agency in a
position to take an overview of community action in their area.
At the simplest level this involves keeping often isolated
groups in touch with each other through a regular newsletter.
This is done on a regular basis by LVSC, MARC, BCC and Tyne and
Wear. As a result, issues of common concern often come to
light where the centres can organise a federation of groups
or campaign around that particular issue. MARC did this in
1977 when it became clear that the Manpower Services Commission
was not going to relax the 52-week rule on employment in the
job creation programme. More recently, MARC organised the
first North West Conference on Dampness in Housing, which was
attended by a considerable number of tenants' groups and advice
workers. (8)

Because the LVSC has to service a population of 7 million
with a large number of community groups, it has decided to use
its staff of eight to provide information, training and support
to particular London-wide groups and campaigns, which are not
funded or resourced from any other source. It therefore
produces a monthly newsletter to keep groups and community
workers informed about policy changes, and training courses
and conferences are also organised for community workers and

activists, where these are not already provided by other
educational institutions. Members of the LVSC also have a
personal involvement in giving assistance and advice to particular projects, for example in fund raising, and also provide
organisational and secretarial assistance to campaigns, such as
the Central London Campaign for Family Housing, the All London
Campaign against school closures and the Campaign to improve
London Transport. In the case of the Campaign for Family
Housing, LVSC gave valuable assistance in helping groups
prepare evidence for the Coin Street planning inquiry and thought
is now being given to ways of setting up a permanent planning
resource centre for central and inner London. From these few
examples, the principle should be clear. Resource centres are,
by providing professional support and services, enabling others
more effectively to participate in decisions which directly
affect their lives.

A further example can be taken from Tyne and Wear where the
resource centre sees the creation of networks and links between
groups as central to its work. For the past three years, for
example, it has undertaken a support and development role in
relation to a regional federation of tenants' groups - the
North East Tenants' Organisation (NETO). Although in the early
stages it was necessary for the resource centre to undertake
a central role in the administration of the organisation, as
the capacity of the NETO executive increased, the resource
centre became free to develop a programme of education and
discussion for the membership. It also plays an important role
in helping the organisation to establish contact with and
service individual groups. Parallel to this, the resource
centre publishes a regular newsletter on issues related to
tenants' and local action groups, which is intended for all
such groups whether they are members of NETO or not, as well
as trade unions and trades councils.

All resource centres see housing as an area where they can
contribute particularly to the development of strong and
united tenants' and residents' groups. SWAPAC has continued
to build linkages between a number of tenants' groups in south
Wales around issues such as direct labour, improvement policies
and recent housing legislation. MARC organised a series of
seminars on housing issues, including the one on dampness
mentioned earlier, which has resulted in the establishment of
a small panel of experts (environmental health inspector,
planner and architect) to advise groups on tactics and
campaigns. It is hoped in the future to build on this
momentum and to launch a more permanent Housing Action project
in the Manchester area.

This long-term strategy of building strong tenants'
organisations at the grass roots level, resource centres argue,
is the only way to oppose the negative effects of the housing
legislation which is expected in coming months.

Development

GARC covers a population of about 30,000 in south-west Glasgow where industrial decline in the Clydeside docks and associated industries has produced some of the highest levels of deprivation, in terms of unemployment, sub-standard housing and vandalism, in the country. Since being established in 1977, the resource centre has developed a strategy whereby the resources available can be placed at the disposal of groups where they can most effectively be used.

In November 1977 an Employment Study Group, composed of interested local people, employed and unemployed, teachers and industrialists, was set up to explore the extent of the problem and to initiate permanent projects to create employment. £1000 was made available to the Group from the centre's funds as loan finance for co-ops and some money has already gone towards setting up a co-operative food store in the area. The feasibility of an electrical workshop, a print workshop and a workspace project have also been considered. GARC has also initiated a local competition for the best idea for a local employment project and is also benefiting from the urban aid funded Local Enterprise Advisory Project, which employs one person to investigate, design and prepare local schemes to provide long-term viable employment in Govan, Ferguslie Park and East Greenock.

Similarly, SWAPAC has been in the past directly involved in exploring ways of retaining jobs and in encouraging local groups to form and to approach central government for funds to set up work creating projects on co-operative principles in the Welsh valleys. A number of projects, such as the small village co-operative Antur Teifi, the industrial co-operatives and workshops of the mining valleys (Rhondda Enterprise and Dowlais knitwear co-operative) and specific local resource agencies like the West Glamorgan Common Ownership Development Agency, have been helped in this way. Similarly, SWAPAC assisted in establishing the North Wales Industrial Resource Centre to develop a community response to redundancy and unemployment in north and central Wales.

SWAPAC now feels that many of these agencies have reached the point where its generalist services are increasingly less relevant to these organisations and that they should move towards providing their own technical support. SWAPAC also feels that, as the industrial crisis worsens in south Wales, its resources should go primarily into providing both short term and long-term research, information and support to trade unions and allied organisations, fighting closures, redundancies and further reductions in living standards. Thus as economic conditions worsen and public spending declines, SWAPAC like a number of other centres, is looking to issues of production as a focus for research, organisation and action.

In a different context, SWAPAC has developed a way in which
the community can help itself in claiming rightful welfare
benefits without recourse to expensive legal assistance. The
Tribunal Access Unit, funded by the Nuffield Foundation and
based at SWAPAC, employs two full-time workers to train those
with limited experience - community activists, the unemployed,
the retired and social workers - in the skills of representation
at Supplementary Benefit Appeals Tribunals and National Insurance
Local Tribunals. A comprehensive information and referral
system is also operated in order to put those in need directly
in touch with those able to offer help. At the time of writing,
a large amount of unmet need has been revealed and regular
training courses are being organised but so far long-term
funding for the unit has not been secured.

Tyne and Wear resource centre has also identified welfare
rights as an area of need and at one time found itself having
to deal with a large number of general inquiries from claimants.
Rather than trying to extend its own resources to cover this
field, which it did not see as its function, it supported the
local trades council in applying for funding for a centre for
the unemployed.

Thus by enabling people to take direct control of the
resources put at their disposal for many different purposes,
some of which have been indicated in the previous paragraphs,
faltering steps are being made towards the long-term goal of
increased local determination and increasing influence over
those responsible for allocating public and private sources of
finance. Steps are also being made towards establishing the
most appropriate form of management for the resource centre
itself. Overall, centres have experimented with a number of
different forms of management, from the formally elected
management group with a carefully worded constitution to the
looser open meeting system. Increasingly centres are involving
activists and others with particular knowledge and experience
to form small committees able to oversee and advise on
particular aspects of the centre's work, as has proved
particularly effective in a number of law centres.

Research and feedback

In pursuing the research and feedback function most centres
use a wide range of channels to communicate their experience,
as well as encouraging community groups to do the same, on
government, local authority and private enterprise investment
policies. These may be through reports, newsletters, the media
or direct contact with councillors or civil servants. A number
of centres have also developed close links with trade unions
and trades councils, and have often carried out research on
particular topics for these bodies on their behalf.

Research in resource centres takes place at a number of

different levels. It may simply involve collating experience
from a number of disparate groups on the effects of particular
policy measures and making this more generally available
through a newsletter or community newspaper. At a more detailed
level, research may be carried out in depth into the activities
of a particular company where redundancies or closure are thought
to be imminent, on housing policies in a particular area or, in
the case of SWAPAC, where a company is proposing to locate a
de-activation plant for chemical waste near a built-up area.

This information is then circulated to community groups and
unions fighting a particular campaign. In some cases, community
groups ask the resource centre to carry out research where it
is known there are experienced members of staff able to do this
kind of work. For example, SWAPAC employs a political economist
who has worked closely with unions and trades councils while
doing research into the organisation and potential of direct
labour organisations and the opportunities these organisations
can provide for training in the building industry. (9) Likewise,
Tyne and Wear has developed strong links with community and
trade union organisations based elsewhere in the Newcastle and
Tyneside area, which are researching and organising in related
fields.

In circumstances where the government is obviously failing to
arrest the decline of particular areas, it is often possible
that a resource centre can stimulate a community response by
providing information or research which can form the basis for
action. In South Tyneside, the resource centre began by
working with two or three active groups but which tended to
operate very much in isolation from each other. With the growth
of NETO groups found they had increasing areas of experience in
common. In 1979 the resource centre with the South Shields
trades council and the services of SCAT set up a research
project to look at housing policy in South Tyneside and the
potential contribution the expansion of the direct labour
organisation could make to employment as well as housing
problems. The report, called 'Demolishing the Myths', was
published early in 1980 and it is hoped that this will form a
useful focus for discussion and action in community and trade
union organisations.

A second example of this community-based research is what
SWAPAC calls the 'Valley City' project. South Wales has for
so long experienced industrial decline - especially the closure
of steel mills and coal mines during periods of recession -
poor housing conditions and welfare services unable to cope,
that this situation is almost accepted as normal. SWAPAC
argued that the valleys really constituted an extended urban
area along the valley floors, which in terms of all the usual
indicators rivalled the traditional 'inner city' areas. It
therefore set out with other community and trade union interests
to marshal all the evidence on the Valley City, on housing
conditions, industrial decline, unemployment and underspending

by local authorities, to emphasise the predicament in south
Wales compared with the more favoured metropolitan areas. The
government's decision in May 1978 to designate only five
districts in the valleys under the Inner Urban Areas Act only
highlighted its failure to make more than a gesture to the
decline of Wales.

Although the Valley City project brought a number of
different groups together and produced some useful publicity
material, the end result did not really justify the amount of
time put into it and most local authorities and government
departments were able effectively to ignore it. The main
problem was that since so many different groups and organisations
were involved and because it involved fairly technical research
work, the whole project got out of hand and top-heavy, so that
many of the smaller groups soon lost interest. From this SWAPAC
realised that much more work was needed in helping groups to
organise at the grass roots before a project on this scale
would be worthwhile.

The way research is carried out and information disseminated
is therefore of vital importance, not only so that time and
resources are not wasted, but so that organisations and
federations around particular issues can grow at their own
pace and are not sidetracked by short-term but fundamentally
empty achievements.

The ideas of research and evaluation can also be applied
to the work of resource centres themselves. Since almost all
of them are developing new methods of operation and techniques,
some based on policy and experience, others pragmatic responses
to new situations, it is essential that developments are
monitored and the direction and strategy of the centre evaluated
at regular intervals. Some centres like the BCC and LVSC have
advisory groups of specialists in the field which can discuss
issues at length, others like MARC, Tyne and Wear and SWAPAC
rely on their management committees, while GARC has set up an
evaluation group made up of both management committee members
and outside academics and practitioners. It is therefore very
much an organisational problem to ensure that the lessons
learnt from previously successful and unsuccessful action and
policy are used to ensure that the centre is more effective and
responsive in future, based on a realistic assessment of what
can be achieved with limited resources.

CONCLUSIONS

It should be clear from these brief examples above that resource
centres, although involved in a wide range of community work
settings, are rarely participating directly with local
authorities or other state agencies. Instead they are pursuing
a much broader objective of working directly with groups which
themselves are seeking a greater degree of participatory

democracy and self-determination in areas where, since the industrial revolution, there has been a history of powerlessness and relative deprivation. The overriding principle is that, wherever possible, decisions which affect a locality should be made at the grass roots level.

The underlying rationale of resource centres is therefore that the articulation of need and participation in the wider society can only take place where those living and working in an area are sufficiently well organised to determine their own needs and make demands which would not otherwise be met. Resource centres are not a replacement for but are complementary to community work at the neighbourhood level and are in business primarily to foster strong and effective groups at all levels. Much of the discussion in the Wolfenden Report and the subsequent response from the VSU has been about the possible functions of local intermediary bodies, many of which are those which resource centres now perform.

Thus from the viewpoint of resource centres, participation is a loaded term implying various degrees of influence, power and control in a society in which these factors are very unevenly distributed. In some areas and by a number of strategies it has been possible for community groups to shift at least temporarily the distribution of power and influence in their favour, but in many others it has been little more than a smoke-screen for local authorities to take unilateral action. The struggle is therefore not only to be consulted and allowed to participate with the state at all levels, in order to make state agencies more sensitive to particular needs, but also to democratise and make accountable those same agencies.

In conclusion, resource centres are applying the principle of participation in its broadest sense not only in their own self-management but also to bring about permanent improvements in living and working conditions, in the following ways:

1 by increasing the total resources available to particular areas by tapping new sources of finance or by setting up new organisations, such as industrial or housing co-operatives, which can draw on investment from new sources;
2 by establishing new mechanisms for decision-making in an area in order to express local views and opinions, act as channels of communication, feedback local experience and needs to policy-makers in central and local government, and disseminate experience and insight to others in the field;
3 by encouraging and supporting those attempting to change the distribution of resources in the public and private spheres in order to benefit the most deprived, or by increasing the total resources available;
4 by enabling and supporting groups and federations which articulate local views about the policies and practices of local authorities and central government, especially

where current practices reinforce systems of deprivation,
whether through ignorance, lack of concern or underspending.

Following from the General Election in May 1979, most of the
four objectives listed above take on increasingly utopian
qualities and the whole field of community action will have to
rethink the relevance of many objectives and strategies in
current circumstances. While urban aid funding has not been
cut by the government, other sources have rapidly disappeared
and the foundations have found themselves swamped with applications. Of the six resource centres under discussion, those
funded by the EEC are hoping to extend their initial period of
funding and thus commit the VSU to paying 50 per cent. Those
most at risk at present are MARC and Tyne and Wear since both
Community Projects Foundations and the VSU are unwilling to
renew the grant; local authorities have so far been unwilling
to fill the gap.

If resource centres are closed in the coming months, not
only will much valuable experience and the achievements over
the last three to five years be lost but working-class
organisations will be unsupported at a time when the recession
and the effects of government policies are beginning to bite
deeply.

NOTES

* This chapter was written with the help and assistance of
   members of resource centres mentioned in the text and as
   a collective contribution by members of the Gulbenkian
   Foundation-sponsored Joint Monitoring Steering Committee.
1 John Lambert, Political Values and Community Work Practice,
   in 'Political Issues in Community Work', Paul Curno (ed.),
   Routledge & Kegan Paul, 1978, p.6.
2 The Group was set up in 1970 and was composed of 55 members
   drawn from a wide range of relevant fields, under the
   Chairmanship of Lord Boyle. The report by the Community
   Work Group is called 'Current Issues in Community Work',
   Routledge/Gulbenkian, 1973.
3 Ibid., p.143.
4 Ibid., p.134.
5 Ibid., p.135.
6 Members of these centres meet regularly to form the
   Gulbenkian-sponsored Joint Monitoring Steering Committee,
   which with funds from the VSU and EEC carries out a mutual
   and co-operative programme of monitoring and evaluation,
   assisted by a research consultant and full-time research
   worker at the School of Social Sciences and Business
   Studies, Polytechnic of Central London.
7 This campaign is reported in 'Community Action', no.37,
   May-June 1978, p.31.
8 In some situations centres have rejected this kind of co-
   ordinating role. MARC has refused to co-ordinate the

voluntary sector in the partnership programme in Manchester, since it might well become a buffer between the local authority and local groups and be forced to make impossible decisions about priorities and funding.

9   In July 1979 SWAPAC and Swansea City Council Joint Trade Union Committee published a report, 'Fighting for Council Services', which drew attention to the achievements of the joint trade union committee of Swansea City Council.

8 The Normanton patch system
Mike Cooper

Individual initiative (in a Democratic Society) that is
leadership, shall be shared by all its members. No formal
devices for government can in themselves provide a people
with a democratic way of life, for the essence of such a
life is the exercise of instructed and effective social
concern. A.N. Whitehead

BACKGROUND

The workers who initiated this development had experienced
community participation in very different ways. Two had
worked with volunteer groups in the Colne Valley. These were
self-run and used the social services department as a resource
and complement to their activities. The aim was to increase
the relevance of statutory social work to the community in
line with the Seebohm emphasis on preventive work. Experience
of volunteer groups had shown the enormous wealth of caring
and expertise, both active and latent, which existed in the
local community. It was apparent that this source of 'caring
energy' often functioned without the knowledge of the statutory
services and where it was known to operate, frequently did so
without aid from these services or even faced hostility from
professionals who saw community self-help and voluntarism as
a dilution of professional expertise. This was particularly
the case at a time when social services were expanding quickly
and there was the general view that given enough professional
staff, buildings and other resources, the statutory services
would be able to cope with the demand.

Direct experience of working with non-professionals indicated
a vast reservoir of ability, good-will and expertise which had
a great deal to offer in partnership with statutory services.
Much of the work bombarding area teams was demands for help
which could as easily be met by lay people as professionally
qualified staff. Moreover, because of the practical nature of
the tasks it can be argued that they should more appropriately

be done by non-professionals. The spin-off for the community
in the form of shared experience and mutual aid is a valuable
addition to community well-being.

The second view developed from direct experience of the
author of the CDP in Batley. The Batley project, like other
CDPs, played out a spectrum of community work activity from a
traditional consensus model through Liberal consensus via
conflict to radical confrontation. (1) Perhaps because none
of these models were ever worked through in a coherent fashion,
or because of incompatibility of goals between individual
workers, the project failed to have any lasting effect on
participative opportunities for the population. This, despite
much rhetoric on the subject. However, useful lessons were
learned about the way different people reacted to different
approaches. Clearly any community workers who expected their
efforts among the grass roots to change the socio-economic
system to favour the underclass were indulging in wishful
thinking. However, the CDP experiment has shown the nature
of the relationship of the political and economic system and
neighbourhood deprivation. An analysis of how the world
works was produced which is relevant to community workers and
social workers alike. What it also showed was that the type
of practiced response available to workers was a matter
almost of individual conscience on the range of options from
full-scale revolutionary activity to helping the worst off
in an unavoidably harsh world. Further, it showed that the
actual practice of even the most radical tended to be in the
helping end of the spectrum rather than the more difficult
social change end. It would seem that a popular revolution
is not on the agenda in the United Kingdom at present. There
were more positive aspects of the Batley CDP, however. Its
support for a local Advice Centre (2) enabled it to purchase
its own premises. This fact alone guaranteed its survival.
It also might have become a viable, locally run alternative
to social services, had it not chosen a more radical path which
put it beyond the pale as far as the local authority was
concerned. Given that it never developed a strongly supportive
local base of any size or influence, its long-term future as
a grass roots organisation was always precarious. It did show,
however, the enormous ability of untrained people to understand
and handle the complex social problems of individuals and
communities and to successfully deal with the bureaucratic
structure of the welfare state. The problem of legitimising
action was seen to be the vital missing ingredient, one which
has also bedevilled many of the community work projects.

We believe a theory of community action which incorporated
these lessons is needed which could encompass the immediate
usefulness of traditional Liberal social work as well as the
analytical basis of radical community work. We wanted to test
whether connections can be made between helping individuals
to cope and creating initiatives for social change. We believe
that participation is a function of politics not administration.

It is about power not organisations and will be achieved when
the power base is strong enough to demand it. To arrive at
such a point requires the support and encouragement of a cross-
section of society. This requires that those who are able to
cope in society become involved with those who cannot.

To involve people for long periods in abstract concepts such
as administration and politics is difficult for all but a few
exceptionally committed people. Our experience was that people
tend to become involved actively in situations when they are
personally touched by them. We suggest that people in general
respond actively to two main stimuli: firstly, to those things
which directly affect themselves and their immediate family,
friends and neighbours; secondly, to things which indirectly
affect the quality of their lives.

An example of the former might be the redundancy of a
breadwinner or the ill health of a spouse or close neighbour.
The latter may be the closure of a school or a housing development scheme. It is obvious to us that the starting point for
social change is the needs of individuals. These can be direct
in the sense of requiring some form of help in their personal
lives or indirect such as wanting opportunities to become
involved in changing the social fabric. The former may well
lead to the latter and may also be caused by it.

The following describes a strategy in which the gradual
drawing together of different interest groups and differently
affected people is being attempted. Working from a local
social services base we began by developing ways of getting
immediate help to individuals and establishing a form of
collective involvement. The next step will be to create
locally a forum or series of forums for debate, and a genuine
spirit of co-operation for action. This is likely to be a
slow process but, hopefully, it will be appropriate to the
needs of individuals. The building of links between people,
ideas and agencies, plus the development of an analysis of
problems in terms of individual's needs is laborious in a
situation where the welfare state is expected to cope alone.

THE FIRST EXPERIMENT - NEIGHBOURHOOD WORK

The first step towards participating with the community was
to make contact. It was necessary to go out to meet people
in villages and housing estates rather than expect them to
make contact with the agency. At the same time for some
workers a form of 'professional distance' from the 'clients'
was seen as a necessary protection and they had to be
persuaded that close contact was desirable and could be
achieved without their being overwhelmed by demands which
they could not meet. It was argued that in any given
population there were a variety of people participating in
caring for others at different levels. Social workers in area

teams have responsibility to understand this reality and to
involve these people in the process of re-defining services to
meet jointly determined needs. To encourage workers to depart
from traditional practice four main hypotheses were presented
which could be accepted as being fair enough and which could
provide acceptable premises for making changes.

The first was to suggest that in order to practise social
work with knowledge of the reality of people's lives, opportunities were needed for people to participate directly in formulating the help they need. To foster this practice it was
decided to place workers in the estates and villages of two
area teams. The prevailing mode of providing services was for
social workers to work with individual cases. We believed in
the value of ordinary people being involved in community care.
The role of neighbourhood worker was therefore given to social
work assistants, and it was deliberate policy for them to make
contact with the public at large, as well as other caring
agents. It meant that people who had not acquired a
'professional mystique' would be at the point of contact. A
corollary of this approach is for problems to be seen primarily
as practical and to be taken at face value. The role of this
worker was to liaise with home helps and wardens, health
workers, postmen, shopkeepers, etc., to 'take the pulse' of a
locality and to be available as the eyes and ears of the
department and as a point of access to departmental services.
Issues which arose were fed back to the area team and
individual problems were either dealt with via the local
network and/or handed on to social workers who would be brought
in to handle delicate or intractable difficulties. In this
way the reality of life in a particular locality was to become
the base-line for evaluating and assessing problems and the
working out of solutions. Participation was expected to
develop in two ways: by the area team workers seeing the need
for a particular form of activity and discussing strategies
with interested local people, or by groups of clients being
encouraged to take forms of action, being helped by members
of the area team as appropriate.

The second hypothesis connects with the first, the logic
being that if the problems of individuals are accepted at face
value and tested directly with the people concerned, then any
person asking for or being referred for help is more likely
to maintain their personal dignity. Bureaucratised and
professionalised authority will, thereby, be forced to justify
those actions which tend to confuse the need for human concern
with administrative or professional necessity.

The third hypothesis was to do with how we thought the role
of the agency should be seen by others, both from inside and
outside. To follow through the notion of the dignity of the
individual the team needed to be accessible and sensitive to
need. It needed to be open so that its processes could be
demystified. Contact with it needed to be easy, pleasant,
useful and equal.

The last hypothesis was perhaps the most difficult to get
across. It is to do with definitions of 'action'. We defined
action in one of two ways. Activity which is about getting
things done according to some external definition of what has
to be done was labelled 'Administrative'. This is concerned
with modes of behaviour, such as following rules already laid
down, either explicitly or implicitly. The second form of
action is about what things should be done, making decisions on
the value of doing a thing or not. This much freer discretionary
area was called 'political' (with a small 'p') and needed to be
the subject of debate and constant revision tested by the
response from the community. Administrative activity, we
postulated, follows from political activity and needs to change
along with it. Political activity is an expression of the
experience of social relationships and can only occur by public
expression and is the only means of articulating reality.
'Private thoughts spoken publicly make them real'. (3) Unless
a problem is articulated it cannot be handled and remains
unrealised. In this context the area team workers as a whole
were thought to have a responsibility to be aware of those
aspects of their work which derived from administrative necessity
and those from an informed appraisal of people's needs. Action
of the 'political' kind was expected to arise when workers
became aware of the inappropriateness of 'administrative'
requirements and when they were able to refer back to their
community the inevitable limitations of the statutory response
for discussion of what to do about it. Herein lay the active
ingredient to participation. Thus participation was seen as
'political' and dynamic rather than as a passive 'administrative'
concept.

Implementation

Armed with these notions of what was a potentially achievable
participative role for the statutory agency new forms of area
organisation were tried in two team areas in 1975. They are
divided into neighbourhoods of about 5,000 population. In each
patch a worker, usually a social work assistant, was assigned
as a neighbourhood worker with the responsibility for making
contact with as many people as possible and to pass on referrals
to the area team to be handled by the domiciliary care organiser
or social workers, etc. A major consideration was to capitalise
on the fact that locally recruited home helps and wardens were
not only Social Service Department personnel, they were often
part of local caring networks. They were thus shown to be a
human bridge across which professional workers could 'mesh
in' with local situations. An unexpected, although predictable,
result of this approach was for home helps in particular to be
seen as capable, caring and intelligent people rather than
skivvies and their perceived status rose enormously. Also the
status of the social work assistant increased as being someone
who could be 'let loose' on the community without specialised
training, and became a valued member both of the team and the
community.

A major disadvantage of separating the functions of
neighbourhood workers, domiciliary care management and casework
was the tendency for these groups to become institutionalised.
Caseworkers were happy to be relieved of a multitude of minor
tasks now performed by neighbourhood workers or domiciliary
workers and tended to become isolated from the activity of the
rest of the team. For some this was considered all to the
good, they were theoretically able to specialise and get on
with 'casework'. In reality, the author believes the general
lack of skill development of social workers left them
professionally marooned, a fact highlighted by the relative
high skill and successful outcomes of many of the tasks
performed by neighbourhood workers. These workers helped with
care for the elderly and handicapped mainly, and worked in well
with health visitors, teachers, education welfare officers,
self-help groups and in general used local helping processes
where possible. Some of the work also involves helping to
create more viable local helping services where none existed.
By using the local knowledge of others and of home helps
in particular a greater understanding and reliance on local
networks was beginning to be achieved. However, bringing
about a closer liaison between the agency and the community
on a participative partnership progress was hampered by the
limited impact that could be made in each area by one worker.
The focus was still largely one of personalised help rather
than participation. While we were happy with an increased
sensitivity to need, this was in the 'administrative' arena
and more thought needed to be put into more dynamic possibilities. Furthermore, in administrative terms the division of
functions into three separate groups of workers served to
reduce the potential impact on the neighbourhoods. In effect
the scheme was 'hoise with its own petard' as neighbourhood
work became a specialism of its own, gradually losing any
potential for involving the agency in combined efforts within
communities. For the agency this might be seen as a perfectly
adequate conclusion were it not for the fact that in practical
terms three or four unqualified social work assistants would
have found it very difficult to survive as brokers for the
community between it, case workers and departmental management
who saw them essentially as helpmeets to case workers.

Given that the fundamental aim was to blur traditional
roles and encourage a collective team 'meshing' with the patch
areas to enhance opportunities for participation, the creation
of new specialisms, however useful, was seen as inhibiting.
A departmental reorganisation in 1976, which meant a move for
the author to lead a different team in Normanton, fortuitously
created an opportunity to reconsider past experience and led
to a change in structuring the neighbourhood idea to include
both ancillaries and qualified workers.

THE SECOND EXPERIMENT - THE NORMANTON PATCH SYSTEM

The town of Normanton

Normanton is a West Yorkshire mining and railway town of 20,000 population. Post war the railways have all but disappeared and the five local pits have closed. The National Coal Board still employs a significant number of the male population but no specific industry is at the heart of the economic base of the town. Some new manufacturing and warehousing has come to a new industrial estate on the heels of the M1 and M62 motorways, which has only had a marginal effect on the economic structure. Workers commute to nearby Castleford and Wakefield and some use the motorways to get to Leeds and other West Yorkshire conurbations. The previous Urban District Council extensively rebuilt the colliery houses and the back-to-backs in three post-war estates and consequently there is no serious housing problem. The population has declined since the war, emigration being by the younger and better-educated for job opportunities and private housing elsewhere, leaving an ageing working-class population. Family networks still exist, particularly among the aged. The older established settlements have not seen rapid changes in population and neighbouring is a normal occurrence. However, the new estates have broken many of the informal networks and in general there is perceptible loosening of informal networks leaving many people bereft of community care.

The area is divided into three patches of 5-6,000 population. Each patch has a team of workers with different skills and abilities. Each patch is led by a patch leader. All roles except (for statutory purposes) that of the patch leader are interchangeable. Home helps and wardens are allocated to patches and clients are assessed for all practical services by the patch workers. The domiciliary care organiser is responsible for the management of the domiciliary services but not for the caring side of the job. The advantages of this structure are various. Opportunities are given for workers of all grades to develop links with people working in the caring field for a defined geographical area on a continuum from informal caring networks, through volunteers and voluntary organisations to other professionals working in the area. It allows for local issues to be illuminated via the problems of individuals. A continuity of awareness of what happens both in the neighbourhood and to individuals over a time span is a main feature which reduces the number of crisis situations which might otherwise culminate in emergencies appearing 'out of the blue'. Thus, problems of individuals can be related to local issues. A better flow of information using the local knowledge of domiciliary workers is achieved. The positive inclusion of these workers in the patch processes cannot be overstated. They act as gatekeepers to the community and also are a source of much voluntary work.

Role of patch leader

The patch leader is a qualified and experienced social worker.
This is possible because Wakefield Social Services Department's
career structure allows all qualified social workers to achieve
the top of the career grade. This is a definite advantage to
the scheme but is not crucial to its effectiveness. It does
mean, however, that the head of the patch team can be expected
to be a well-informed, wide-thinking person able to conceptu-
alise the needs of individuals and see them as part of a
community structure. This role is gradually being evolved
and has several interlinking aspects. The patch leader has
accountability for statutory cases and is the only worker in
the patch with a caseload. However, he or she is not expected
to do direct work with all the cases and is used as a
consultant by both the patch workers and members of the wider
community including other agencies. It is assumed that in the
majority of cases clients' needs have practical elements,
such as housing, income maintenance, child care. Once these
issues are tackled with some degree of success the psychological
effects of 'diswelfare' may well be able to be dealt with by
the client via his own personal networks, personal strength
and the help of professionals and other organisations as
appropriate. In this analysis the patch leader is responsible
for supervising the patch worker's effectiveness in dealing
with practical situations and developing effective liaison
with other agencies as an advocate for clients within the
patch. Thus he or she is a manager and supervisor of staff,
a consultant and an advocate. For those cases where assessment
reveals the need for a more traditional casework relationship
such as in marital problems, the management of delinquency
and mental health work, the patch leader is expected to undertake a casework role using other patch resources as appropriate.
Over and above work with individuals, they are expected to be
aware of community issues and to organise, in conjunction with
the Assistant Community Liaison Officer, Area Officer and
others, ways of handling, explaining and understanding them.
In this respect they act as community workers. Examples of
the community work aspect of the role are the setting up of
a youth club, the formation and support of a volunteers' group
and the exposure of conditions on a gypsy caravan site for
which remedial action is promised.

Role of Community Liaison Officer

The Community Liaison Officer acts on several levels also. He
is a link between the patches, encouraging community development
and highlighting areas of community involvement. He has been
a central point for mediation between the domiciliary care
organiser and patch team members and has helped to create a
high level of patch interrelations over town-wide issues.
He has acted to prevent the parochial and individualised
concerns of patch workers from being blinkered to wider

concerns. He works as a team liaison person with local
organisations, sitting on committees, encouraging new groups
and generally acting as ambassador for the team in the community,
backing up the work of the patch teams.

Patch workers

Four out of the seven in post are loca-ly recruited and policy
has been to seek such recruitment. It is envisaged that
ultimately all patch workers will be local people. These tend
to be women in the age range of twenty-eight to fifty years,
who have had a wide life experience and possess a level of
maturity enabling them to cope with the demands expected of
them. Three of them have been recruited from home helps or
wardens and were doing voluntary work. Their work includes
assessments for practical departmental services, including home
helps and wardens, and much of their time is spent with the
elderly and infirm. They are also involved in practical aid
to defined cases under the guidance of patch leaders. Their
different aptitudes, work preferences and experiences are
used as a basis for allocation of tasks. Opportunities are
available for broadening their experience in such areas as
welfare rights, community liaison, group work. They also work
closely as colleagues with home helps and wardens.

    The best way of describing these workers is to think of
them as 'paid relatives'. They undertake the kind of tasks
most families would expect of a competent close friend or
relative and they have become known as friendly, well-informed
and available people in their patches. An example of this is
evidenced by reference to the coincidence of two workers
having the name of Sylvia. A client when coming to the
department for help said that he wanted a Sylvia to be
allocated to his problem. The first name had become synonymous
with the role. Also they are developing a critique of the
welfare services and act as advocates in the community.
Another example is the way one patch group alongside neighbours
and volunteers helped to organise the move of an established
community from old housing to a new estate.

Volunteers

Each patch team is responsible for identifying and attracting
people who will help. The process is via word of mouth and
street contact. There is no system of accrediting volunteers,
the tasks they perform are considered to be for and on behalf
of the neighbourhood.

    All requests for help, whether received formally or
informally (informal requests are increasingly becoming the
vehicle for requesting help), are passed to the patch teams.
Each patch uses its knowledge of the community to determine

who does the work and the degree of involvement necessary. This
is done at regular patch meetings under the auspices of the patch
leader. Patches call meetings as appropriate to co-ordinate
individual problems or initiatives about community issues.
Issues which concern the whole town or cases requiring new
initiatives or negotiation with other agencies involve the
Area Officer, Assistant Community Liaison Officer and other
workers as appropriate. The whole team meets weekly and the
patch leaders, Assistant Community Liaison Officer, Intermediate
Treatment Officer and Senior Social Worker also meet weekly with
the Area Officer to discuss casework issues and techniques and
co-ordinate and plan future developments. The patch leaders
are individually supervised by the Area Officer and Senior
Social Worker.

Results

By putting the three previously separated functions into each
patch the inter-weaving of roles has been accomplished. Status
problems, however, still persist due to salary differences as
a residue from the traditional job demarcation. The only
reason these differences are not destructive of the team is
because of the enhanced personal status of the workers and
their vastly increased levels of job satisfaction. That this
is exploitative of the unqualified staff is undeniable and it
is hoped that eventually the relevant authorities will recognise
this situation.

    The concept of individual case loads has been significantly
altered. A situation is only thought of as a case for two
reasons: if it has a statutory element or if it needs
intensive work. All other situations concerning individuals
are simply classed as people known to the team and a minimum
of recording is made. Involvement with local networks appears
in most cases quickly to alert the patch team to changes in
people's circumstances and identifies common problems and early
intervention has the effect of taking the pressure out of
crisis. The team caseload has halved in the three years since
the inception of the patch system. In particular, service to
the elderly and handicapped is more immediate and comprehensive
and people are maintained in the community who might otherwise
be in residential care.

THE FUTURE

The team's progress towards active participation is necessarily
slow. Time scales are long; false trails are followed without
immediate tangible results. Change appears to happen mostly at
the margins of issues rather than centrally. In many ways the
'patch' model has been an attempt to orientate a Social Services
Area Team towards seeing the community as the place where it
does its job and to work with citizens, whether clients or not,

in a joint effort to solve problems and create and develop new opportunities in a genuine participative enterprise. The team is now beginning to work in ways which demonstrate the potential for participation and has only recently begun to make concrete some of the theoretical aspects of the philosophy. In any event, the posture of the team has enabled an integration of workers of different descriptions and made them aware of the need and value of participation for themselves and for the community and have begun to uncover some of the pathways towards genuine co-operation. The patch approach has rendered staff 'vulnerable' to ordinary people, it being hard to remain professionally or bureaucratically aloof from people when you rub shoulders with them on a daily basis. Being vulnerable appears to produce more honesty about what cannot be done and has a levelling effect, tending for the workers to de-label stigmatised groups, communities and individuals. It makes patronising responses hard to sustain.

Now the team, as a working unit, has established an ethos which accepts sharing of tasks and contemplation of issues with different lay people in the community; a more practical emphasis is being developed, aimed at achieving an analysis of local needs and in co-operation with local people to find opportunities for planning future activities. Some of this planning will inevitably involve politics and some conflict is likely. We are developing strategies which we expect will have broad-based local support and which will allow us to function with integrity as local government employees and as professionals inside conflict-laden situations, especially in a period of cut-back in resources.

The means to do this effectively is coming from a drawing together of the three levels or strands of the patch team structure. Firstly, those individual cases which are amenable to help by better liaison with other agencies and constructive criticism of our own department are being consciously brought to the notice of the relevant authorities and where results are not evident we are consciously bringing in local people, councillors, doctors, etc., to take up cases with us. Thus by this means we are opening up debates on issues relating to the health service and the education system.

Second, issues within patches are being pursued by the patch teams, local volunteers and local associations of various kinds such as tenants' associations. One such is a link between the tenants on a district heating scheme which is struggling with the Council about high heating charges and also general concern about the poverty of the environment on the estate. Other issues come up via individual cases and are taken up as a matter of principle by a loose association of staff, clients, voluntary workers, councillors and the local press.

Third, town-wide issues are being taken up by more active

voluntary groups. For example, the Old People's Welfare
Committee are encouraged by the team, local councillors,
voluntary workers and the clergy to tackle difficult housing
problems for the elderly. A recently formed development group
has joined the forces of clergy, Age Concern, councillors,
social workers and others to create a day centre for the
elderly and has persuaded the town council to donate a large
sum to enable it to get off the ground. The collection of re-
cyclable waste is beginning to become a town-wide issue and it
is hoped to create a co-operative effort to turn this into a
regular income source for the town as a whole. To bind this
activity into a recognisable whole, so that all the issues,
activity and information can be clear to all who wish to
participate a local forum in which any person or group, lay or
professional, can bring a grievance, suggestions for help, or
information, is being set up. The basic philosophy behind this
body is the notion that everybody in the town is responsible
for being aware of what is happening in the world they locally
inhabit as residents or workers and are jointly responsible for
dealing with what is discovered, however uncomfortable that
may be. This local forum will be known as the Social Care Assembly
for Normanton (SCAN).   Membership will be open to any adult
living or working in the area (there will also be a junior
membership) and delegates from every group and organisation in
the town will be eligible as members. It is hoped to encompass
the political, statutory, religious, mutual aid, voluntary,
recreational, fund-raising, sports, youth, industrial and
commercial enterprises as participants. It will enable people
to attend as employees of statutory organisations or if they
prefer, as private individuals. It is already clear that some
people in official roles would welcome the freedom to participate
not as representatives of their employing body but as private
citizens. This applies equally to elected representatives.
There will be no executive committee, merely a secretariat
and a president who will act as an impartial chairman. No
decisions of the council can be binding on any constituent
member or individual. It is designed to perform as a local
'united nations' and can only work within a consensus based on
factual realities. The council, it is hoped, will take up
local issues and encourage a high degree of problem sharing.

On a less grandiose scale but highly significant for the
patch scheme is the reorganisation of the warden system which
is taking place. It is proposed to place wardens for the
elderly in patches. The significance of this move is to create
eighteen instead of three patches, thus opening up communications
right into the heart of neighbourhoods. Wardens will have as
their main task the care of the elderly. They will also be
encouraged to enlist the aid of the immediate neighbourhood
in the task. At the same time peripheral knowledge of what is
happening to people in the neighbourhoods will be greater,
which will have the effect of clarifying the problems and lead
to greater accuracy of communications about hardship and thereby
make it less easy for the effects of cuts or other policies to

be obscured. This, linked to the wider patch contacts and the
Community Care Council, should go a long way to making tangible
the statement of Hannah Arendt referred to above.

   To conclude, it must be said that the work of an area office
is a team effort. Without the faith, confidence and willingness
of all concerned to take and create opportunities, this initiative
may well have been another interesting idea strangled by the red
tape of bureaucracy and obscured by professional mystique.
Unless more creative possibilities are explored with official
sanction both of these factors in our view threaten to obliterate
the human face of practical social and community work.

NOTES

1   H. Rose and J. Hamner, Community participation and social
    change, 'Community Work Two', London, Routledge & Kegan
    Paul, 1975.
2   M. McGrath, For the People by the People: A Resident Run
    Advice Centre, 'BJSW', vol.5, no.3.
3   Hannah Arendt, 'The Human Condition', University of Chicago
    Press, 1959.

9 Community education in Scotland

Charlie McConnell

PRIMING THE PUMPS

For readers south of the border a few comments concerning recent historical developments are necessary in order to appreciate the important contribution adult education is making towards public participation and community work in Scotland.

1975 saw the publication of the Alexander Report 'Adult Education. The Challenge of Change'. (1) This report is of particular significance for adult educators in Scotland. Three major changes were recommended by Alexander.
1 That adult educators should prioritise their work within areas of multiple deprivation and with disadvantaged groups. This following the recognition that only 4 per cent of the adult population participated in adult education and that this was dominated by middle-class socio-economic groups.
2 That adult educators should positively discriminate towards working-class communities, for example by offering a free adult education service as developed since 1975 in Strathclyde.
3 That adult educators should adopt a community development approach in stimulating demand for and participation in adult education by working-class people. This meant (a) a more flexible approach to learning calling into question traditional didactic approaches and emphasis on classes and class numbers; (b) developing problem-solving education where people's problems were seen as powerful motivating forces for learning and the starting points for educational development; (c) democratising education whereby education becomes a lifelong learning process with potential for facilitating the politically and critically conscious participatory democracy. Utilising here the dialogical and predominantly libertarian methods developed in community work.

Administratively Alexander called for the integration of informal adult education, youth work and community work provision under the new heading of community education, and for employing bodies and training agencies to respond to this

change.   To a large extent in the past five years statutory,
voluntary and training bodies have responded accordingly and the
community development model of work now predominates at the
level of rhetoric at least! (2)

The following case study, the Strone and Maukinhill Informal
Education Project, covers the period 1973-78, during much of
which I was the action/research worker with the project.   This
project has already attracted significant interest in Scotland
and Professor Alexander has himself written of the project:
'I see the project as a small part of a group movement for and
by people who, through lack of an effective power base, were
by-passed and neglected by those operating the machinery of
local and national government.' (3)

The use of social indicators to designate certain 'areas of
need' or more pejoratively 'areas of multiple deprivation' is
standard practice in Strathclyde Region.   One such area is to
be found in the Inverclyde district of Strathclyde.   It was a
'labelled' area many years prior to the introduction of social
indicators.   Known simply as 'The Strone', the area is more
correctly Strone and Maukinhill.

In the field of neighbourhood community work the main inputs
in the area during the time of the case study project came
from the Local Authority Community Development Unit and The
Rowntree Trust.   The Community Education Service was a late
arrival on the scene in Strone and Maukinhill.

The Community Development Unit in Inverclyde is now the
largest in Strathclyde.   Since its inception in 1972 it has
grown to a team of a dozen community workers plus secretarial
staff and a recently developed Fieldwork Teaching Unit with
one full-time Fieldwork Teacher (an ex-CDP worker).   The Unit
is part of the Strathclyde Regional Social Work Department
and is formally accountable through the district management
structure in Inverclyde.   It operates throughout the district
(independent of but in co-operation with area social work
teams on the basis of the principle of positive discrimination).

With the background of this official approach to community
development we should place the other major input, the Rowntree
Trust-financed Strone/Maukinhill Community Action Project
(SAMCAP) out of which developed the Strone and Maukinhill
Informal Education Project (SMIEP).   The Rowntree project was
initially independent of the local authority and thus one
could assume less tied to the corporate planning model adopted
by the Local Authority Community Development Unit.   The
possibility of a more radical model working in the community
alongside the local authority input thus existed.

In much of the community work literature there is reference
to the greater freedom of action for workers not employed by
the bureaucracy they seek to challenge.   This was not really

the case for this project. The origins of the Rowntree input
lie with a local councillor who successfully applied for the
finances. Besides Jo Grimond MP as symbolic but absent
chairman, the councillor, also Convener of Social Work, along
with the Director of Social Work were on the management
committee alongside a priest, a vicar, a doctor, an academic
and two residents. It seems that most of the committee knew
little of community development except for the director and
convener. They thus tended to view the process as one within
the sphere of social work with the additional belief that it
could lead to improved dialogue with and through the local
councillor.

A point of interest here for would-be organisers of management
committees was that the community action project, though tackling
issues of education and later, quite significantly, housing,
never tackled the social work department.

A final point on setting the community development scene in
the area is that the relations between SAMCAP and the Social
Work Department Community Development Unit have never been
particularly good. In recent years the various workers in the
field have rarely worked together, and, in fact, have often
consciously worked against each other. There is certainly
evidence to suggest that community work inputs in the area
have been somewhat divisive, with the Community Development
Unit setting up groups and the Community Action Project Worker
working with others. Although some conflict may be inevitable,
or even desirable, it would seem that for community workers,
whoever their employers may be, some clarity and unity over
the issues and their work with a community is crucial.

ADULT EDUCATION NEEDS LOCATED

If the Local Authority Community Development Unit and SAMCAP
were largely the brainchild of the Labour Convener of Social
Work and the Director of Social Work, the Strone and Maukinhill
community development experiment in adult education, SMIEP,
clearly emerged from the grass roots, developing from the
growth of community groups and being identified as important
by them.

The Strone and Maukinhill Informal Education Project
developed from almost two years of community work inputs in the
area. Of primary importance in this respect was the work of the
SAMCAP community worker. She considered that her task was to
encourage residents to work together for various social and
environmental improvements which were important to them, whilst
at the same time promoting a spirit of optimism in the area.
This was simply translated into making herself available to any
group of residents who wanted to start collective action.

By summer 1973, there was a range of new activities and

associations, attracting residents who had not previously been
involved in the existing tenants' association. 'Not all groups
were successful and relations between groups were not always
harmonious but nevertheless a mood-for-action was developing.
People were becoming involved in the organisation of the
groups - writing letters, planning meetings, reading council
minutes; government reports, legislation.' (4)

It was at this time that an identification of a need for
particular knowledge and skills began to be articulated. It
was thus suggested to participants within these groups, by the
community worker, that they might like to join an English FE
class run by a local further education lecturer in the local
community hall. In other words introducing more structured
learning experiences alongside community action. Several
people joined this group, including a 76-year-old. Of this
the local press wrote 'it enables people in the area to take
up further education in surroundings familiar to them.... In
fact, its aim is to bring education to the people rather than
have the people go to the education centres.' (5)

It was this aspect more than possibly any other that made
SMIEP an extension of the community development process. From
the outset its aims was to de-institutionalise and demystify
education and to elicit demand without pre-empting response.
These points are seen most clearly in the process by which
this almost insignificant English class grew by Autumn 1974
into a unique experiment in community adult education in
Scotland.

In March 1974 a short, open-ended questionnaire was put to
the participants of the class to test opinions as to extending
this experiment. From this questionnaire evidence for a
significant 'demand', initially from local activists, was
located. The SAMCAP community worker, a college lecturer and
a number of her colleagues in the English and General Studies
Department, then approached the college principal to seek
approval for extending the principle of adult education located
in a community. Thus the FE college would be seen as a
teaching resource centre and its lecturers as advisers/community
workers. The support of the college authorities was secured
and the Regional Education Department's support for this scheme
came through in the early summer of 1974.

ASSUMPTIONS CHALLENGED

In a report on the project prepared by the college lecturers
involved, (6) they say that this change in attitude by a
college towards a community was important because it challenged
many assumptions and traditions of the educational establishment
including:
  1 that education must be conducted within an educational
     institute;

2 that education must be controlled by an educational
   institute;
3 that further education establishments are limited to
   certain types of courses;
4 that classes should bear no relation to need.
With these assumptions now challenged the next hurdles were
public participation and resource support.

The debate as to financial support will be dealt with later,
but one area, the 'selling' of the SMIEP idea to the community
highlights the role and style of this community worker.
Initially the community worker had a meeting with the English
lecturer and her colleagues in the English and General Studies
Department to discuss:
1 how best the community might be approached and involved;
2 the structure of any possible community committee;
3 the relationship of the committee to the college and
   the Community Action Project;
4 selling the project to the different community groups
   and organisations within the area, publicising in particular
   the idea of the college coming into the area as a local
   resource.
The college's direct approach to the community was absolutely
crucial, it being felt that the success or failure of the
project depended on the skill and sensitivity with which this
was tackled. To this end the community worker arranged
meetings between representatives of the college and existing
groups in the area, from which emerged a committee.

The majority of the new committee were from the English
class students, with the 76-year-old acting as honorary
chairman. It must be added here that this committee structure
concept was itself debated; the danger of potential cliques
emerging which could be unrepresentative of the community was
acknowledged, and the requirement for a regular turnover of
officers and an annually rotating chair was written into the
constitution.

The committee had three main functions. Firstly, it aimed
to perpetuate the project through obtaining necessary finance,
and satisfying existing demand as well as stimulating further
demand. Secondly, it had to administer its finances to provide
for all classes (accommodation, equipment, texts, materials)
and to liaise with the college administration, through whom
teachers were paid by Renfrewshire Education Department.
Lastly, it had to decide with the advice of the heads of
department and the principal upon the staff to be employed
for each class.

The aims of SMIEP by 1974 were:
To elicit and respond to the needs, individual and collective,
of the community, and to enrich, enlighten, develop and
involve on a practical, political, social, cultural, and
academic basis. The types of education offered aim to appeal

to individual needs and interests, community needs and
interests, practical needs and interests, and to prepare
people for future education/employment. Further, all classes
offered aim to develop their members emotionally and
intellectually through sharing and challenge, and hopefully
to further confidence as well as offer new vision of and
for themselves and their children. This stimulus cannot
help but lead to the action necessary to create a more
inspiring environment. (7)

With an organisational structure, and these aims SMIEP as an
embryonic English class became a potential community development
and adult education medium for Strone and Maukinhill.

The next major step was to get participants and to choose
courses. It was agreed that if it was essential to elicit
demand without pre-empting response then the list would have to
avoid at all costs looking like a set of classes that the
middle classes thought the working classes ought to be interested
in. At best that would be patronising, at worst, disastrous.
Education should be relevant to the needs of the community and
where desired related to social action. It was decided that
three approaches at publicity and demand elicitation could
occur. 'The View', a newly formed community newspaper run by
the SAMCAP, community worker and some of the students of the
English class, would include a tear-off questionnaire section
to try to obtain some idea of what might be wanted. Alongside
this a little brochure was produced by the committee listing
some ideas, telling people of the project and giving the venue
and date of an enrolment night. This brochure was then
distributed by committee to all the houses in the community.
The community newspaper questionnaire and the brochure contained
only two sentences for completion by would-be students.
1   'I wish I could...................'
2   'I wish I knew how to............'

Although the response rate of returned slips was not great,
almost all the responses contained constructive if somewhat
traditional suggestions - typing, car maintenance, English,
home maintenance, dressmaking. The major litmus test was to
be the enrolment night, however. Held in a local hall and in
conjunction with a free film show and tea three hundred adults
and unnumbered children turned up - and in the event 223 adults
enrolled for twelve classes.

It seems that this number exceeded all expectations and
necessitated a search for tutors. Besides the college teachers,
two local residents volunteered as tutors, plus some local
teachers and their wives. As to other resources, typewriters,
etc. were provided by the Education Department, some classrooms
in a local primary school were utilised, and two local halls.
These resources were, however, often inadequate, e.g. at the
primary school desks and chairs were too small for adults;
the project had only one cupboard for storage; the local halls
were at the same time used by numerous youth clubs, luncheon
clubs, social events etc.; and SMIEP had to compete for its

limited use. The janitor for the largest hall was a committee
member which proved crucial.

A question must be answered concerning the relative success
in attracting the community along to that enrolment night. The
considerable publicity has already been discussed. The interest
in the English class was important, as without doubt was the
word of mouth network within the community. The tacit support
of the other community groups brought with them considerable
interest, whilst the location of the project was of major
influence, located as it was within the centre of the community.
But alongside these the question of finances cannot be ignored -
not merely the considerable expense of travel to the FE College
as an alternative, but also and chiefly, a no-fees policy of
SMIEP.

The first English class had always had as a hallmark the
fact that it should be free. The SAMCAP community worker,
college lecturers and primarily those early interested tenants
were fully aware of the constraints inherent in fee-paying
education and its equation with educational opportunities. All
these early participants would term themselves 'socialistic',
although within a broad political spectrum on the left. In
common, however, was a clear commitment that any education
experiment should be free, and any minimum attendance levels
applicable at the college should not apply in areas of need - in
other words a real commitment in positive discrimination. This
belief has remained a central tenet of this project (and as a
precedent has possibly been SMIEP's greatest influence upon the
development of the community education service throughout the
region).

Until 1975 the community worker had secured Rowntree Trust
financial support for the SMIEP venture of £500, but this was
only of a temporary nature and in order for this project to
continue, a project which was by now reaching hundreds of
people, security in terms of finances was necessary. Although
tutors were paid for out of the college and later the 'community
education' budget, non-tutoring costs, e.g. for equipment,
books, hiring of theatre groups and primarily the payment of
rents for the use of community facilities, were not covered.
In all, these accounted for several hundred pounds - nearly
half going on the rent paid for the use of the halls alone.
With the support of their regional councillor (also secretary
of Strathclyde Labour Group and a significant factor in the
project's development) the SMIEP committee approached the newly
formed Strathclyde Regional Education Department in early 1975
for financial assistance.

It has been stated already that the ruling Labour party in
Strathclyde were heavily committed to positive discrimination
and community development and following this meeting with
SMIEP the following clause was passed on 16 April 1975 by the
Regional Further Education sub-committee in relation to areas of
need:

The education service should provide adult courses and
tutor service wherever the need arose be it within or without
education authority premises and that in such cases no fees
be charged, the education service being responsible for
providing a 'tutor service' and paying the tutor's fees. (8)
A few months later an annual grant of £1000 was assured. Although
this precedent set by SMIEP did not cover those non-tutorial
costs mentioned, it was a crucial precedent that in subsequent
years has enabled community education both from the statutory
and non-statutory sector (e.g. Worker's Education Association)
to make inroads in areas of need.

The financial grant given to SMIEP and this commitment to
positive discrimination was only half of the package required
by the project in its approach to the regional authority. The
position of the Rowntree Trust and the College of Further
Education towards SMIEP had led to a situation whereby control
and finance were in the community's hands. This of itself was
a significant innovation, behind which was the belief that,
as the 'SMIEP committee grows in maturity, the college loses
more and more of its monopoly of educational expertise'.

The policy of the Rowntree Trust to SMIEP was that 'The
Trust does not attempt to control operations which it funds
other than having the theoretical right of suspending any
grant made.... We also receive reports on the progress of the
Projects, as they are prepared. But essentially control
remains with the Project Committee.' (9)

And even when the funding body after one year became the
Region these principles were accepted by the Education
Authority with direct funding being made available to the
committee to allow them to continue and develop their programme;
although the local authority have insisted upon regular
auditing, querying the various purchases and vetting the
accounts in considerable detail. One should add that although
this funding was only on an annual basis,considerable time and
energy was taken by the committee in having constantly to
justify themselves during the subsequent years.

EXPERIMENTING

By 1975 SMIEP witnessed a shift towards experimenting with
less traditional media for learning - moving away from what
Alexander had called didactic methods of somewhat formalised
classes towards increased community action, political theatre,
video, etc. This change was the result both of dialogue
between the students, the committee and the community
educationalists and of an increasing influence of experiments
from elsewhere, particularly Ashcroft, Jackson and Lovett in
Liverpool and Freire in Latin America, (10) and recurrent
education theory, especially the analysis of the importance
of 'language' for the educationalist; SMIEP having also begun

to identify that words such as school, course, class and even
teacher seemed to stifle interest.

In her book 'Adults Learning', (11) Jennifer Rogers discusses
what motivates adults to education and suggests several reasons:
1 vocational, 2 self-development, 3 captive wives, 4 social
motives, 5 remedial, 6 the facilities; and one could add a
seventh - social action.

It would seem for SMIEP that the preponderance of traditional
leisure activities, e.g. dressmaking, initially desired by the
participants was of importance to them for many of the first
six, but could these classes be translated into catalysts for
social action?

The committee felt this was possible and desirable. Dressmaking, for example, was also used as an approach to consumer
education, as a way of cutting costs for many participants, and
as a potential forum for women's studies. In terms of a greater
political content both 'Writing for the Press' and a series of
meetings on understanding local government and community
councils were sharing with the participants necessary skills in
producing a local paper or in setting up pressure groups.
Discussion groups, sometimes held in pubs or people's homes,
about industrial democracy or the work of John McLean (a
socialist educator of the early twentieth century), and the
introduction to some groups of 'neighbourhood action packs',
all developed knowledge, confidence, political consciousness
and experience of the participants. And one important area
of experimentation was political theatre put on by the project
and the 7:84 groups which attracted audiences into the hundreds
on several different occasions.

The 7:84 theatre company was set up in Scotland under the
direction of John Magrath in 1973. They were a clearly
socialist political theatre company (7 per cent of the population own 84 per cent of the wealth) who used the theatrical/
music hall genre to politicise their audience. SMIEP, along
with other community groups in Scotland, have utilised this
approach on a number of occasions, covering issues such as
multi-nationals in Scotland and alcoholism. On each occasion
over 200 local folk have turned up. It seems that one element
in the success of this group has been the utilisation of a
language that people understand. Through music and dialogue
placed in a working-class milieu crucial issues, often complex
economic and political issues, are discussed.

On the question of alternative educational media, reference
should be made to the projects' use of audio-visual aids. In
early 1976 an opportunity arose for access to video equipment
from the Scottish Council for Educational Technology at very
little expense. (12)

Because of the ease with which anyone could be taught how to

use it local people in Strone and Maukinhill were able to film
their community as they saw it - producing 'instant television'
of the community by the community, for the community. This
process at the same time helped to demystify film production
and in a very short time one could observe individual confidence
growing amongst the users. On the other hand the very fact of
seeing one's neighbour walking around with a film camera could
produce both interest and entertainment.

One of the films on the question of housing was also
utilised by community workers in the area to present and 'bring
home' important issues to some of the senior officials and
elected members at the council offices. The researcher attended
this meeting and undoubtedly the showing of this film at the
end of a somewhat turgid meeting led to great interest and an
uncomfortable defensiveness on the part of the Director of
Housing.

In the early days of SMIEP a community newspaper, 'The
View', was begun by the SAMCAP community worker. This paper
was utilised in a number of ways by the project:
(a)   to include questionnaires on SMIEP,
(b)   publicity and advertising,
(c)   arranging courses in 'writing for the press' for contributors
      and producers alike,
(d)   as a learning medium itself.
It has been noted elsewhere by Ensor (13) that community
newspapers emerged as a reaction to the complacency of the
provincial press. From the outset the SMIEP committee and the
other community development experiments saw it as a reaction to
blatant political bias in the local press and thus as an
alternative source for information and comment. But also to
counter the constant labelling of this community by the local
press. The reputation of the area, for example, on issues of
vandalism or alcohol problems or 'scroungers' was felt to be
largely the creation of the press. Thus, for SMIEP in particular
the question of 'image projection' was crucial if any changes
in local authority attitudes were to occur.

In addition, through involvement in the community newspaper
and on the 'writing for the press' course several residents
emerged as confident and articulate spokesmen for the area
through the publication of letters in the local press and this
was undoubtedly not a small influence on the interest taken by
the rest of Greenock, and indeed Scotland, in this project.

ACTION RESEARCH

During most of the period covered by this experiment
there was a monitoring input by a research worker. To a large
degree the researcher's own close involvement had an effect
upon this project's development. Indeed this was in part
intentional if the evaluative action research process is

correctly understood. (14)   Some examples highlight this.

In drawing up questionnaires the researcher worked closely
with the committee over design and implementation. The
undertaking of door-to-door surveys and interviews was a communal
process with the researcher sharing his skills with the
committee's intimate knowledge of the people and of the area -
a two-way process. The co-option of the researcher as a non-
voting observer of the committee led to numerous occasions
where opinions of the researcher were sought. This opinion-
seeking was of influence on the question of the relationship
of the project with industry, with the local schools, and over
experimenting with alternative media.

In 1976 the researcher, following interviews with local
trade unionists and members of the Trades Council, made
suggestions to the committee that some educational links between
the community project and the trade unions could occur. An
interesting discussion followed and these ideas were brought
together in a document. A course was then run on the theme of
Industrial Democracy and an open debate in the local community
hall was prepared.

A local environmentalist gave a session of talks and slide
shows on pollution in the area - relating this to immediate
issues like dirty laundry and pollution in the Clyde. And one
result of this was the drawing up of a list of all responsible
authorities, phone numbers and addresses so that the project
might act as a watchdog.   As to numbers coming along, on each
occasion up to twenty adults and children got involved.

On the topic of profits and commerce in general the 7:84
theatre group appeared with their production 'Honour Your
Partners', this play being about the role of multi-nationals
in the Scottish economy, and of particular relevance to this
area in terms of employment.

The concept of 'action research' adopted by the researcher
has become increasingly common as a methodology for community
development. Lambert has written (15) that the criteria for
good research are:
1 'care' in a search of inquiry,
2 'science' guiding the endeavour of discovery,
3 'criticism' informing any investigation.
Yet, as he notes, there is a dilemma here for the researcher
in a community project between the action and the research.
Care and insistence on method means that the researcher cannot
be too hasty, yet the action worker or community group often
needs information urgently. As to the scientific nature of
social inquiry one repeats that communities are not labora-
tories, 'facts' don't necessarily speak for themselves and
the claim that methods can be divorced from values and
ideology (both the researchers and his employing agency), is to
be doubted, whilst critical investigation through elaborating

on the nature of questions and answers can only aid rather than remove difficult decisions about what needs to be done. (16)

Research findings are not neutral since intelligence and understanding are a part of control and power. It was this awareness plus a wish for the research itself to reflect the community development process of encouraging participation and demystifying that 'power centre' that led me to the action research methodology.

A close affinity between the activities of community work practice and social research has already been acknowledged in much of the recent professional literature. Rapoport (17) describes 'action research' as aiming to contribute both to the practical concerns of people in an immediate problematic situation and to the goals of social science by joint collaboration within a mutually acceptable ethical framework. This type of research does not therefore merely provide a purely detached assessment over time of some aspect of performance but rather sets up a dynamic interaction between the researcher and the practitioner as part of the ongoing experimental process.

At its roots this approach also aims to engage practitioners, volunteers, action groups in enquiries about matters that are of interest and importance to them. Thus for example, the use of a questionnaire survey engaged over a dozen local residents in drawing up the questions and processing the questionnaire with the researcher. In this process the participants were encouraged to think and work systematically and with clarity. Research method is as a result demystified and seen to be available to all. Research becomes a form of action that is no longer merely the domain of experts but of the people who themselves must act. In this defining of problems and finding of facts research itself becomes a form of empowerment and action.

For this reason action research has a high potential for becoming political; the simple phrase 'knowledge is power' is crucial. Anyone who has ever watched an unprepared community group without information and facts at their fingertips, confronted by experts from the council, is witness to this. Knowledge is power therefore in the sense that it gives a group real confidence to participate.

There are difficulties for the researcher here, but possibly Rapoport's concept of 'mutually acceptable frameworks' meets these. There is the obvious danger of the researcher having over-biased support for the community he is working with, particularly if he uncovers 'evidence' which it is not 'political' to publish.

Fortunately the goals of this project were ones with which I could work - relatively clear and not, for example, as

ambiguous as those set for CDP. But the techniques of evaluation
are problematic; for example, where one used existing sources of
data great care had to be taken. Frequently data had only been
recorded haphazardly. Often availability of data was the result
of accessible evaluative material done on some poor experience,
whilst good experiences were unrecorded. One should add here
that almost the first input of the researcher here was to
suggest regular, well-kept recording of the project.

EVALUATION

It is necessary now to make some brief comments upon the
effectiveness of such a project. We have noted already some of
the processes involved and the roles and activities of the
various 'professional' workers - for example, the community
worker and the action/research worker - in stimulating and
sustaining participation of various kinds. Does the SMIEP
experiment and others like it have anything to tell us concerning
participatory democracy and political education? I would wish
to argue that community education community development has a
major contribution to make in this respect. Community education
workers, whether termed community workers, adult educationalists
or even action research workers, accomplish change by enabling
the people in a particular community to clarify their own
objectives, improve their own relationships, and overcome for
themselves any obstacles in their way.

   Community educationalists are not leaders inspiring people
with their goals but they can be catalysts helping groups to
diagnose, clarify and implement their own goals. This has
been termed the non-directive approach. Community education
involves, therefore, the sharing of knowledge, skills and
experience in language and form people can relate to. There is
a recognition inherent in community education that to be
committed to participatory democracy the community educator
must not indoctrinate or condition, because to indoctrinate
would involve treating the group as a means and not an end.
For SMIEP the relationship to participants, whether it be the
committee or others involved, was one of dialogue and respect
between equals.

   Hampton, in the journal 'Teaching Politics', (18) remarks
of this process that 'in some cases the adult educator may
attempt to create the community atmosphere which will encourage
political action as a basis for educational activities.' In
all this, says Hampton, the educator must be concerned with
the growth of the learner's self confidence to engage in
social or public activities. In this sense all community
education is political, although not all community education
is about politics. It recognises that politics is life and
that for the community educators, whether working with young
people on an adventure playground, or tenants over the
publication of a community newspaper, education is geared to

social action, to individual and communal creativity and
participation in the decisions which affect everyone's life.
However jargonised, this is clearly an ethos of liberation;
that is to say 'the creation of a social order in which there is
maximum feasible equality of access;   for all human beings to
economic resources, to knowledge and to political power, and the
minimum possible domination exercised by any others. The
striving for such a state of society is not only the concern
of the working class, but of many other groups and organisations
in present-day society',(19) and the development of such groups,
e.g. of students, community educationalists, the women's movement,
community groups and many others in relation to the traditional
labour movement,has the potential for an even more profound
influence upon social change in the 1980s.

NOTES

1   Alexander Report, 'The Challenge of Change', London, HMSO,
    1975.
2   See especially 'Discussion Paper No.1', Scottish Community
    Education Council, 1979, and the Worthington Report on
    Community Development Services in Strathclyde, Strathclyde
    Regional Council, 1978.
3   K. Alexander, Foreword to C. McConnell (ed.), 'The People's
    Classroom', Dundee College Publication, 1979.
4   B. Darcy, 'The Relationship of S.M.I.E.P. to Community
    Development', 1973-74, S.M.I.E.P., 1977, page 2.
5   Greenock 'Telegraph', 24.8.74.
6   M. Kay and J. Jackson, 'A Greenock Experience', September,
    1975.
7   Ibid.
8   Strathclyde Regional Council, Education Minutes, Clause 5,
    April 1975.
9   The Joseph Rowntree Social Trust Ltd, letter to Researcher
    7.3.77.
10 B. Ashcroft and K. Jackson, Adult Education and Social
    Action, in D. Jones and M. Mayo (eds), 'Community Work
    One', London, Routledge & Kegan Paul, 1974; T. Lovett,
    'Adult Education, Community Development and the Working
    Class', London, Ward Lock Educational, 1975; P. Freire,
    'Pedagogy of the Oppressed', Harmondsworth, Penguin, 1973;
    V. Houghton and K. Richardson, 'Recurrent Education',
    London, Ward Lock Educational, 1974.
11 J. Rogers, 'Adults Learning', Harmondsworth, Penguin,
    1971, chapter 1.
12 This type of equipment is now much more readily available
    in Scotland - see 'Video in Scotland', Scottish Film
    Council, 1976.
13 Ensor, 'Community Newspaper Kit', Community Service
    Volunteers, 1976.
14 R. Lees, 'Research Strategies for Social Welfare', London,
    Routledge & Kegan Paul, 1975.

15 J. Lambert in C. Briscoe and D. Thomas (eds), 'Community
    Work: Learning and Supervision', London, National Institute
    and George Allen & Unwin, 1977.
16 Ibid, p.114.
17 R. Rapoport, The Dilemmas in Action Research, 'Human
    Relations', vol.23, no.6, pp.499-513.
18 Hampton, Adult Education and the Teaching of Politics, in
    'Teaching Politics', no.6, 1977, p.139.
19 T. Bottomore, Socialism and the Working Class, in
    L. Kolakowski and S. Hampshire (eds) 'The Socialist Idea:
    A Reappraisal', London, Quartet, 1977, pp.132-3.

10 Negotiating a new tenancy agreement

Dudley Savill

> We shall enhance the rights and status of public sector
> tenants, to whom we offer for the first time, a tenants
> charter. The charter gives a comprehensive framework of
> statutory rights. It will make a profound difference to
> public sector housing in this country first and foremost
> to the tenant and his family.

This grandiose claim was made by Michael Heseltine during his
speech introducing the second reading of the Conservative
government's Housing Bill. He had filched the previous Labour
administration's 'tenants' charter' proposals and dressed them
up with the 'right to buy' in his attempt to dispose of vital
public assets. The provisions he was offering to tenants
were but a pale shadow to those in the 'charter', conceived
with so much 'sweat and tears' by the National Tenants'
Organisation. However, the Bill contained two ambiguously
worded clauses providing tenants with a written tenancy
agreement and the right to be consulted on specific housing
management matters. This can be seen as a tentative advance
for the status of tenants or a poor trade-off for spiralling
rent increases and greatly reduced services. A lot may depend
on how the 'consultation arrangements' are put into effect.
Therefore, management faces an enormous task of producing a
framework for effective 'participation' in decision-making
with their six million council tenants in Great Britain. This
case study analyses a specific system of 'participation'
through which a tenant federation negotiated a new tenancy
agreement with its landlord - the Greater London Council.

THE AGENCY

The Greater London Council Group is a federation of tenants
affiliated to the London Tenants' Organisation (previously
known as the Association of London Housing Estates). (1)
This is a confederation of tenants' associations which is now
the London Region of the National Tenants' Organisation. It

196

has twenty-two years of campaigning and servicing the interests
of tenants behind it. A measure of its success is that in
1978/9 the organisation had some fifteen federations affiliated
to it, a budget of £170,000 and a staff of twenty-three. It is
an important model for providing council tenants with a forum
for participation as well as being one of the few community
work agencies controlled by member groups.

THE OBJECTS OF THE EXERCISE

    The conditions governing the tenancy of the dwelling are
    fundamental to the establishment of a satisfactory landlord/
    tenant relationship.

Because of the continuous housing shortage, would-be tenants
are prepared to put up with almost any conditions to obtain a
council tenancy. They do not examine very closely the terms
of any contract they are party to. Understandably, they are
only too pleased to sign a tenancy agreement and get the keys
to their dwelling. Tenancy agreements add to the legal power
local authorities have over their tenants. The importance of
the agreement is that it sets down what behaviour the council
expects of its tenants, with the implication that if the canons
are not adhered to there are sanctions to bring offending
tenants into line. The National Consumer Council report on
'tenancy agreements' 1976 pinpointed most agreements as being
so one-sided that there was only one party to them. What is
more, the mood of them is so paternalistic that the agreements
were more suited to the last century than to this. This was
especially the case with the Greater London Council 'Conditions
of Tenancy' in 1973. This document laid down a whole series
of terms under a number of headings 'The Tenant shall do this
or that, the Tenant shall not without written permission...'.
Nowhere did it spell out management's obligations. The final
sentence of the agreement warned tenants that 'any infringement
of the Regulations would lead to a termination of the tenancy'.
During the period of 1975/6 the Greater London Council issued
150,000 'notices to quit' a year and evicted 517 tenants mainly
for rent arrears.

STRUCTURES OF PARTICIPATION

The Council has 532 estates, half of which are known to have
organised tenants' associations. When the tenancy negotiations
started in 1973 there were some 70 associations affiliated to
the ALHE; by the time they were completed in 1977 there were
more than 100.

ALHE/GLC Sub-Committee

In 1973 the scope for member GLC estates in ALHE's activities

was limited to a sub-committee structure of the organisation.
Membership of the sub-committee was restricted to elected
representatives of the ALHE executive committee and up to
fifteen co-opted members from the estates. It was a very
haphazard affair, with attendance at committee meetings being
rather intermittent. The life span of the sub-committee was one
year and it reformed annually following the first meeting of
the organisation's newly appointed executive committee. Usually
three or four members from affiliated GLC estates were elected
to the ALHE executive committee and they were the core of the
sub-committee structure. These four members would elect their
own officers and decide who they wanted to join them as co-opted
representatives from the estates. Following the election of a
Labour administration to County Hall in 1973 the ALHE were
invited to appoint two tenant representatives to sit on the
Council's Housing Management Committee with full voting rights.
These two delegates were elected by the sub-committee.

ALHE Group or Federation of GLC Estates

The limited sub-committee structure within ALHE proved
ineffective in meeting the aspirations and expectations of
member estates. There was a growing demand from affiliated
associations to be involved in shaping the organisations's
objectives in its relationship with the GLC. Following mounting
pressure from the estates, it was decided by ALHE to form a
group. This group would act as a federation harnessing all
member estates. The group was inaugurated in June 1976 with
thirty representatives from twenty-four estates present.
Members decided on a forum of participation with affiliated
estates represented by one delegate at the bi-monthly general
meetings. This structure evolved into a policy-making body
of the organisation with a small executive committee appointed
to act on decisions between meetings. The executive committee
consisted of eight members selected on a geographical basis,
with London being broken down into four regional areas.
Furthermore, two of these members were the elected delegates
to the GLC housing management committee. Finally, the executive
committee was responsible for briefing the two delegates prior
to the Council's housing management committee meetings.

Consultation machinery with GLC housing management committee

The Council consulted tenants' associations through machinery
set up with the ALHE group of member estates. It was represented
by the chairman, vice-chairman and opposition leader of the
housing management committee and serviced by chief officers
from the management and maintenance departments. The tenants'
delegates were the executive committee of the federal
organisation. The tenants selected the agenda, submitting
items in advance of the meeting, so that the Council officers
could present reports, and brief the chairman. Occasionally,

following the chairman's instructions, the Council would provide
papers dealing with specific aspects of policy and tenants'
views would be sought before the housing management committee
discussed it. This could range over such areas as estate
amenities, transfer and allocation systems, repair costs and
rents. However, although tenants' views were taken into account,
very few changes in policy decisions are made.

ROLE AND PRACTICE OF COMMUNITY WORKER

Background

The process of negotiating a new tenancy agreement covered a
period of four years. The role and practice of the community
worker changed considerably as the different stages of participation evolved. The first stage was working with the GLC sub-
committee as its secretary. At that time there was a tradition
in the ALHE of paid staff members servicing the organisation's
various sub-committees. The community worker would be
allocated a sub-committee and act as its secretary. This role
limited the worker's influence, as he was perceived as being
the committee's servant rather than its adviser. At times
this could produce a rather confusing situation. For example,
if the worker in his advisory capacity was trying to widen the
debate on a resolution and this upset some members, they
might claim that it wasn't his business, as he was employed to
carry out instructions. However, the worker did possess
influence by the act of producing the working papers for the
meetings. This set the boundaries for the discussion on which
policy recommendations were eventually made. The drafting of
papers could result in a number of arguments going unchallenged,
as the tenants didn't grasp the points being made or lacked the
confidence to question the worker. Through his knowledge and
access to information the worker was in a good position to
direct the work of the committee. The mechanism of making him
secretary to the committee was one way of checking and
restricting the community worker's influence.

Stage 1

The ALHE approached the Conservative party chairman of the GLC
housing management committee asking for the tenancy conditions
to be revised. He responded immediately by inviting the
association to submit its proposals. This way of proceeding
gave the tenants a valuable advantage, as they had the
initiative for establishing the terms of subsequent discussions.
Furthermore, the officers were placed on the defensive, as they
were expected to react to papers rather than prepare them. The
sub-committee instructed me to draw up documentation outlining
proposals for a new tenancy agreement.

   The existing agreement contained twelve lengthy clauses

spelling out in detail the obligations of tenants but saying
nothing about management responsibilities. Alas, there was no
comprehensive report in existence providing information about
the various forms of agreements being used by housing authorities
so I had to start from scratch researching relevant legislation
of housing and public health acts. I needed to be better
informed and, having briefed myself on section 32 of the 1961
Housing Act which refers to local authorities' statutory
responsibilities for repairs, I drafted proposals for a new
agreement. I attempted to provide a balanced document taking
account of views from those who wanted clauses strengthening
sanctions against 'erring' tenants, to those who wanted fewer
restrictions. It was not an easy matter to reach a consensus,
particularly when touching on such a divisive issue as the
right of tenants to keep dogs. This item in itself can tear
an association apart. My draft was vigorously debated by the
sub-committee and after making a number of amendments it was
sent to all affiliated estates for comment. Associations were
given plenty of back-up material and were asked to respond
within a period of six weeks. However, this was insufficient
time for the estates to recognise the importance of the
exercise and to grasp the implications of a complex issue.
Therefore it was no surprise that only five estates submitted
views and amendments. These were considered by the sub-
committee and those which were accepted included in the
proposed new agreement. The result of this activity was to
produce a document which added seven clauses to the Council's
existing agreement but deleted the all-important sentence
'termination of tenancy'. The new clauses outlined details of
the Council's obligations and the range of services it supplied.
This exercise had taken place over a period of four months.

Stage 2 Council working party

The tenants' document was referred to a working party of senior
officers. They invited the ALHE sub-committee to appoint a
number of tenants' delegates to be involved in the working-
party discussions. The objective of the meetings was, in the
words of a council employee, 'to establish common ground with
the Association'. The tenants selected three of their members
and a community worker as an adviser to sit on the working
party. However, this mechanism was nothing more than a mask
for an astute piece of obstruction by the officers. They
employed all their experience to spin a web of ever-decreasing
circles. Their tactical strategy was masterly - delay at all
cost. Under the pretext of legal complications, they spread
the meetings out to only two in the course of a year. When
that produced little response, the tenants had to apply
considerable pressure to get the working party to commit its
findings in writing. The officers, who were clearly on the
defensive, at last provided a document deleting most of the
tenants' proposals. However, they agreed in principle to add
a section headed' statement of intent'. This would indicate

a moral responsibility of the Council towards its tenants but one which had no legal liabilities.

A further three meetings were then arranged over a span of three months. The officers' team was now led by the assistant director of estate management, a man of forty years' experience in local authority housing. The meetings were held in his office with a number of other officers present. The tenants had strengthened their team with the inclusion of a lawyer well versed in landlord/tenant matters. This had been done to counteract the variety of obstacles which the officers were expertly raising in the discussion. There was a noticeable change in the officers' attitudes, one of deferring to an equal. They were back on the defensive, having to spell out their reasons for why this or that wasn't possible. No longer could they use their knowhow to blind the tenants. Furthermore, the tenants' confidence increased, and they were contributing fully to the debates and using their wealth of experience to indict the council's failings on service standards. At the end of the third session, the tenants felt that they had countered the officers' objections, and their case for a revision of the agreement was proven. But within a fortnight a letter was received by the sub-committee stating that the director of housing could not recommend acceptance of the tenants' proposals to the housing management committee. It set out in considerable detail the grounds for his refusal. His prime objection, which pinpointed the real fears of his officers, was that 'to convert Council's responsibilities based on procedures and practices into a contractual agreement could lead to serious difficulties with tenants, including litigation in the courts'.

The sub-committee set about lobbying all the councillors on the housing management committee. They sent letters, copies of their proposals and the detailed reply drawn up by the lawyer answering the officers' objections to the revised agreement. The reply dealt with the 'use' of litigation argument pointing out this would be overcome if they agreed to the setting up of 'arbitration machinery' to act as a clearing house before either party could resort to legal action. However, this strategy did not achieve the required response as the councillors neither grasped the relevance of the issue nor considered it much of a priority. In fairness to them, they were very occupied with other matters, and changing a piece of paper was not an important item on their agenda. Nevertheless there was something of a breakthrough when the vice-chairman of the housing committee, buttonholed at a meeting by tenants, agreed to arrange a time to discuss the ALHE proposals. However, a succession of events, not least impending rent increases and cuts in housing services, prevented this from taking place. These became immediate issues deflecting tenants from any real follow-up. Eventually the tenants bombarded the chairman of the housing management committee with a series of acrimonious letters. He continued to play safe and delegated

the assistant director of housing management to answer on his
behalf. This he did in masterly fashion, devising a skilful
letter full of apologies for the delays.

Stage 3

The protracted discussions had been going on for two-and-a-half
years. At last the tenants' persistence paid off when the
chairman, exasperated at the constant delays and criticism, took
the matter into his own hands. He set up a sub-committee of
the housing management committee consisting of his vice-chairman,
one other majority party member and the shadow chairman of the
minority party. It was given full delegated powers to negotiate
a new agreement with the tenants.

   However, the sub-committee also took its time to gather up
information and complete the consultation process with the
district committee chairmen. The federation's executive
committee embarked on a campaign of harrying the housing
committee chairman, determined to pin him down. At last, after
eight months' work, the sub-committee produced its own report
which the chairman seized upon and promoted during a radio
interview as a new deal for 'London's tenants'. This was a
so-called tenants' charter, granting a number of important
rights, including some form of 'security of tenure'. This was
a considerable advance on the tenants' proposals submitted
three years previously. The housing committee endorsed the
document drawn up by its sub-committee as a basis for negotiation with the tenants' federation. All Greater London Council
tenants' associations were sent a copy of the document and
asked to return their comments within a month. The ALHE
Federation was invited to submit its own 'collective views'
and discuss them at a meeting with the Council's sub-committee
in early December.

   The Council, through producing its own proposals for a new
agreement, was for the first time on the offensive. The onus
was now on the tenants to respond and they were being asked to
react within a very short time period. The federation called
a series of meetings of all members to discuss the document
and to plan a campaign strategy. These meetings were comparatively well attended by some twenty estate representatives
and produced a very high level of debate. There was a much
greater understanding of the issues involved, people were more
informed about legal implications and there was a growing
consciousness of the need for a statement of tenants' rights.
My role was by now a very peripheral one. I was only expected
to intervene in discussions when my advice was specifically
requested. The federation executive committee was delegated
to negotiate new conditions of tenancy with the Council's
sub-committee. Its members were well briefed and highly
informed and in full agreement on the tactics to be employed
in the discussions with the Council.

When the Council's sub-committee representatives met the
tenants' delegates for the two lengthy sessions of negotiations
in December and January, it found itself facing a well-disciplined,
experienced and highly articulate group of people. The Council's
representatives were accompanied by solicitors, clerks and the
assistant director of estate management. I was present not so
much as an adviser but as a notetaker for the tenants. The
following incident reflects this situation rather well. The
chairman of the Council's sub-committee following the practice
employed by the chairman of the housing management committee at
the quarterly consultative meetings opened the discussions by
addressing his remarks to me. He asked me by name to put the
tenants' case. The leader of the tenants' delegation intervened
to point out that I was not a spokesman but was there as an
official of the group. He then got me to hand out to the
councillors and their officials the federation's documents
outlining his members' response to the council's proposals.
He then spoke to the document, thus focusing the sub-committee's
attention to the arguments contained within it. This was a
psychological ploy throwing the councillors and officers off-
balance and putting them on the defensive. The chairman over-
ruled his officers' objections and accepted the documentation
as the framework for the ensuing dialogue.

The tenants' delegates argued their case well, they were
accommodating and conciliatory to some of the objections to
their main proposals. They were very much aware that within a
few months new elections to the Greater London Council would
be held. They knew this could result in a change of party
controlling County Hall, one that would be much less sympathetic
to their interests. Since the minority party was giving its
blessing to the 'new agreement' which had been the subject of
the sub-committee's report to the Council's housing management
committee the tenants realised they must give no excuses for
obstruction. There were a number of principles that had to be
fought for, but many of their reservations were on minor
matters. They were ready to be flexible if it was clear that
the council would resist certain changes. The real struggle
concentrated on clauses dealing with security of tenure,
repairs and the attempt to build in arbitration machinery.
Throughout, the assistant director of estate management used
his experience and reputation to undermine the tenants'
proposals. He pointed out that, by trying to strengthen certain
clauses, the tenants were expressing a lack of confidence in
the work of the officers. He claimed this was an unjustified
attack on their record of service. Shrewdly he put the chairman
on the spot by trying to get him to declare himself in the
defence of the officers. However, the chairman remained
impartial and made no statement on the matter. At the end he
summed up by saying 'there had been strong and tough negotiations which were the very stuff of democracy'. He would do
his best to make provision for the differing views expressed
by both the officers and tenants' delegates.

The Council's sub-committee presented its findings to the
housing committee at its final session in March. These proposed
a number of changes to the agreement, reflecting some of the
views put forward by the tenants during the negotiations. The
two tenant delegates on the committee managed to obtain a major
amendment to the document at the meeting before seconding the
proposal for its acceptance by the Council. There is no doubt
that the tenants influenced the substance of the agreement
which emerged from the March 1977 meeting. The sub-committee's
report included twenty-eight amendments and additions to the
clauses of the agreement which had been recommended as a basis
for discussion to the housing committee in October 1976. From
these no less than sixteen were due to the proposals and
modifications submitted by the tenants during the conferring
period.

CONCLUSION

There are a number of lessons to be drawn from this case study.
One of the most important is the need for 'working-class' groups
such as tenants' associations to gain control of resources
necessary to support their participation. This means in
particular full-time staff. Tenants have so many demands on
their voluntary contribution to community life that to sustain
numerous campaigns is very difficult. Furthermore, there are
so many immediate issues to divert tenants' attention that a
lengthy project can soon drain limited time. When becoming
involved in sophisticated structures of consultation with
trained officers and elected representatives, tenants'
organisations must have back-up assistance. This would be in
the form of supplying information, dealing with paper work,
helping to clarify issues and the preparation of strategies.
Therefore, staff directly employed by the tenants from grants
or subvention from rents are an essential resource. The case
study illustrates some of the benefits gained by the tenants'
group from having their own staff worker servicing it from the
outset of the project. Clearly, as the negotiations proceeded
the tenants' delegates moulded themselves into an effective
team. They found their confidence, mastered the subject
matter and by sheer persistence matched the manoeuvrings of a
highly trained group of officers.

An issue which arises out of the employment of staff by
tenants' organisations is worker accountability. How do people
from a different cultural background effectively control the
service they are paying for? There is no doubt that trained
and articulate community workers can manipulate and direct
groups. They may do so for a variety of different reasons
such as their personal motivation, ideology, shortage of time
available or as a strategy for achieving objectives. Furthermore, they may feel that to direct the group is the best
service they can give in the circumstances. Therefore, some
community workers exploit their knowledge, experience and time

to assume a leadership role at the expense of being catalysts.
Unfortunately, there are numerous examples of community workers
being unwilling to relinquish roles usually associated with
initiating a project and this has damaged the development of
the group rather than enhanced it. I am not suggesting that
all community workers operate in this way, but this is a
problem that one should be aware of. I have made a point in
the case study of assessing my role as worker with the group.
At the beginning the tenants were reliant on my expertise and
access to information to draw up the documentation. They
regarded me as a specialist and expected me to act as a spokesman. This somewhat reinforced my leadership role within the
group and in the early meetings with the Council I was in the
forefront of the discussions. However, as the group became
more cohesive and experienced under a change of chairman my
role was diminished. I was required to carry out instructions
instead of initiating activities. In the closing stages of the
meetings with the Council sub-committee my contribution was
limited to making comments when prompted. This happened on
four occasions over a period of seven hours' debate. This
shows the importance of the community worker being able to
adapt to the changing needs of the group even to the extent
of accepting a relatively insignificant role towards the end
of a project. Indeed this could be a measure of his achievement.

The final lesson to be learnt from the study concerns the
relative power bases of people in the local authority decision-
making framework. Who is in control and who ultimately determines
the Council's policy? Our experience clearly shows the enormous
influence wielded by the officers in 'participation exercises'.
Although we were dealing with a number of skilled, shrewd and
highly ambitious politicians the officers always controlled
events. They succeeded in prolonging the debate for years
when it could have been sewn up in months. They blocked
progressive provisions in the agreement contrary to the wishes
of the councillors and ourselves. They somewhat watered down
the final version of the agreement from the radical document
that at one stage looked likely to emerge. However, in the
end the tenancy agreement did contain a number of major
innovations and was an important step forward for tenants.
It was the product of a compromise of views between elected
representatives and tenants' delegates. Although the officers
had to give ground under political pressure, they never weakened
their overall stance that a little change may be all right but
too much change is dangerous!

Another salutory lesson for tenants is never get involved
in Council working parties without the inclusion of elected
members. Officers are particularly adept at deferring issues
in the absence of councillors when the pressure is off them,
and there is no one in authority present to override their
objections. I will close the case study quoting the words of
the chief officer involved in the project when he paid a
tribute to the tenants' contribution: 'The tenants have

obtained more than I expected, more than I advised and as much
as an institution as powerful as the Greater London Council can
give in the circumstances.'

Surely, this is what participation should be about!

NOTES

1   'An introduction to the Association of London Housing Estates',
    a booklet on the organisation, obtainable from London Tenants
    Organisation, 17 Victoria Park Square, Bethnal Green, London
    E2 9PE.

11 Promoting participation through community work

Bryan Symons

Earlier articles in this book have discussed how community work
can help promote participation. The case studies have looked
at what has actually happened in various areas, and though they
reveal some successes, they have been limited; in most places
achievements are even less. The reasons for this are many.
The achievement of real participation requires basic structural
changes in our institutions, and even its limited development
tends to be resisted by many politicians and civil servants
unwilling to see a diminution of their power. However, some
of the failure can be blamed on community work itself. Workers
have frequently lacked the necessary skills and knowledge to
make use of the opportunities that are available.

To help groups influence decision-making is an extremely
difficult task. Most decisions are not made at the neighbourhood level but in the town hall, in parliament, in the civil
service and often in the offices of multi-national organisations.

The achievement of effective participation by local groups
requires a leadership capable of running an often quite complex
organisation, of negotiating with, and possibly opposing, the
institutions of the state and of realistically appraising what
are the options available and how much can be achieved in a
particular situation. The group needs a structure which can
democratically respond to the needs of the community it
represents, control its leadership and prevent the co-option
of those dealing with the authorities.

To help a group develop to this stage, community workers
need to have the practical skills required for running a
community group, to know how decision-making groups work, and
to be capable of intervening in them in such a way as to help
their development. They need a good grasp of how local and
central government operates in practice, the nature of
bureaucratic institutions, and a wide range of social legislation. Most of all, they need to have the ability to pass all
this knowledge and experience on so that the groups they help

207

can operate as effectively as possible without outside direction.
This article will examine in detail what knowledge is needed,
how it can be learnt and the operational structures necessary
for supporting the worker.

The term 'community worker' is used to mean someone who is
employed to assist community groups or voluntary organisations
to operate more effectively. The worker's role is to stimulate
action and participation by groups of which they are not
themselves members. They are not politicians or themselves
community leaders or activists.

DEVELOPMENT OF COMMUNITY GROUPS

Workers assist organisations of all kinds, from small informal
groups mounting opposition to a road scheme to large voluntary
organisations employing a number of workers. But all groups
need to develop through certain stages and to learn certain
tasks, and those groups who are attempting to participate in
the decision-making process of the state need to work out the
best method in their own situation. The skills can be
illustrated by outlining the stages a group must go through to
become an effective representative body, to make tactical
choices when relating to the authorities and to be able
constantly to reassess its objectives and policies. These
stages do, of course, overlap and the 'tasks' achieved in them
must continue to be carried out in an effectively functioning
group:

1 People coming together need to identify the prime objects
   that the group will pursue.
2 They need to actually form a group and develop some form of
   group identity and cohesion.
3 They need to work out a structure suitable for the nature
   and activity of the group.
4 Members of the group need to develop differentiated roles
   to pursue their objectives effectively.
5 The group needs to develop a relationship with the community
   from which its members come. If it is a representative body
   like a tenants association it should develop a democratic
   and representative structure and organisation, not only
   formally through annual elections but by having a membership
   that is actually involved.
6 Following from this, the group requires effective leadership
   which ensures that it does not become dominated by a clique
   or individual and so closed to influence by its membership.
7 At times a group will benefit by using outside expertise,
   but it needs to develop the confidence to use that expertise
   intelligently and critically. It should neither reject
   opinions that do not suit its own prejudices nor simply
   follow the advice of some 'expert'.

If a group wishes to participate it has to develop the most

effective relationship with the authorities to ensure its
objectives. The example of the range of possibilities open to
a tenants' association dealing with a local council over the
housing conditions on an estate provides a good example of the
options open. The level of least involvement is for the
association occasionally to meet officers or councillors to
discuss specific grievances. This does not tie the association
and does not build up the personal relationships between the
individuals in the association and in the council, which can
make conflict more difficult. However, an association operating
like this always has to respond to problems and can never be
actually involved in making policies. Fixed regular meetings
concerning the estate can allow the examination of wider issues,
but as many decisions are made at higher levels than that of
the estate this still does not allow much influence on policy
formulation. Borough or even city-wide consultative meetings
between councillors, officers and a number of associations are
frequently arranged and can be extremely influential, as an
intelligent council is not going to ignore the advice of its
consumers, but such meetings do not actually give groups a
formal say in decisions. Some tenants' associations and
federations have therefore got their representative on to the
council's housing committee or they participate in a formal
sub-committee. On these committees they have a vote and
receive all the information that officers give to councillors.
This does mean decisions can be influenced at an early stage
and information can be got out to associations. The representatives may, however, come to accept council thinking, and can
become divorced from the groups they supposedly represent.
Moreover, the right of representatives can be used by a council
to say that it has carried out consultation.

The difficulty with all participation within the council
structure is that few people are involved and they are easily
absorbed. Such participation also moves away from what local
people know and understand. Real involvement at a local level
in decisions eventually enables more effective participation
centrally, as more people gradually come to understand the
issues. Perhaps the fullest form of participation is control
of estates through a tenants' management arrangement or a
co-op. This is still fraught with difficulties, however. Many
estates are in too bad condition to be taken over, while on
better estates the leadership can become enmeshed in management
and can be blamed by other tenants for problems, when in
practice such problems cannot be tackled locally, and may be
caused by a basic lack of resources. None of these alternatives
preclude groups campaigning against the council, though the
more they are involved in council structures, the more difficult
this can become. The options then are complex, and none are
ideal. The case studies have shown some of the problems that
arise. A group must be able to assess the situation, respond
to changes and bargain hard and effectively, knowing when to
compromise.

The worker must enable the groups to work through the stages and assess the options. He or she must also be able to supply information and guidance on actual subjects under negotiation.

SKILLS AND KNOWLEDGE NECESSARY

An effective underpinning of the work requires a good under-standing of the social and political framework, and the practical possibilities and potential achievements of community work. This means not only a general political awareness but ideally specific knowledge of sociology - an understanding of the nature of class and community, of deviancy theory and the ways that sections of the community are stigmatised, and of ethnic and women's studies, for example. To influence the local institutions of the state, knowledge of organisation theories and the nature of bureaucracy is essential. Increasingly, too, as community work concerns itself with economic issues, workers need to be able to advise on their implications, or at least know where such advice can be found. They therefore require some understanding of these issues in general, and of inner city and other deprived areas in particular.

This more theoretical knowledge base provides an essential background for a worker, but the most important skill is to be able to help the growth and development of the group. Sometimes help is required in very basic areas. The worker needs to explain how committees work, and to help people to share responsibilities, to carry out specific committee roles and to develop a mechanism for ensuring that decisions are implemented.

Workers also need to be able to help the committee relate to, and involve, the rest of the membership. This can be achieved partly by helping to ensure a clear constitution and election procedures, but also by helping the group to draft newsletters and leaflets in such a way as to be read easily and understood. It may be useful to help groups organise regular general meetings and develop a structure based on them. As groups need adequate finance, a worker should also be able to help treasurers organise their budgeting and accounts at the appropriate level of sophistication. Particu-larly if community workers and other staff are employed by a community group, budgeting becomes of crucial importance as large amounts of money are involved, and there will be a number of creditors to deal with - staff themselves, inland revenue, stationery suppliers, public utilities, etc. Certainly finding someone who can handle these problems in working-class communities is not easy, and the workers may have to do much themselves and spend considerable time training local people.

Fund-raising (e.g. organising events like raffles, bazaars and jumble sales) is another crucial aspect of financial management. The worker therefore must be able to help groups organise events, as well as help prepare grant applications, assist in negotiations with the fund-providers and develop suitable contacts in the relevant agencies (state or charitable).

If workers have developed the necessary range of skills, knowledge and contacts they should be able to help groups develop through the growth 'tasks' outlined earlier. It is regrettably true, however, that many workers lack some of these basic and essential skills. This lack is even more evident when we turn to the skills and knowledge necessary to help groups understand the powers and internal machinery of statutory authorities.

THE LOCAL AUTHORITIES

While local councils have limited powers, none the less they do have direct control over the issues most local groups tend to deal with - housing, recreation, redevelopment, social welfare and education - and they do give planning permission on issues of concern to groups such as roads and office development. Encouraging negotiation with them and pushing for participation in local government decisions is therefore the main concern of community workers concerned with participation.

Workers thus need to know how local government works, and the different powers and responsibilities of the local authorities that cover their areas. They need to understand the roles of committees, and the working groups where real decisions are often made and which may be held in secret. They should also understand the relationship between different service committees and the central policy and finance committees. At the officer level they need to know what sections in what departments deal with the various issues of concern to their groups, and they need to understand the different powers and responsibilities of officers. This knowledge is not something that can be taught in the abstract, since there are differences in every authority. The most complex part of this is not formal powers, but informal. Useful advice to a group must be based on knowing the actual influence particular officers have (which may have little to do with their formal powers); what the political groupings are within the majority political party; what the 'pecking order' is between councillors (a leader or chairman of committee may have limited power and real influence may reside elsewhere); and crucially what the balance of power is between officers and councillors.

CONTACT WITH OFFICERS AND COUNCILLORS

Workers must develop contacts with councillors and with officers so they can give concrete advice to groups about who to see or negotiate with. A network of friendly officers in relevant departments is vital because the worker can help

ensure that groups deal with these officers. It also enables the
worker to find out what is happening and to develop an early
warning system so that a group can be alerted to issues before
they come up for discussion. The converse of knowing your
allies is, of course, also true - the worker needs to be able
to advise groups about less sympathetic and hostile officers
and to be able to give some advice on how to handle or out-
manoeuvre them.

Support from influential officers and councillors at
committee meetings can be crucial, and informal discussions
with them by members of the community or, if necessary, the
worker, can be very important. So close contact with councillors
should be developed where possible. In some cases, however,
councillors may be hostile to community groups, because they see
them as usurping their role, or to community workers (especially
in their own ward) because they are doing a job that some
councillors believe is theirs. Community workers often write
off such councillors, even though they may be close to a
number of local groups.

In some cases suspicion can be allayed by making clear to a
councillor that the job of representing constituents and making
political decisions is not in conflict with the task of a
community worker, who is advising groups about how to organise
and how to use both the council and local councillors.
Inevitably, though, if the worker helps a group in conflict
with the policies of the councillor it may not be possible to
overcome the distrust.

LOCAL GOVERNMENT FINANCE

It is not sufficient to know where to get support and who to
deal with. A worker must be able to advise on what is actually
possible, and must therefore understand the whole complex
subject of local government finance. A full account of the
subject is obviously outside the scope of this article, but
its importance is clear. A group needs to know how much is
actually available and how that amount can be increased. The
worker has to be clear about how the local authority budget is
made up, and how the different elements both in the capital
and revenue account are raised. The need to understand the
process by which committees decide on their spending priorities,
and what options they have within them, is paramount.

A worker also needs to be aware about various special grants
available to councils from central government, as these may be
able to be used to help the groups. An understanding of local
government finance is also necessary if broad-based campaigns
are to be mounted. In inner city areas campaigns need
developing around a reform of the rate support grant to ensure
more resources are available from central government. In
country areas, where authorities often underspend, workers need

to know whether councils are using all the resources available
to them, or if they are accumulating reserves. If so, the
authority may actually receive less the following year.

OTHER ORGANISATIONS

The local authorities will be the major statutory organisation
that a community worker helps groups to relate to, but they are
not the only ones. Groups may want to influence the health
authorities, so they should be in contact with the community
health council and have some idea about their policies and
activities. In general, the worker needs to develop contacts
and relevant knowledge with regard to all the statutory
organisations with which the groups will deal. They also should
find out what services and help can be offered by other
voluntary and community organisations, such as law centres,
councils for voluntary service, community relations councils,
neighbourhood councils and tenants' federations.

TACTICS AND CAMPAIGNING

The more controversial the issue the more likely it will be that
extensive lobbying of councillors will be required. This
should preferably not be carried out by workers, but by local
people in order to show local support for the issue. But
people should be aware that, while a reasoned and well-argued
case is important, many people in authority are not open to
reason - they may fear for their position or simply be blinded
by their own prejudice. When lobbying, tactful reminders of
adverse publicity, or hints of support from the opposition in
a marginal council can be more potent than a superbly argued
case.

    As a general rule, an attempt should always be made to bring
about change without conflict. Only if this fails should there
be an escalation and a campaign - either local or broad-based -
built up. In this way it is more likely not only to involve
militants, but also people who see that a reasonable attempt
at negotiation and compromise has been tried and has failed.
It will also ensure that the authority cannot say that the
'proper channels' have not been used, or that 'we are always
ready to discuss if the issues are presented in a reasonable
manner'.

    If a full-scale campaign is actually needed people can most
easily be mobilised around concrete and local issues - tenants'
groups can gain massive support for attempts to improve repairs.
Local parents will organise around attempts to provide play
provision. People - not unrealistically - are prepared to come
together if they can see some benefit to themselves and can
see a real chance of success. It is not easy to bring people
together around vague and unclear issues. Any broad-based

campaigns have to have this in mind. As a general rule it is
the left-wing activists who become involved in such campaigns,
not ordinary working-class people. Leaders of these specific
campaigns can meet, co-ordinate activities and ensure that they
do not play each other off. Broader-based campaigns are most
likely to emerge from these concrete struggles.

   Before a community worker advises people to go into any
serious campaign an assessment should be made of the chances of
success, as defeats demoralise people and make future campaigns
more difficult. In a campaign, groups have few real sanctions
available, so it is important that publicity is well organised.
The local radio, TV and newspapers are very important, so
workers should develop sympathetic personal contacts in the
media. Even when a press release is put out it should be
followed by a phone call. The release itself should be succinct
and punchy, making the main points early on.

   Demonstrations can be helpful in getting publicity, showing
the strength of feeling and level of support, and in creating a
spirit of unity among those in a campaign. They are, however,
of only limited use, and too many 'demos' simply devalue their
use; after a while people cease to turn up. Finally, direct
action can be taken - for example, occupation of a housing
department by homeless people, a rent strike or work-ins at
places threatened with closure. These can have useful publicity
value and can embarrass local authorities. Those taking the
action need to be very committed and prepared to take the
consequences of breaking the law - which means that they need
to be aware of what their legal position is. It should be
borne in mind that direct action is not an end in itself, but
another means of publicity and a way of embarrassing the
authorities.

   No campaign will be totally successful and the community
leaders need to learn the art of negotiation and compromise
and so, at times, do the workers both to advise people and
where necessary to negotiate themselves. Campaigns can be
effective, but the community does lack power. Workers should
consider advising groups to develop links with local political
parties, particularly ward Labour parties who supposedly
represent the local working-class community. It may also be
wise to encourage people to join them; after all Ward parties
select candidates, which is a real sanction available to
control councillors. Even when community activists themselves
become councillors, however, they can be absorbed as easily
as anyone else. Activists need to maintain a permanent pressure
through the Ward party if they are to use if effectively, and
to use all the other non-party political means that have been
outlined.

PERSONAL QUALITIES

Community workers, then, need a broad grounding in the social

sciences; knowledge of a wide variety of legislation; a detailed
understanding of local government in their particular area; the
ability to develop a wide range of contacts and allies among
bureaucrats and politicians; experience and knowledge about the
working of committees and groups; the judgment to intervene in
group meetings in such a way as to help the group work out
policies but not to dominate them; and a sufficient understanding
of tactics to be able to supply advice on dealing with the
authorities.

Certain personal attributes are also necessary for successful
community work. A worker requires a practical ideology based
on a belief that people are capable of controlling decisions
and should be encouraged to control their own lives, and a
conviction that this can most effectively be achieved in a
co-operative and collective way. A belief therefore that flows
from this is that resources should be distributed more equally
in society than at present. Without a firm commitment to these
ideas it is difficult to see someone making a really effective
worker. This is not the same as saying the worker should be a
heavy ideologue. Indeed, such people generally make extremely
bad workers as too often they are concerned to impose their own
views on the community, and not to encourage it to learn for
itself.

But 'correct' political attitudes and understanding are not
enough. Community work is a long-term process. It is concerned
to enable people not just to demand and get things now but to
enable people successfully to organise in the future. Community
work is partly a way of encouraging people to learn, and the
best way of learning is through experience and understanding
rather than having ideas imposed by someone such as a highly
educated community worker, who is articulate and able to impose
his or her views. Similarly, workers who attempt to speak and
demand on behalf of a community that they do not represent not
only undermine the credibility of community work, but
provide people with little experience of organising for
themselves. Community workers therefore need the ability to
help other people develop and grow. This is a slow process -
patience and a willingness to do without instant results is a
necessity.

One other related quality should perhaps be referred to -
the ability actually to stay in a job for long enough to
achieve results. This is actually one of the most difficult
tasks! The work is exhausting, often depressing and requires
a good deal of evening work. But it takes time to build up
trust in a community, time really to get to know how a particular authority actually works and time to build up contacts.
Many of the personal qualities cannot actually be taught; good
training can, however, certainly encourage the development of
certain aspects of the personality and can help develop many
of the skills necessary. The management, organisational setting
and support services can also help encourage good work practice.
These will be examined, in terms of what has been discussed earlier.

COMMUNITY WORK AS AN INDEPENDENT DISCIPLINE

Community work training is often a part of the training for
other disciplines such as social work or youth work. Social
work courses in particular have often been seen as a sufficient
basis for people to become full-time community workers. While
social workers may well have community work aspects to their
job, particularly if they are working with self-help or community
care groups, such courses do not generally provide an adequate
grounding for a full-time community worker, particularly if the
work they do is concerned with helping groups influence
decision-making.

   This is partly a matter of time - a complete knowledge base
cannot be offered in both social work and community work on a
two-year course, given the need for adequate field-work place-
ments ‾and partly a matter of orientation. The main task of
social work is to help individuals cope more adequately with
society, in those aspects of their lives in which they need
that support. The main task of community work is to assist
decision-making groups who wish to improve their environment,
and increase the power and resources available to their
community. Where social workers do work with groups, their
concern tends to be in therapeutic objectives, rather than in
helping groups to make collective decisions and relate to the
power structure. Ideally, therefore, full-time community work
courses are required. In practice, in the present atmosphere
of cuts, new ones are not likely to be created and already
established ones could be under threat. It is therefore
important for people engaging in community work after completing
social work courses to realise that their training is unlikely
to be complete, so that subsequent in-service training is
extremely important. The next section will look at the training
that should be offered on full-time community courses to ensure
that workers can help groups to influence decision-making.
Community work options provided as part of social work, or
indeed youth work, courses can only offer as much of this as
is practical.

SELECTION AND TRAINING

The core of any training for community work has to be that
which allows the worker to help groups to operate effectively
and assist them in negotiating and participating in decision-
making (i.e. the skills to do the work discussed earlier),
even where students intend to concentrate after their course on
working in fields such as play, or under-fives. Self-help
groups need to develop as clear a structure as a group primarily
concerned to promote the improvement of local conditions, and
self-help groups spend a considerable amount of time negotiating
for resources. Many groups have both self-help and pressure
functions.

   Many of the skills can only be learnt in practice. Ideally, therefore, on a full-time course, over half the time should be spent on placement, with one long placement of a year's duration to give sufficient time for the student to develop a proper project. This would enable the student to gain the requisite experience. The placement would need backing with one or at most two days in college, drawing out the lessons of the work and learning to work with groups and committees. An under-standing of the working of the local state and of relevant legislation is also essential, as is an examination of relevant case studies and the rather meagre community work literature.

In-service training

Workers continue to need training after they have finished a formal course. However, an untrained worker can engage in community work, provided there is proper support. Ideally, this means a number of workers with a supervisor and at least one day for academic work. The minimum situation that should be acceptable for taking untrained workers is that the post is properly supervised and supported, and adequate time given to attend the various courses provided by academic institutions and the large support agencies such as the National Council of Voluntary Organisations.

Under no circumstances should an untrained and untested worker be put in an unsupervised situation. For reasons stated earlier bad workers can harm the community, community work - and themselves. Yet frequently people from other backgrounds with no experience of community work are given jobs running neighbourhood projects in a totally unsupervised situation. A research worker, a planner, a trade union activist or a social worker is not necessarily a good community worker. This cannot be emphasised too much. Proper on-the-job training therefore does require a commitment from the agency and the supervisor, and should not be undertaken lightly.

Selection

Clearly, selection is a difficult subject to generalise about as the jobs in community work vary so much. None the less, it is vital. People come to community work from a variety of backgrounds and with a variety of interests, and often have very little idea about what is actually involved, but selection often tends to be inadequate and crude. Short interviews - as in many other spheres - tell one little and either community activists or uncomprehending management do not necessarily provide the best interviewers. Considerable time and trouble needs to be given to interviews, particularly for workers in unsupported and unsupervised situations.

ORGANISATIONAL SETTING

Much debate has taken place over whether or not workers should
be in local authorities or voluntary organisations, and if they
are in local authorities what department they should be in and
how should teams be organised. There is no right answer - it
depends on the work to be carried out, the particular situation,
the level of experience of the workers and so on. Workers need
support, new workers in particular need to be operating under
supervision, and there must be an opportunity for people to
exchange ideas and discuss issues and problems. Controls need
to exist to ensure that workers cannot go off and do as they
like without reference to anybody, and there must be a means of
ensuring continuity.

Voluntary agencies

One of the supposed advantages of voluntary organisations is
that they are independent of councils and can oppose their
policies. In practice, fund-raising or trusts can provide
some money, but they do not provide a regular source of income.
Council support has in most cases been essential for organisations employing workers. The independence of an agency rests
ultimately, therefore, on the willingness of an authority to
allow it to continue. Many of the advantages for workers in
voluntary agencies are not, however, in this broad independence,
but in day-to-day matters. Workers in statutory authorities
generally have supervisors, often not community workers, who
may have little sympathy for the work and not want too much
trouble. Workers may thus have to face the hostility of
colleagues if they assist groups confronting their department.

   Voluntary organisations have much more freedom to experiment
with different forms of staff structure and, most importantly,
in some organisations workers can be controlled by the
representatives of the groups they are servicing. Workers in
voluntary organisations also have greater freedom to develop
new projects and new approaches without going through a whole
hierarchy to get agreement. In terms of directly influencing
and changing local authority structures the advantages of
workers in voluntary agencies is that they tend to have easier
access to councillors and senior officers than people in the
local authority, though this will vary from authority to
authority. Voluntary agency workers can also much more openly
co-ordinate campaigns - within the limits mentioned earlier.
These advantages mean that, in any overall council-wide policy
on community work, grant-aid to enable voluntary organisations
to employ workers is essential if participation is to be
encouraged.

Management in voluntary organisations. In most voluntary
agencies there are two aspects of management - the committee
and the internal staff organisation:

Committees. The role of a management committee is to ensure
the overall direction of the agency, to decide on policy, to
lay down guidelines within which the staff work, to be involved
in fund-raising, to control the finance, ensure the staff are
adequately supported, and to hire and fire staff. Very rarely
is there any consideration of how to help the committee to
fulfil these tasks, or to ensure that the right people are
selected.

If the direction of a local community agency is to be
genuinely decided by the community served by the agency, then
a high percentage of the members must be local. In some cases
a neighbourhood group may directly employ a worker to help
them. Many local projects are more broadly based and composed
of representatives of local groups. However, groups can
sometimes be parochial and committee members may resent the
project working with 'undesirable' (say, squatter) groups, or
even with any new group. If a new project is being set up by
another agency or by the council, a support group needs
developing first in which members can be encouraged to develop
an understanding of the aims of the project. Only after the
project has been in existence some while should power be
transferred. None the less, it is essential that all community
projects develop management committees to ensure community
control. Without them, decisions are made either by workers,
who have no mandate, or by distant agencies. Of course,
management committees can be, and frequently are, weak, and it
is difficult to disagree or over-rule workers who are in post
all the time. The workers themselves have to be able and
willing to encourage the process.

Local people may well not have all the necessary skills and
experts may need to be co-opted - people with community work
skills, people with financial skills and so on. If community
workers are, however, really concerned to promote control by
ordinary people of institutions which influence them, then they
should start with themselves. Such arrangements are important
in that they provide an opportunity for people to gain
experience in running bodies with relatively large funds and
employing professional workers.

Internal staff organisations. In small voluntary organisations
an adequate support to workers is very important. One- or
two-person projects face grave difficulties in providing this
and worker networks, involving workers supporting each other
across various organisations, are vital. These small
organisations should only recruit experienced and self-
motivating workers. Slightly larger groups with a number of
workers generally benefit by appointing a co-ordinator to
provide support and guidance to the other workers. This
allows less experienced workers to be taken on and helps
continuity when workers leave. Completely collective structures
can work, but tend to require the appointment of experienced
staff with a strong commitment to providing mutual support and

a willingness to face criticism from other team members. Too
often these preconditions have not existed and the workers have
achieved little and harmed their organisations and the people
they work with.

Type of voluntary organisation. None the less, small community-
controlled structures are the ones that seem most desirable
for voluntary organisations. Once they become large the benefits
of community control and flexibility are lost, and the organisation tends to become just another alternative bureaucracy.
Bodies like CVSs or CRCs are particularly susceptible to this
process. They set up and administer neighbourhood projects
which have little community involvement, and the central unit
becomes a purely administrative body for local projects. The
same pattern applies to national community work agencies like
CPF, which needs to encourage local projects to become community
controlled as soon as possible.

A comprehensive and developed system of community work in
the voluntary sector requires a clear understanding of the
different roles required of different agencies, and the workers
in them. The neighbourhood projects will inevitably be primarily
concerned with their own locality, though workers should still
be helping groups to push for participation and consultation.
Workers for 'umbrella' groups - CVSs, CRCs, Age Concerns,
tenants' federations and play associations - should, however,
be helping groups come together and pressurising for basic
structural changes in order to allow real participation and
control. This was discussed more fully in chapter 1.

Small agencies do, however, face a number of problems. In
particular, fewer staff and less experienced management
committees means less support is available for workers. This
is generally made worse by inadequate financial resources to
provide an opportunity for staff to go on courses and receive
other forms of training. Larger bodies such as CPF are of
value in helping set up projects. They need to be willing to
continue to supply in-service training and support after a
scheme goes independent. For small agencies with a number of
staff the problem of resources reinforces the need to recruit
someone with a leadership and support brief. For one- or two-
person projects it is important that experienced staff are
recruited. It is also essential that staff are encouraged to
get together in support networks. This is discussed below.

Statutory-based work

The great advantage workers in the statutory sector have is
access to information often not generally available, possible
power to recommend on grant-aid to groups and, most importantly,
the power to put forward from the inside ideas for changes in
local authority structures and ways of relating to local groups.
Therefore an overall strategy for promoting participation

requires both statutory workers and workers in voluntary
organisations.

However, an adequate structure for statutory community work
is important. Many workers have felt it useful to be in a
particular service department, in a comparatively junior post.
They have argued that no one will notice them and they can
assist groups (even in conflict with the local authority)
without it being realised. This argument has some short-term
validity. But no one is invisible. One of the great mistakes
of community workers is to believe that they can act undetected
for any length of time. Moreover, an isolated worker in a
team of other workers often feels completely unsupported.
Colleagues do not really understand what they are trying to
do and feel resentful because the worker has not got a clear
job that they understand.

They also face the problem that they may be encouraging the
community to oppose the decisions of their colleagues and
superiors, and may be put under pressure because of this.
Equally the council committee overseeing their department may
resent one of their officers causing opposition to them. The
other main problem is that by working in a particular department,
with the resources of that department, the worker can most
valuably encourage action on matters relating to the department,
but this is not the same as engaging in general community work.
It makes sense for housing departments to employ liaison
officers and planning departments to have development workers,
as long as it is clear that their briefs are limited and
concerned with promoting participation and it is recognised that
they may not be the best workers to help groups in a real
conflict.

The same principles apply to workers in social services
departments. They are particularly useful in helping community
care groups and self-help organisations· In some authorities
the social services department has attempted to become the main
community work department, but it is not a suitable base for
this. If social workers try to take on general community work
they face grave difficulties because of the immediate demands
of a caseload, and because the role of social workers, with
their statutory powers over people, is different from that of
a community worker. Therefore, in any service department full-
time community workers need to have specific and limited roles,
though other staff may have community work aspects to their
jobs.

Generalist departments. General community work in a local
authority needs to be concentrated in a specialist section
without so many vested interests. Such sections have been set
up in a number of authorities and they, of course, do have
their own problems. They are very much 'out front' and their
actions are very open. Central department community workers
are better at providing more superficial assistance to a number

of groups, assistance to authority-wide agencies, information
about council policy, and advice and support to other community
workers. They can also be extremely influential in looking at
council structures and ways of relating to the public and
recommending changes, and in commenting on policies being
developed from the point of view of participation and better
consultation. Neighbourhood projects, on an estate for example,
have generally been attached to social services teams, but they
would be far better as part of a central community work team,
because of the support available from other workers. Indeed,
it would provide maximum support to statutory community workers
to go further than this and develop a structure which allows
all community workers to be part of a central team, 'seconded'
where relevant to different departments, regularly attending
training sessions and staff meetings for all council community
workers. Such structures are not likely to be developed in the
near future, so that adequate training on the available courses
and good support networks are very important for both statutory
and voluntary sector workers.

WORKERS' NETWORKS

Workers need to be able to come together and work out their
problems; network groups provide a way of doing this.   ACW
has attempted to encourage a country-wide development of these
groups. In a few areas they have worked well as training and
support organisations, and at times they have been successful
pressure groups for community work, but on the whole they have
not been successful.

    There are a number of reasons for this - rivalries between
different agencies and workers is one cause. Sheer lack of
self-discipline is another - the meetings become a chance to
meet and chat. If there are many workers in small voluntary
agencies, or isolated in council departments, the development
of support networks is crucial. The biggest disadvantage that
the model of community control for voluntary agencies faces is
that in many cases only one or two people will be employed.
Networks which can examine workers' projects in detail, share
knowledge on the workings of the local authority or examine
local government finance (for which there is little written
information available), organise sessions on developing areas
of work, or on changes in the law, are vital. But they do
require people to commit themselves to them and, for a real
examination of work, mutual trust has to be developed and this
does take time. The co-ordination of such a network and
adequate preparation of issues for discussion is also time-
consuming, and this may be another reason for their failure.
A suitable body to take on this role could well be a CVS,
provided that it has the confidence of the workers. Another
possibility could be a local college community work department,
which has happened in a number of areas. The successful scheme
in Islington is referred to in chapter 2.

Effective networks do need to be developed as so many issues
are not capable of simple answers, but need wide discussion.
Since workers are operating inside and outside the bureaucracy
and at many different levels, only by exchanging information
can workers gain a full picture of developments in their area,
and how they can most effectively promote change.

CONCLUSIONS

The ideal environment for community work to operate in to promote
participation requires a situation in which there is a willingness for public bodies to fund training, and for local councils
to be interested in promoting community action and in involving
local people in decision-making. The councils need to be
prepared to fund workers in both voluntary organisations and
in the statutory sector, and to accept that groups that are
funded may criticise the council and engage in conflict with
them. In the present era of public expenditure cuts this is
a difficult case to make. Community work is seen as peripheral,
voluntary organisations can be cut without too much trouble
from unions, and to pay workers to help people demand better
services as the funds available decline can seem the height
of folly. General community work departments and voluntary
organisations are particularly vulnerable and there are
advantages in the present circumstances for workers to be in
many different departments and not too visible.

However, in one area there is hope. It is possible that
over the next few years we will see an increasing number of
radical Labour councils, committed to fighting the Tories,
taking power in the town halls. If they are to win the support
of working-class people for public expenditure and persuade
people to campaign against the government, they must ensure
that the services are far more under the control of the people
that use them, and that people are far more involved in the
decisions that the Council takes than at present. Community
work could play a vital role in helping people to participate
effectively,and to learn the skills to take over and run
services. The employment frameworks discussed in this article
would provide the most efficient structure for them to operate
in. A consequence of this type of development, however, would
be that community workers could be seen far more clearly than
at present as political appointments, and might not expect to
survive a change of administration at the town hall. In a
period of increasing ideological conflict this is a choice
that community work may have to make if it is to continue to be
involved in promoting participation.

In many areas and in many situations the position will not
be so clear-cut; community workers will survive, though in
reduced numbers, and they will be engaged in a variety of work,
part of which will be concerned with participation. Their
support structures and networks will be vital if they are to be

as effective as possible. As state funding becomes more precarious we also need to consider developing independent and self-funding arrangements. Tenants' federations are perhaps the one type of community organisation in Britain that might be able to employ workers through contributions by the community. In Islington, for example, if only 40 per cent of families in council property contributed £10 a year to a federation, the federation would have an income of about £64,000.

If developments such as these took place it would transform community work and the role of community workers. But, while the next few years are going to be very different from the period since the mid-1960s, when community work started expanding, the lessons learnt about the ways in which community work can operate most effectively still remain valid. They will need to be applied to the extent and in the ways that they can.